T0320802

State-Firm Coordination and Upgrading

State-Firm Coordination and Upgrading

Reaching the Efficiency Frontier in Skill-, Capital-, and Knowledge-Intensive Industries in Spain and South Korea

Angela Garcia Calvo

OXFORD

UNIVERSITY PRESS

Great Clarendon Street, Oxford, OX2 6DP,
United Kingdom

Oxford University Press is a department of the University of Oxford.
It furthers the University's objective of excellence in research, scholarship,
and education by publishing worldwide. Oxford is a registered trade mark of
Oxford University Press in the UK and in certain other countries

First Edition published in 2021

Impression: 1

Published in the United States of America by Oxford University Press
198 Madison Avenue, New York, NY 10016, United States of America

British Library Cataloguing in Publication Data

Data available

Library of Congress Control Number: 2021935698

ISBN 978-0-19-886456-1

DOI: 10.1093/oso/9780198864561.001.0001

Printed and bound by
CPI Group (UK) Ltd, Croydon, CR0 4YY

Preface

This book grew up of dissatisfaction with three methodological aspects of the political economy literature. The first is a view of the world that distinguishes between advanced and developing countries. In such a neat division, countries that successfully navigate the transition from developing to developed economies usually fall through theories' cracks and are either ignored or treated as exceptions. I believe there is a distinct logic to the transformation of such countries in the middle, and that it requires its own framework, for its own sake, and for the purpose of providing signposts for other countries. The second is a tendency to develop separate frameworks to explain processes of industrial transformation in Western and Asian countries. I believe that this is a bias that makes theory formulation weaker because it leads us to ignore different, yet viable, ways to solve the same or comparable problems during the same period of time. The third is a tendency to separate the political economy of industrial transformation from industry. As a jurist and an applied economist by training, I was educated to see economic institutions and industry as two sides of the same coin. Two decades of professional and academic experience have galvanized the perspective that the dynamics of state–firm interaction are the key to successful economic transformation. Economic change cannot take place in the absence of a significant industrial overhaul but firms' transformation depends on leveraging support from their home country's institutional environment.

Over the course of this project, I was asked many times why I chose to explore economic transformation through a comparison between Spain and Korea. This book argues that the comparison makes methodological sense. However, ideas also come from strange corners of our personal lives. In my case, the comparison stemmed from an TV documentary I watched with my parents as a child and which contrasted the decline of Spain's manufacturing sectors with the upward trajectories of Korea's firms in the same industries. The notion that Spanish ship, steel, and auto manufacturers were competing with and being beaten by Korea's firms despite the fact that the two countries were half a world away, blew my mind away. Many years later, several interviewees for my doctoral thesis about Spain spontaneously mentioned the same idea to me, prompting me to learn more about Korea and to develop this project.

A fascinating part of the comparison is that starting from a similar industrialization base, from the 1980s the two countries pursued different strategies to become advanced economies. Spain, which ached to be accepted by "Europe," welcomed foreign direct investors and relied on foreign technology. Korea, which longed for recognition and autonomy from unwanted foreign intervention, built its technological capabilities from the ground up and defended its industry from foreign interference. The cover of this book illustrates the two perspectives nicely. At the top is a picture of Madrid's Gate of Europe. The two contemporary, twin, inclined towers, frame the northern entrance to Madrid's Paseo de la Castellana, the capital's business artery, in an open welcome. At the bottom is a picture of Seoul's Namdaemun gate (officially known as Sungnyemun). The fortified, fourteenth-century gate used to welcome foreign emissaries to the capital. Today, it stands as a striking symbol of Korea's identity in a sea of traffic and modern buildings.

Having a good idea and finding a gap in the literature is relatively easy. Gathering the resources, finding the right support, sustaining the effort for years, and turning it into a completed manuscript is another matter altogether. I could not have done it without Bob Hancké and Saul Estrin, my mentors at the LSE, who provided insightful feedback, encouragement, sensible career advice, good humor, and showed considerable patience and understanding as they read through numerous versions of the material in this book. Working with Bob and Saul was a pleasure and I could not have asked for a better team. I have a special debt with Bob, who, in addition to mentoring me through this book, also guided me through my PhD thesis and has seen me turn from student to author.

Special thanks also go to the scholars and institutions who hosted me throughout the development of this project and encouraged me to pursue it. Stephan Haggard hosted me at UC San Diego and provided valuable advice on how to organize my thoughts effectively while helping develop my skills as a qualitative researcher. Larry Summers and Robert Z. Lawrence, welcomed me to the Kennedy School of Government and provided much appreciated mentorship and practical advice. Yang Jae-Jin and Choi Young Jun graciously welcomed me to Yonsei university and made my research in Korea possible, while providing valuable insights about the country. Kim Sun Joo, Carter J. Eckert, Chang Paul Y., and Susan Lawrence hosted me at Harvard's Korea Institute, provided a nurturing environment for research, and introduced me to Harvard's Korean community. Peter Hall acted as my informal mentor at Harvard's Center for European Studies, read parts of the argument, and provided helpful advice throughout. José Manuel Martínez Sierra hosted me at the Real Collegio Complutense at Harvard. Margarita

Estevez-Abe welcomed me at the Collegio Carlo Alberto in Torino, validated my idea of pursuing a comparative analysis between a European and an Asian country at a time when most people saw such comparison with skepticism, and introduced me to vital contacts in the US and Korea that made this project possible.

Additional thanks go to Suzanne Berger, Choi Chul, Alvaro Cuervo-Cazurra, Steve Coulter, Pepper Coulpepper, Mauro Guillén, Kahee Jo, Kang Nahee, Kang Myung Koo, Sean McGraw, Sebastien Lechevalier, Lee Munseob, Sean McGraw, Carol Mershon, Sophus Reinert, Sebastian Royo, Marco Simoni, Tim Sturgeon, Robert Wade, and Denise Walsh. They listened to or read different versions and parts of the argument, raised questions, provided useful suggestions on what to do with the material, and generally encouraged me to pursue this project. In addition to these scholars, I extend my thanks to the many Spanish and Korean civil servants and private sector managers who shared their time and expertise generously.

Further thanks go to the team at Oxford University Press, who turned this manuscript into a book. Adam Swallow kindly accepted my proposal for publication, Jenny King managed the production process and graciously let me provide input on the cover, Nivedha Vinayagamurthy, managed the production process, and Martin Noble polished the language and patiently waded through the massive bibliography section.

Several institutions provided financial support to complete this project. I gratefully acknowledge help from the European Union's Horizon 2020 research and innovation programme under grant agreement No 747943, the Real Collegio Complutense, the Collegio Carlo Alberto, the London School of Economics, the Santander Mobility Scholarship, and the European Social and Research Council.

Lastly, I want to thank the colleagues, friends, and family that stood by me through this process or parts of it, held me through the ups and downs, celebrated the milestones, and reminded me to go out and enjoy life. Among them, I especially want to thank Pilar Castillo, Nikki Davis, Nuria Fernández, Carlos Javier García Calvo, Gail Elise McLaren, Cristina Pérez, Eva Sánchez, Liesbeth Wiering, Eun Yang Song, and Eun Yang Young.

My biggest debt, however, is to my parents Isabel Calvo Jiménez and José Luís García Liso, whose unconditional love and support made me who I am. This book is dedicated to them.

London,
January, 2021.

Contents

List of Figures and Tables

Figures

Tables

List of Abbreviations

3G	Third-Generation
AMETIC	Electronics, information technologies, telecommunications and digital content trade association (Asociación de empresas de electrónica, tecnologías de la información, telecomunicaciones y contenidos digitales)
ANFAC	Spanish Association of Automobile and Truck Manufacturers (Asociación Española de Fabricantes de Automóbiles y Camiones)
ASD	Aerospace and Defense
AV	AutonomousVehicle
BcN	Broadband Convergence Network
BoS	Bank of Spain
BT	British Telecom
CASA	Constructiones Aeronaúticas SA
CDMA	Code-Division Multiple Access
CEMFI	Center for Monetary and Financial Studies
CEO	Chief Executive Officer
CNC	Computer Numerical Control
DACOM	Data Telecom Corporation
DGTel	Directorate-General for Telecommunications (Dirección General de Telecomunicaciones)
DS	Developmental State
EADS	European Aeronautic Defence and Space Company
EPB	Economic Planning Board
ETRI	Electronics and Telecommunications Research Institute
EU	European Union
EV	Electric Vehicle
FCEV	Fuel-Cell Electric Vehicle
FDI	Foreign Direct Investment
FEDEA	Foundation for Applied Economic Studies
FTTB	Fiber To The Business
FTTC	Fiber To The Cabinet
FTTH	Fiber To The Home
FTTP	Fiber To The Premises
GDP	Gross Domestic Product
GFCI	Global Financial Center Index
GM	General Motors
GSM	Global System for Mobile
GVC	Global Value Chain
HCI	Heavy Chemical Industry

HMC	Hyundai Motor Company
IAEA	International Atomic Energy Agency
ICE	Internal Combustion Engine
ICT	Information and Communications Technologies
IEA	International Energy Agency
IMF	International Monetary Fund
INE	National Statistics Institute (Instituto Nacional de Estadística)
ITP	Industria de Turbopropulsores
KAERI	Korea Atomic Energy Research Institute
KAICA	Korea Auto Industries Cooperative Association
KAIST	Korean Advanced Institute of Science and Technology
KAMA	Korea Automotive Manufacturers Association
KDB	Korea Development Bank
KDI	Korea Development Institute
KEPCO	Korea Electric Power Corporation
KHIC	Korea Heavy Industries and Construction Company
KIET	Korea Institute for Industrial Economics and Trade
KII	Korea Information Infrastructure
KISDI	Korea Information Society Development Institute
KITECH	Korea Institute of Industrial Technology
KOPEC	Korea Power Engineering Company
KPN	Koninklijke PTT Nederland
KT	Korea Telecom
MIC	Ministry of Information and Communication
MT	MachineTools
NBFI	Non-Bank Financial Institutions
NGAs	Next Generation Access Networks
NPS	National Pension Service
OECD	Organisation for Economic Cooperation and Development
OEM	Original Equipment Manufacturer
OICA	International Organization of Motor Vehicle Manufacturers (Organisation Internationale des Constructeurs d'Automobiles)
PP	Popular Party (Partido Popular)
PSOE	Spanish Socialist Party (Partido Socialista Obrero Español)
PTO	Public Telecommunications Operator
PTT	Public Telephone and Telegraph
R&D	Research and Development
RCEP	Regional Comprehensive Economic Partnership
SEPI	State Agency for Industrial Investments (Sociedad Estatal de Participaciones Industriales)
SETSI	Secretary of State for Telecommunications and Information Society (Secretaría de Estado de Telecomunicaciones y Sociedad de la Información)
TDMA	Time-Division Multiple Access
TDX	Time Division Exchange

TEDAE	Spanish Association of Technology, Defense, Security, Aeronautics, and Spacefirms (Asociación Española de Empresas Tecnológicas de Defensa, Seguridad, Aeronáutica y Espacio)
UK	United Kingdom
UN	United Nations
UNCTAD	United Nations Conference on Trade and Development
UNESA	Unidad Eléctrica
US	United States
WTO	World Trade Organization

1
Economic Development, Upgrading, and Coordination

1.1 Becoming an Advanced Economy

I begin this book with an empirical puzzle: How did Spain and South Korea upgrade to reach advanced country status? How did they come to host firms that are globally competitive in skill-, capital-, and knowledge-intensive industries? In the post-1980s context, upgrading involves progressively shifting from lower to higher value-added activities within global value chains (GVCs) (Gereffi et al., 2005). The process increases value creation and capture, which are expected to translate into higher living standards (Sen, 1999).

When a country starts from very low levels of development, upgrading is relatively achievable. Increased participation in GVCs correlates with a drop of over one billion in the number of people living in absolute poverty between 1990 and 2013 (World Bank, 2016). However, reaching the highest echelons of the global division of labor to become an advanced economy is much more difficult. If we define advanced economies as those with an income per capita level that is above 50 percent of that of the United States (US), then, since 1980, only 21 countries have become advanced economies (Garcia Calvo, 2021). What is more, only a third of these countries have reached advanced country status by increasing the complexity of their productive structures, and by becoming the home base of at least one lead firm that controls the process of design, production, and distribution of a global production network, has global market power, and a recognizable brand name.

Spain's and Korea's journey to become advanced economies and reach the efficiency frontier in complex industries is not only remarkable but also intriguing. The two countries industrialized in the 1960s and 1970s on the basis of state-directed efforts that supported the development of a similar set of mature manufacturing industries including shipbuilding, steel, chemicals, consumer electronics, and the automotive industry. In the decades that

State-Firm Coordination and Upgrading: Reaching the Efficiency Frontier in Skill-, Capital-, and Knowledge-Intensive Industries in Spain and South Korea. Angela Garcia Calvo, Oxford University Press. © Angela Garcia Calvo 2021. DOI: 10.1093/oso/9780198864561.003.0001

followed, they reached comparable levels of economic development and standards of living but their productive structures diverged significantly. Spanish firms in complex service sectors such as banking and telecommunications reached the efficiency frontier, but manufacturing capacity declined sharply. By contrast, Korean firms in existing manufacturing sectors such as electronics and motor vehicles moved upward within the value chains of their respective industries but many services remained underdeveloped or underperforming.

By studying Spain's and Korea's upgrading processes, this book offers more than a detailed analysis of two fascinating stories. The comparison between these two countries' economic transformations offers an opportunity to test conventional positions on late development and industrial upgrading and to question existing categorizations. Interpreting Spain's and Korea's upgrading from a liberal angle as the result of solid macroeconomics, market liberalization, integration in the global economy, and state retrenchment is tempting (Hayek, 1944). However, liberalization alone cannot explain how firms from late industrializing economies gained access to the socially embedded resources and capabilities they needed to reach the efficiency frontier and become globally competitive. A developmental state (DS) perspective in which national governments set the course for transformation, empowered by the information provided by firms (Weiss, 1998), can also be persuasive. However, the DS perspective is a theory of state power (Weiss, 1998) that minimizes the agency of large firms based in late industrializing economies. The DS literature also tends to equate the developmental approach with strategies based on "the pursuit of local manufacturing capacity, technological autonomy, and export competitiveness" (Thurbon, 2016, p. 16), but there is no reason to think that this is the only viable pathway to late-stage development.

In addition, the comparison between these two countries offers a chance to question conventional categorizations. Most political economists, economists, and development practitioners tend to see the world through the lens of either the world's most advanced countries or developing economies. However, neither the definitions nor the frameworks derived from the empirical analyses of very advanced or developing countries are well suited to characterize countries that stand in the middle, such as Spain and Korea. Their complex economies, higher standards of living, sophisticated welfare systems, and global standing clearly set these countries apart from developing economies. On the other hand, their trajectories of recent industrialization based on learning rather than innovation (Amsden, 1989), and their concentration of activities in a relatively small set of competitive, complex industries distinguish new advanced economies from the world's most advanced countries and make frameworks based on advanced industrialized economies ill-suited to explain Spain's and Korea's institutional environments or the economic challenges they face.

The argument developed in this book changes our perspective in at least three ways: from markets or states as alternative explanations of industrial upgrading to state–firm coordination as a driver for economic transformation, from one pathway to upgrading based on technological self-sufficiency to at least two different pathways based on either technological autonomy or regional integration, and from a world divided into emerging economies and world leaders to a more nuanced perspective that recognizes the perspectives of countries in-between.

The analysis of Spain's and Korea's upgrading has implications beyond these two cases. The argument about state–firm coordination and the importance of state activism in enabling firms to develop the resources and capabilities they need to become globally competitive is applicable to other countries trying to achieve advanced country status. Similarly, the characterization of two viable pathways to upgrading offers contemporary emerging economies possible options to consider, depending on their existing production strategies, the strength of their governments, and their ties to more advanced economies.

The remainder of this first chapter sets the stage for the rest of the book by justifying the choice of Spain's and Korea's cases, discussing the problems with competing explanations, and outlining the alternative argument adopted in this study. It consists of four sections. The first assesses the comparability of the Spanish and Korean cases and describes the contours of their upgrading. The second outlines the broader debate on economic transformation and its implications for developments in Spain and Korea. The third articulates the book's argument and shows how it helps understand the Spanish and Korean cases. The final section presents a preview of the rest of the book.

1.2 Comparing Spain and Korea

Spain and Korea are not often studied from a comparative perspective but neither is it unheard of. From a business perspective, Guillén (2010) used a comparison between Spain, Korea, and Argentina to cast doubt on conventional views about globalization. In addition, León, Choi, and Ahn (2016) use similarities in the characteristics of Spain's and Korea's labor markets and welfare regimes to study the policy determinants of female labor force participation.

My empirical focus on these two countries is motivated by two factors. The first is size. With populations of about 50 million each, Spain and Korea are the only two large countries to have overcome the middle-income trap. Large countries can host manufacturing production plants and have sizeable internal markets, which increase the range of upgrading strategies and production specializations they can pursue. Large economies also require a solid, scalable institutional structure capable of fostering transformation simultaneously across a broad range of industries with diverse needs. The complexity of these institutional structures and upgrading strategies makes Spain and Korea important cases to develop a general framework to understand upgrading. The second and more important factor involves a combination of analytically useful similarities and differences. The two countries faced comparable economic and social challenges simultaneously and achieved surprisingly similar outcomes in terms of the size of their national economies and income per capita levels. However, Spain and Korea appear to have reached these outcomes through different pathways that have resulted in diverse productive specializations in complex services and manufacturing respectively.

Spain's and Korea's modern, large-scale industrialization started almost simultaneously. Spain's took off with the 1959 Stabilization Plan, which ended the two decades of autarky and international isolation that followed the end of the Spanish Civil War and General Franco's accession to power (Sánchez Domínguez, 2001; Pérez, 1997). Korea's industrialization started in 1961 with the military coup that brought General Park Chung Hee to power with a mandate to end corruption and ensure Korea's autonomy from foreign powers (Haggard, 1990). At the time, Spain and Korea were poor agricultural societies (Sánchez Domínguez, 2001). The two countries were also poorly endowed in terms of natural resources, had deficient infrastructures, and exhibited little semblance of technological, organizational, or skill leadership. Although Spain's average standard of living was higher than Korea's (US$369 vs. US$155 per capita income) (World Bank Development Indicators, 2020), Korea's potential for growth far exceeded that of other countries of the same income level. Korea's high levels of social and educational development and the breakdown of the old regime's rigidly stratified society offered a fertile environment for economic development (Amsden, 1989). In addition, the participation of Koreans in the economy during the Japanese occupation had been greater than that of local populations subject to European colonial rule (Jones and Sakong, 1980). Finally, unlike most post-colonial countries, Korea had experienced a relatively short occupation, had a rich cultural background, was conceived as a historically cohesive unit, and had a very homogeneous society (Jones and Sakong, 1980).

Spain's and Korea's industrialization processes in the 1960s and 1970s were based on absorbing rather than generating innovation. Local innovation consisted mostly of knowledge transfer, learning, and applied improvements based on local demand conditions (Adanero, 2006; Kim, 1997). Spain's and Korea's activist governments structured their industrializations around multi-annual development plans that followed in the footsteps of Spain's and Korea's respective precursors: France and Japan (Haggard, 1990; Smith, 1998; Pérez, 1997). These plans supported the expansion of mature, heavy industries and concentrated on a similar set of sectors. Spanish plans prioritized steel, chemicals, shipbuilding, and automotive (Sánchez Domínguez, 2001). Korea's industrialization initially concentrated on light industries, but during the Heavy-Chemical Industry Drive (HCI) of the 1970s, Korean plans concentrated on six sectors: steel, petrochemicals, shipbuilding, electronics, general-purpose machinery, and non-ferrous metals (Sakong, 1993), in addition to automotive (Korea Institute for Industrial Economics and Trade [KIET], 2014). By the end of the 1970s, both countries specialized in the production of mid-quality, relatively undifferentiated products (Bloom, 1992; Rico González, 2006).

Spanish and Korean plans delivered rapid growth. Between 1961 and 1974, Spain's gross domestic product (GDP) grew by an annual average of 9 percent and Korea's by 7 percent (World Bank Development Indicators, 2020), but the oil crises of the 1970s brought to the surface a host of problems in both countries, including competitive deficiencies, liquidity problems, high debt levels, current account deficits, rampant inflation, and, in the case of Korea, a misallocation of resources, overcapacity, and underutilization (Jwa, 2004). The first shock was felt at a delicate political moment in both countries. In 1973, Franco's age and declining health heralded the end of his rule (Preston, 1986). In Korea, growing social opposition and security concerns led Park to transform the country's formal democracy into a full dictatorship in 1972 (Haggard and Moon, 1990). Therefore, neither Spain nor Korea responded immediately with contractionary policies.

The second oil shock in 1979 forced both countries to take specific measures to address the crisis. However, by the early 1980s, broader changes were also in the cards, as the governments of the two countries expressed their ambitions to join the ranks of advanced countries and integrate fully into the global economy. Both countries articulated these objectives explicitly; the Spanish 1982–86 government program aimed to "situate Spain in its rightful place in the international community" (Spanish Socialist Party—Partido—Socialista Obrero Español [PSOE] 1982, p. 6), whereas Korea's fifth economic and social development plan (1982–86) acknowledged that "Korea will have to nurture its capacity to participate more actively in the world economy" (Economic Planning Board [EPB], 1981, p. 5). The two countries also took symbolic steps to showcase their prowess and their brand-new democracies to the world; Spain hosted the FIFA World Cup in 1982 and Korea, the 1988 Olympic Games.

Joining the ranks of advanced countries was no small undertaking; in the mid-1980s, the two countries were still far from the world's leading economies. In 1985, Spain's income per capita was 35 percent of that of the US, whereas Korea's was only 22 percent (Table 1.1). Infrastructure in both countries lacked much to be desired. Telecommunications services, a basic indicator of development, fared badly in terms of coverage, network equipment, investment, and profitability. Access to telephony service was not universal, and the number of access channels was below that of other developed economies. For instance, in 1985, only 52.2 percent of Spanish homes had a telephone, whereas in the US, 90 percent of homes had a telephone by 1960 (Telefonica, 1985; Faulhaber, 1995). Low telecommunications penetration in both countries came hand in hand with lack of coverage, especially in rural areas, long waiting lists for new lines, and deficient service (Rico, 2006; Larson, 1995). Finally, low-income levels and lack of buyer sophistication in both countries favored the production of mid-quality products whose most attractive feature was usually their price. This became an obstacle as the two countries started to export. For instance, in 2010, an article in Canada's *The Globe and Mail* described the Hyundai Pony, a model that the Hyundai Motor Company (HMC) started to sell in Canada in 1984, as a "Honda Civic built in a back alley by an inebriated blacksmith." (Cheney, 2010).

Table 1.1 Income per capita as a percentage of the US

Country	1985	2016	Percentage of US IPC (1985)	Percentage of US IPC (2016)
United States	33,024	53,015	100%	100%
Sweden	22,781	44,371	69%	84%
Germany	21,377	46,841	65%	88%
France	20,830	38,758	63%	73%
United Kingdom	20,712	39,162	63%	74%
Italy	19,859	34,989	60%	66%
Japan	19,017	36,452	58%	69%
Israel	17,976	32,494	54%	61%
Ireland	12,874	55,653	39%	105%
Spain	**11,538**	**31,556**	**35%**	**60%**
Singapore	11,342	67,180	34%	127%
Portugal	9,784	27,726	30%	52%
Republic of Korea	**7,322**	**36,151**	**22%**	**68%**

Source: Maddison Database Project (2018) Data in US$.

Yet by the 2010s, Spain and Korea had significantly narrowed the gap with the world's leading economies and were more integrated in the global economy than they had been at any previous point in their modern histories. GDP growth followed a rapid upward trajectory (Figure 1.1). Income per capita levels in both countries were well above 50 percent of that of the US (Table 1.1). Spain and Korea boasted excellent infrastructures, including some of the world's most advanced next-generation access networks for telecommunications (Table 1.2). Both countries were also home to globally competitive firms operating across a range of complex (skill-, capital-, and knowledge-intensive) industries, such as telecommunications services, retail banking, electronics, motor vehicles, nuclear energy, renewable energy, aerospace, machine-tools, and civil engineering. Firms in these industries no longer relied on costs and scale alone to compete but on complex advantages based on processes, organizational efficiencies, and product features (Porter, 1990).

By 2009, Spanish banks have climbed to the top of international rankings in terms of market capitalization, efficiency, and productivity (European Central Bank Statistical Data Warehouse, 2009). By 2011, Spain's incumbent telecommunications operator was the world's fifth largest integrated operator by revenue, the third most profitable (Organisation for Economic Co-operation and Development [OECD] Communications Outlook, 2013), and one of the most efficient and best managed (Giokas and Pentzaropoulos, 2008). Similarly, in 2016, Korea's Samsung Electronics was not only one of the world's largest producers of semiconductors (memory chips) and liquid crystal displays, but also one of only two profitable manufacturers of smartphones (Reisinger, 2016). Furthermore, in 2018, Korea was the world's fifth largest automotive producer (International Organization of Motor Vehicle Manufacturers—Organisation Internationale des Constructeurs d'Automobiles [OICA] Production Statistics,

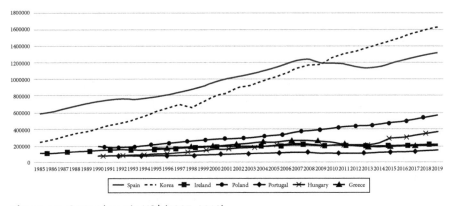

Figure 1.1 GDP volume in US$ (1985–2019).

Source: OECD Economic Outlook 2019 (GDP volume in US$ (million), constant exchange rates.

Table 1.2 Percentage of fiber connections in total fixed broadband (2019)

Country	2019
Korea	81.65
Japan	79.03
Sweden	68.95
Spain	62.53
OECD	26.81
France	19.78
United States	15.55
Ireland	8.76
Italy	6.04
Germany	3.58
United Kingdom	2.33

Source: OECD, Broadband Portal.

Definitions: Fiber subscriptions data includes FTTH, FTTP, and FTTB and excludes FTTC and FTTN.

2018) and the only late industrializing economy to have become the home base of a globally competitive local automotive assembler.

However, even if both countries made it to the *big league* of advanced countries, Spain and Korea followed different pathways. Spain's strategy emphasized foreign direct investment (FDI), technological outsourcing, and regional integration within the European Union (EU) along the lines of what could be called an integrational approach. As can be seen in Table 1.3, in 2018, Spain received 3.4 percent of the world's inflows of FDI even though it only accounts for 1.7 percent of the world's GDP. Spain's gross domestic investment in research and development (R&D) was only 1.2 percent of its GDP, which is half the OECD's average rate. Finally, intra-EU trade accounted for 67 percent of Spain's exports and 62 percent of its imports in 2016.

By contrast, Korea's strategy prioritized self-sufficiency and technological autonomy along the lines of what Thurbon (2016) calls a techno-industrial approach. Thus, in 2018, Korea received only 1.1 percent of the world's FDI, even though the country represents 1.9 percent of the world's GDP, and its stock of FDI was about a third of Spain's. Korea's emphasis on technology is evident from its gross domestic investment in R&D relative to its GDP, which, at 4.5 percent, is the world's second largest rate after Israel's (OECD Main Science and Technology Statistics, 2020).

These strategies have had a significant impact on the production structures of the two countries. Although in the 1960s and 1970s Spain and Korea industrialized on the basis of a similar set of mature manufacturing industries, they have since veered toward production specializations in complex services and manufacturing respectively. In 2018, only 12 percent of Spain's output

Table 1.3 Inward foreign direct investment (2018)

	Spain	Korea
FDI inflows in USD million	43 591	14 479
FDI inflows as percentage of world	3.4%	1.1%
FDI stock	659,038	231,409
FDI stock as percentage of world	2%	1%
GDP in current prices	1 424 996	1 619 928
GDP as percentage of the world	1.7%	1.9%
Gross domestic expenditure in R&D* as percentage of GDP	1.2%	4.5%

Source: UNCTAD.

Data in US$ in millions.

* OECD main science and technology indicators.

Data for 2018.

came from manufacturing, whereas the corresponding figure for Korea was 29 percent (OECD National Accounts, data for 2018). In fact, since 1985, the share of Spain's manufacturing output has declined sharply from 25 percent (National Statistics Institute—Instituto Nacional de Estadística [INE] regional accounts, 2013), whereas Korea's has risen by two percentage points (OECD National Accounts, data for 1985 and 2018).

The two countries' trade balances also showcase their specializations (Table 1.4). Spain shows a significant deficit in manufacturing but a surplus in services. The opposite is true for Korea. Specializations in services and manufacturing are also evident at the industry level. For instance, in 2018, services and software accounted for 83 percent of Spain's information and communications technologies (ICT) production (Electronics, Information Technologies, Telecommunications, and Digital Content Trade Association—Asociación Multisectorial de Empresas de Tecnologías de la Información, Comunicaciones y Electrónica [AMETIC], 2018). By contrast, in the same year Korea's electronic equipment represented 74 percent of the country's ICT output (Korea Information Society Development Institute [KISDI], 2019).

1.3 Competing Explanations

How should we understand Spain's and Korea's upgrading? Why did two countries that pursued comparable industrialization strategies and had comparable productive structures in the early 1980s respond to the same challenge through different strategies that led to diverse productive specializations? Were these two different pathways equifinal? The comparative political economy literature and the specific literatures of Spain and Korea offer two ways

Table 1.4 Spain's and Korea's trade balance (2018)

	Spain	Korea
Merchandize trade balance in USD million	−42 878	69 657
Services trade balance in USD million	63 776	−27 661
Current account balance, percentage of GDP	0.90	4.72

Source: UNCTAD.
Data in US$ in millions.
Data for 2018.

of understanding this process of transformation: economic liberalism and the DS approach.

1.3.1 The Liberal Perspective

The liberal perspective can be traced back to the work of Hayek (1944) and it is based on the neoclassical belief that the market is the most efficient allocation mechanism. The liberal perspective understands economic development and sustainable economic growth as the outcome of a market-embracing approach involving balanced macroeconomics, market liberalization, the restructuring of ailing industries, state retrenchment from economic production, and an export orientation (Smith, 1998). In the post-1980s context, economic development also involves growing participation in GVCs and upgrading, or the progressive shift from lower to higher value-added activities to reach the higher echelons of GVCs (Gereffi et al., 2005). Following Porter's Stages of Development, upgrading requires that firms transition from competing on the basis of factor endowments, costs, and scale to competing on the basis of complex advantages based on processes, organizational efficiencies, and product features.

In the 1990s and 2000s, the liberal approach was a part of the standard Washington Consensus advice issued by development practitioners in international organizations to emerging economies (Rodrik, 2006). The interpretation also found strong adherence in Spain and Korea (Smith, 1998; Coe and Yeung, 2015). The liberal argument does explain a series of reforms undertaken by Spain and Korea in the 1980s and 1990s. However, it does not necessarily tell the whole story.

1.3.1.1 The Liberal Perspective in Spain
The first transformational measures adopted by the early Spanish democratic governments aimed to reinforce the powers of the Bank of Spain (BoS),

Spain's central bank, to conduct monetary policy, develop effective bank supervision mechanisms, and set the basis for the liberalization of financial markets (Fuentes Quintana, 1985). A severe banking crisis also prompted the decisive restructuring of the banking industry (Dziobek and Pazarbasioglu, 1998; Martín Aceña, 2005).

The able management of macroeconomic reforms and the banking crisis showcased the strength and credibility of a group of orthodox economists trained at the BoS (Termes, 1991; Malo de Molina, 2012). During the governments of the PSOE from 1982 to 1996, talent from this group of economists came to dominate Spanish economic policy making and provided continuity to liberal reforms (Pérez, 1997; Smith, 1998). The governments' liberal penchant is reflected in a series of actions undertaken throughout the 1980s.

First, they embarked on an austerity program involving wage restraint, tight monetary policy, and the reduction of the fiscal deficit to control inflation. By 1985, the annual rate of inflation was reduced to 8.8 percent (down from 14.4 percent in 1982) (Economic and Social Council [ESC], Labor statistics, data for multiple years). Second, they tackled the industrial crisis. Royal Decree Law 8/1983 of November 30 established the legal framework for a restructuring program that privatized and let unviable firms in 11 large sectors fail. Most of these sectors had been preferential industries under the development plans of the two previous decades. Therefore, the strategy signaled the end of the state-directed industrialization era. Third, the orthodox economists liberalized product markets by introducing legislation that enabled foreigners to invest in most manufacturing industries under the same conditions as resident Spaniards (Royal Decree Law 1,265/1986 of June 27). Fourth, during this period, the government initiated a program of partial or full privatizations. Among the privatized firms was Telefonica, Spain's incumbent telecommunications operator and the country's largest publicly listed firm (Garcia Calvo, 2021). Fifth, Spain's shift toward economic pragmatism and integration in the world economy was manifested in the PSOE's impulse for EU accession.

Market-conforming measures found continuation in the conservative party (Popular Party–Partido Popular [PP]) governments that took over the PSOE between 1996 and 2004. The most notorious liberal measures during this period were a round of privatizations involving 60 firms for a value equivalent to 6.7 percent of Spain's GDP (Estefanía, 2010). The firms that were privatized during this period included some of Spain's most prominent companies in the fields of telecommunications, energy, tobacco, and banking.

However, these accounts only tell part of the story. In sharp contrast to its liberal stance toward financial markets and most manufacturing sectors, the

Spanish government sheltered complex service sectors such as banking and telecommunications from foreign competition for a critical period during the 1980s and 1990s. Protection gave local firms precious time to address their competitive deficiencies and undertake internal restructuring. For example, Royal Decree 1,388/1978 of June 23 enabled the establishment of foreign banks in Spain, but limited to three the number of branches they could open, established a cap on the amount of funding they could obtain from foreign markets, and restricted their ability to invest directly on Spanish firms. Furthermore, authorization for the entry of foreign banks depended on the discretional authorization by the government. Not considering this enough, in 1984, the BoS placed a moratorium on foreign bank entry, arguing that "financial markets had reached a point of saturation by foreign banks (arbitrarily set at 14 percent of the credit market)" (Pérez, 1997, p. 147). Restrictions were not fully lifted until 1993, giving banks over a decade and a half since the start of the banking crisis to restructure and prepare for a fully competitive environment.

Similarly, the liberalization of telecommunications, which took place in 1998 under an international World Trade Organization agreement, was managed in ways that protected Telefonica, the incumbent operator. Although the government sold half of its stake in the operator between 1985 and 1987, the 1987 Communications Act left no doubt that Spain was not moving toward an arm's length model by stating that telecommunications continued to be "essential services, owned by the state, and managed by the public sector" (Law 31/1987 of December 18, Article 2.1). In fact, the state continued to exert control over Telefonica's strategic direction by continuing to appoint its CEO. After Telefonica's full privatization in 1998, the state also maintained a degree of control over the operator through the enactment of a golden share (Law 5/1995 of March 23), which enabled the government to veto any purchases of 10 percent or more of Telefonica's capital. The government used Law 5/1995 in 2000 to block a proposed merger between Telefonica and KPN (Vitzthum, 2000). The golden share rule was only revoked in 2003 by a European court ruling (*Commission of the European Communities vs. Kingdom of Spain CASE C-463/00*) that the government did not transpose into Spanish law for an additional three years (Law 13/2006 of May 26).

It would be tempting to see the temporary sheltering of complex services, such as banking and telecommunications, as an exception within a broader pattern of upgrading driven by restructuring, liberalization, and privatization. However, this becomes difficult to sustain when one looks at the types of industries in which Spanish firms have become globally competitive.

In 2020, 28 out of the 35 firms listed in the IBEX 35, Spain's blue-chip stock index, operate in complex services such as banking, telecommunications, utilities, software, media, and civil engineering. Only seven of the 35 listed companies operate in manufacturing sectors.

1.3.1.2 The Liberal Perspective in Korea

The liberal argument also explains three waves of liberalization measures adopted by Korea in the 1980s and 1990s. The first wave, in the early 1980s, involved prize stabilization to address the consequences of the oil crises and the excesses of the HCI drive. These measures included an initial rise in interest rates, currency devaluation, price controls, a wage freeze for civil servants and industrial workers, and decreased subsidies and tax benefits to large firms (Sakong, 1993). In addition to macroeconomic stabilization, the first wave of liberalization involved a battery of additional measures to severe direct ties with banks, reduce firm dependence on policy loans (public loans to manufacturers at very low or even negative interest rates), diversify firms' sources of capital, liberalize product markets, and change the direction of industrial policy.

Between 1981 and 1983, the state sold its shares on all nationwide commercial banks, issued licenses for two new commercial banks, and relaxed the requirements for establishing non-bank financial institutions (NBFIs), leading to the creation of 69 new NBFIs between 1982 and 1983 alone (Park, 1994). Furthermore, the government initiated the phasing out of policy loans while introducing financial market reforms that enabled firms to tap into new sources of capital. Thus, in 1982, the state unified all bank loan rates into one, which made policy loans less attractive, and in 1984, the state froze the total amount of bank credit available to the top five *chaebol*, Korea's large, diversified business groups, and set ceilings for the top 30 (Park and Kim, 1994). To diversify corporate sources of credit, from 1984, the government required firms to repay bank loans with funds raised through stocks and bonds, which compelled firms to become publicly listed. From 1985, Korean firms were also allowed to issue bonds in international markets (Park, 1994).

The Korean government also took some steps to liberalize product markets and incentivize competition. Within Korea, the government signaled its intention to support competition through the creation of the Fair Trade Commission in 1981 (Law No. 3320, December 31, 1980). Market liberalization took place primarily through incentives for inward and outward FDI. To encourage inward FDI, the Foreign Investment and Foreign Capital Inducement Act (Law No. 3691, 1983) shifted from a list of pre-approved sectors in which foreign investors were able to invest, to a negative list system of sectors in which foreigners could not invest. It also simplified administrative processes for investors and introduced investment incentives, such as tax benefits and guarantees on the repatriation of dividends. These measures halved the number of industries in which foreigners were unable to invest between 1980 and 1985 (Nicolas, Thomsen, and Bang, 2013). To encourage outward FDI, the government eliminated permissions for outward investments of less than US$2 million, increased ceilings for overseas investment credits provided by the Export-Import Bank of Korea, introduced overseas investment insurance policies, and created the Overseas Investment Research Institution to provide information and consultation on foreign investments (KIET, 1989). Finally, the 1986 Industrial Development Act shifted the direction of industrial policy by moving from industry-specific inducements to activity-specific fiscal and financial incentives in areas such as R&D, training, and energy-saving, irrespective of economic activity (KIET, 1989).

Under the *segyehwa* (globalization) label, President Kim Young Sam launched a second wave of liberalization starting in 1993. The liberal penchant of Kim's government is reflected in the dismantling of the Economic Planning Board (EPB), the super ministry responsible for Korea's multi-annual development plans, in 1994 (Wade, 1998), the liberalization of short-term capital flows in 1993, which brought in a torrent of foreign low-cost credit (Shin and Chang, 2003), and plans to further liberalize FDI as part as Korea's commitment to join the OECD in 1996 (Kim and Wang, 1996).

These measures, particularly the liberalization of short-term inflows of capital, were the main causes of Korea's debacle during the 1997 Asian crisis (Shin and Chang, 2003). The crisis forced the Korean government to seek financial assistance from the International Monetary Fund (IMF), launching a third wave of liberalization (Eichengreen, Lim, Park, and Perkins, 2015). Measures adopted in the late 1990s included macroeconomic tightening (higher taxes, lower government spending, higher real interest rates), structural reforms in the financial sector, labor markets, and corporate governance, and further liberalization of the trade regime (Wade, 1998; Chang, 2006). The drop in Korea's FDI Regulatory Restrictiveness Index between 1997 and 2003 from 0.532 to 0.148 illustrates the extent of these changes (OECD FDI Regulatory Restrictiveness Index, 2020).

As was the case in Spain, however, the liberal argument only tells half the story. Policy measures to transform the banking sector, introduce elements of market competition, and restructure the chaebol during the 1980s were not far reaching, and their implementation was often halting and incomplete (Amsden and Euh, 1993; Shin and Chang, 2003). Although the government formally privatized large banks in the early 1980s, it continued to influence them indirectly through methods such as discounted lending from the Bank of Korea, Korea's central bank, controls over the banks' lending interest rates, and the practice of appointing managers to large banks (Ubide and Baliño, 1999). These and other measures enabled the government to continue using the banking system to channel credit to productive industry until the third wave of reforms. The 1997 financial crisis and the ensuing reforms did not spell the end of financial activism either. On the contrary, in the 2010s, state-owned banks accounted for 25 percent of all loans in the Korean financial system and made low-interest loans to Korean firms, usually on the basis of performance (Thurbon, 2016).

Similarly, although trade restrictions were relaxed in the 1980s and then again in preparation for accession to the OECD in 1996, in 1997, Korea still ranked second after China in terms of regulatory restrictions to FDI (Nicolas, Thomsen and Bang, 2013). In fact, the country generally continued to discourage FDI (Shin and Chang, 2003). Trade liberalization accelerated after 1997, but in 2018, Korea still ranked sixth among OECD countries in terms of regulatory restrictions, with a restrictiveness index that is more than twice the OECD average (OECD FDI Regulatory Restrictiveness Index dataset, 2020). FDI stocks and inflows are also significantly lower than would be expected for a country the size of Korea. A preference for purchasing local products and the persistence of numerous behind-the-border barriers contribute to Korea's limited inflow of FDI.

Not only does the liberal argument not tell the whole story, but it also fails to unpack the mechanisms through which Korean firms in complex industries managed to develop the set of skills, capabilities, and resources they needed to shift from competing on the basis of costs to competing on the basis of advanced product features, complex processes, and efficient organizations. For example, in 1985, consumer products and parts and components accounted for over 80 percent of Korea's ICT production and the lion's share of exports (Electronics Industry Association of Korea using data from the customs office, 1985). Local innovation consisted mostly of knowledge transfer, absorption, and adaptation to local production conditions (Ernst, 1994; Kim and Wang, 1996). Even if liberalization was responsible for upgrading, market opening alone does not explain how Korean firms developed the research capacity necessary to generate rather than assimilate and adapt innovation, addressed shortages of specialized talent, developed sufficient knowledge of R&D management, established channels to process and disseminate innovation, and gained access to the international innovation networks necessary to develop knowledge-intensive equipment for telecommunications networks.

1.3.2 The Developmental State Perspective

The limitations of the liberal argument have led other scholars to turn to the DS argument to explain Spain's, and especially Korea's, upgrading. Authors writing along these lines criticize the liberal view for downplaying the role of government in mobilizing and allocating resources in late industrializing economies (Rodrik, 1997, 2017; Chang, 2002, 2011; Gerschenkron, 1962). Instead, they present a view of upgrading based on proactive states, coherent bureaucracies, and linkages to business (Johnson, 1982; Amsden, 1989; Evans, 1995; Haggard, 1990, 2018; Wade, 1990, 2018). The DS argument is also associated with transformation strategies that pursue the development of "local manufacturing capacity, technological autonomy, and export competitiveness" (Thurbon, 2016, p. 16).

1.3.2.1 The Developmental State Perspective in Spain

The DS argument is consistent with the salience of Spain's high corps of civil servants in the country's economic transformation. Paramount among within the structure of the civil service is the High Corps of State Economists and Trade Experts, possibly the most prestigious of Spain's elite civil service branches. This corps attracts highly qualified economists who are responsible for the elaboration and implementation of economic and trade policies. Civil servants from this corps were responsible for the elaboration of the 1959 Stabilization Plan that led to Spain's membership in the Breton Woods institutions, the developmental plans of the 1960s and 1970s, and the implementation of the Moncloa Pacts (1977), the political agreements that contained the main lines of Spain's economic transformation into an open economy. Individuals belonging to this corps have also played a pivotal role in Spain's transformation since the 1980s. One of them, Luís Angel Rojo, recruited and mentored the cohesive group of orthodox economists who held the reins of Spain's economic transformation (Garcia Calvo, 2016). Rojo's position as sub-governor and then governor of the BoS (1988–2000), together with the rise of his mentees to prominent positions within government, ensured a high level of coherence between the government's economic policymaking and the BoS's monetary policy.

The DS argument is also consistent with the presence of deep linkages between Spanish government officials and decision makers in the private sector. These linkages are especially strong with Spain's large private banks (Pérez, 1997; Pons Brías, 1999, 2002). In fact, until the enactment of Law 30/1980 of 21 June, there was no explicit system of incompatibilities between public and private employment in the banking sector, and it was common for professional bankers to take up positions in the governing organs of the BoS (Pérez, 1997). Public–private symbiosis continues to be a defining feature of the relationship between Spanish economists and the banking sector. For example, microprudential supervision is based "on the principle of establishing a close relationship to the firms through trust and knowledge exchange" (Bank of Spain, 2009). In practice, and until supervisory functions were transferred to the European Central Bank in 2014, this principle was operationalized through a team of inspectors who worked full-time at the supervised banks (Bank of Spain, 2009). Two additional institutions provide the basis for continuous interpersonal relationships and dialogue between public and private bankers. The first is the Foundation for Applied Economic Studies (FEDEA), a research foundation financed by the BoS along with large banks and other Spanish corporations. FEDEA's strength is its ability to bring together economists affiliated with top higher education institutions around the world. The second is the Center for Monetary and Financial Studies (CEMFI), a private postgraduate educational foundation created by the BoS in 1987 in response to the need for highly qualified specialists in economics at the central bank and elsewhere in the Spanish economy. CEMFI is a direct source of talent for the central bank and the private sector (Garcia Calvo, 2016).

Within a DS logic, these features help explain Spain's upgrading in complex services sectors such as banking. However, several other features of Spain's trajectory turn the DS argument on its head. One of the most salient features of the economic architects of Spain's transformation was their economic orthodoxy and their explicit rejection of the developmental approach through which Spain had industrialized in the previous decades (Pérez, 1997). In addition, the argument does not unpack the mechanisms through which the state used protectionism in complex services to compel large, publicly listed firms to upgrade rather than remain complacent and enjoy the benefits of their sheltered position. This is particularly puzzling given that Spain's upgrading took place in highly concentrated sectors in which individual firms exercise a fair degree of market power. For instance, in the case of banking, the largest seven banks had a decades-long history of operating as an organized cartel (Pérez, 1997). The question is even more obvious in telecommunications services, in which, unlike banking, the country did not have either a specialized ministry for telecommunications or a high corps responsible or knowledgeable about telecommunications, and policy decision-making was delegated directly to Telefonica's employees by virtue of a 1946 contract between the operator and the state (Garcia Calvo, 2021).

Even more conspicuously, Spain's upgrading in complex services and the country's rapid loss of manufacturing capacity contradict the expectation that upgrading should take place through manufacturing. The early and thorough liberalization of product markets, a chronic trade deficit in manufacturing, high rates of inward FDI, and low levels of R&D investment compared to other advanced nations also fail to conform to the expectation of pursuing upgrading through technological autonomy and export competitiveness. Finally, because the argument does not expect a pattern of upgrading that deviates from the techno-industrial approach, it also cannot gauge whether Spain's strategy was equivalent, better, or worse.

1.3.2.2 The Developmental State Perspective in Korea

The DS argument explains well the continuation of Korea's industrial policy in complex industries such as electronics. Korea's strategy for ICT consisted primarily of a series of large-scale technology development projects that aimed to foster "technological and manpower development" (EPB, 1981, p. 14). As predicted by the argument, these plans were designed by a proactive state. From the early 1980s, the Ministry of Communications assumed an elevated status within Korea's ministerial structure. The minister and the vice-minister were trained engineers and had a direct, open line to the president (Oh and Larson, 2011). The ministry's plans were implemented by a cohesive, high-caliber, specialized civil service, many members of which had been educated in US schools and worked in some of the world's most advanced electronic research labs, including the iconic Bell Labs (Kim, 2012). Plans were also supported by the resources of the EPB until its dissolution in 1994 (Oh and Larson, 2011) and by a tight-knit network of ministry-affiliated think tanks, public research institutions, and a world-class engineering school (Kim and Leslie, 1998). The implementation of this strategy is directly related to Korea's upgrading in electronics manufacturing and the emergence of two large competitive firms: Samsung Electronics and LG (Garcia Calvo, 2021).

In addition, the DS argument justifies the limited impact of public bank privatizations in the early 1980s and the revival of credit activism in the aftermath of the 1997 crisis via a network of public financial institutions, such as the Korea Development Bank and the Export-Import Bank of Korea (Thurbon, 2016). More broadly, the DS argument and its characterization of techno-industrial upgrading is consistent with Korea's pattern of upgrading in complex manufacturing sectors such as electronics and automotive. It also correlates well with the country's low levels of FDI stock and inflows, its high levels of R&D relative to GDP, the slight increase in manufacturing as a percentage of GDP since the mid-1980s, and Korea's sustained commercial surplus in goods.

However, as in the case of Spain, the DS argument does not explain the whole story. The DS literature cannot explain how the state managed to compel privately-owned, publicly listed, increasingly sophisticated firms in industries such as electronics or automotive to follow its direction, especially as the development and liberalization of capital markets and internationalization made firms independent and increased their market dominance. This is particularly true after 1997, when Korea unraveled the connection between the state, large banks, and large firms, which had been at the core of the country's developmental system (Shin and Chang, 2003). In addition, the argument does not explain how the state continued to make itself useful as firms developed in-house innovation capabilities and therefore required less external support. Finally, while the DS argument can connect the role of the state with positive upgrading outcomes in manufacturing industries, it does not explain why state activism seems to have been counterproductive to the development of complex services such as banking.

1.4 State–Firm Coordination and Upgrading

Understanding the process through which Spain and Korea upgraded to reach advanced country status and came to host firms that are globally competitive in skill-, capital-, and knowledge-intensive industries requires that we overcome the market versus state dichotomy by identifying both states and large firms as necessary but not sufficient to foster upgrading in the post-1980s context. We can then focus on exploring why and how states and firms coordinated their actions and chose their strategies, enabling firms to move up GVCs and Spain and Korea to become advanced economies.

To do this, we need a bottom-up perspective that starts with an understanding of the productive structures of the two countries, the resources and capabilities Spanish and Korean firms needed to upgrade, and the reasons why they required state support to access or develop those resources. We can then switch to analyzing the characteristics, motivations, and goals of states to understand why they cooperated with firms, and why Spain's and Korea's governments adopted different strategies for upgrading.

The construction of this argument proceeds in four steps. The first is to situate firms at the center of the analysis and acknowledge firm agency

(Hancké, 2001; Hall and Soskice, 2001). Reaching advanced country status depends on the ability of local firms to move up within GVCs. Firms are responsible for generating and capturing the additional value-added that translates into sustainable growth, high-quality jobs, and higher living standards. Therefore, understanding firms and the resources they need to compete globally is essential to understand how Spain and Korea became advanced countries.

Not all firms are equally important. During their industrialization, the Spanish and Korean governments relied on close partnerships with a small community of large, local firms to further their developmental goals. In return, these governments bestowed benefits that enabled large firms to thrive (Amsden, 1989; Pérez, 1997). Today, these firms play a central role in the Spanish and Korean economies and dominate the types of industries in which the two countries have become globally competitive. The book concentrates on these large, systemic firms.

Competition usually takes place at the level of the industry. This means the skills, assets, and incentives that firms need to upgrade are determined at the industry rather than at the firm level (Porter, 1990). Accordingly, the book examines the trajectories of large firms within the context of the sectors within which they operate. The research focuses on upstream sectors characterized by high capital and skill intensity, concentration of activities in a few large firms, dense connections to other sectors, and centrality to a country's economy. Sectors with these characteristics are more likely to accelerate the rate at which a country can absorb ideas and new knowledge and, therefore, the speed of both upgrading and development. Amsden (1989) argues that low-capital and low-skill sectors, such as textiles, have a limited capacity for upscaling because they can maximize and sustain their profit over relatively long periods of time through capacity expansion rather than through costly qualitative process changes, skill improvements, or investment in the latest-generation equipment. In addition, low skills are difficult to apply to other activities and thus offer low potential for diversification. Zysman (1983) adds that sectors dominated by a few large firms are more likely to contribute to national changes in competitive advantage because they are more prone to unraveling investment patterns in physical or market infrastructures in order to establish a competitive position in the market. These investments accumulate over time, leading to changes in comparative advantage and, ultimately, upgrading. Zysman (1983), Hausmann, Hwang, and Rodrik (2006), and Hidalgo and Hausmann (2009) also argue that deep linkages to other sectors make certain industries more likely to transform a whole economy by transmitting change through proximity and interdependence mechanisms. Finally, Whitley (1999) tangentially mentions centrality to a country's economy or control of key resources within a national institutional context as a key attribute for wealth generation.

Specifically, the research is based on in-depth analyses of three sectors that are central to the economies of Spain and Korea and illustrate fundamental aspects of the two countries' models. The three sectors are banking, information and communications technologies (ICT), and the automotive industry. The structure of credit markets is a fundamental component of different forms of capitalism. Spain's and Korea's different underlying perceptions of the banking sector as either an industry on its own right or an instrument to support productive industry are at the center of a fundamental difference between the two countries' approaches to upgrading. ICT's combination of services and manufacturing showcases incompatibilities between the needs of firms operating in complex services and manufacturing even within a single industry, the tradeoffs national governments face in supporting either type of industry, and their impact on national productive specializations. The complexity of the auto industry, and Spain's and Korea's different structures within it serve as a platform to explore the role of external linkages in shaping industrial specialization and their contribution to define the two country's production structures.

After large firms are brought to the center of the argument, the next step is to establish the types of capabilities and resources Spanish and Korean firms needed to upgrade and whether the state was necessary to support that process. This analysis requires a deep understanding of competition mechanisms within each of the three industries selected, and the situation of large Spanish and Korean firms at the time of the analysis. The research finds that firms faced important constraints in terms of technology and product development capabilities, experience with fully-fledged competitors, organizational and management capabilities, and infrastructures. Furthermore, they were unable, on their own, to develop or acquire these capabilities and resources autonomously because they depended on firms' ability to coordinate with other external actors operating at the national level, including other firms in their industry, financial entities, and legislators. However, these actors were unable or unwilling to provide firms the resources they needed to upgrade. By contrast, national governments, with their responsibility toward building and maintaining the economic architecture of the nation and with their unique powers, were uniquely positioned to bridge this gap and provide firms access to the specialized resources they needed to upgrade.

Once we establish that firms needed cooperation from the state to upgrade, the next step is to investigate why Spanish and Korean governments supported upgrading and why they pursued different strategies. To do this, the focus shifts toward the motivations and characteristics of the state. I argue that the Spanish and Korean governments supported upgrading because it enabled them to further economic goals that they could not accomplish without cooperation from firms. These goals included universalizing and overhauling basic utility infrastructures, ensuring macroeconomic stability, maintaining high levels of employment, gaining political acceptance by the international community, and increasing levels of national self-sufficiency. The result was that upgrading became a quid pro quo arrangement in which firms operating in industries that could directly contribute to the fulfillment of public goals obtained the resources and capabilities they needed to upgrade. In exchange, governments obtained cooperation from firms to further their own objectives.

Despite the common need for state–firm coordination, Spanish and Korean governments adopted different pathways to upgrading: one based on FDI, technological outsourcing, and regional integration, and another based on technological autonomy and self-sufficiency. These strategies were shaped in the first instance by the structure of the two countries' national governments and the identity and capabilities of decision makers. The DS literature shows that economic development is linked to the presence of coherent bureaucracies with well-defined career prospects (Johnson, 1982; Evans, 1995), supportive adjacent agencies (Weiss, 1998; Hall and Soskice, 2001), and elites who share a common background (Breznitz, 2007; Hancké, 2001). Industrialized economies that stood at the level of Spain and Korea in the early 1980s already had the type of coherent, highly trained bureaucracies with well-structured career pathways described by the literature. However, there remained enduring differences in the structure of their governments, the background and specialization of policy makers, and the quality and characteristics of supportive adjacent agencies. Such differences affected decision makers' perceived priorities and the capacity of the Spanish and Korean governments to implement different types of upgrading strategies.

I characterize Spain's government as generalist and Korea's as techno-industrial. The first can be described as a government in which most economic decisions are taken by ministries with broad economic powers headed by individuals with training in social sciences, such as economics and law. Because of their background and training, these policy makers tend to prioritize broad economic objectives, such as macroeconomic stability, but they often lack the specialized knowledge necessary to develop complex technical plans that support capability development in technology-intensive manufacturing industries. This effect is amplified when specialized technology competencies reside within peripheral agencies that play a vicarious role in economic decision making.

By contrast, a techno-industrial government is one that tends to have high-profile ministries headed by individuals with technical backgrounds, such as engineering or physics. Such backgrounds translate into a view of development that is associated with increases in technological capacity. Accordingly, the upgrading strategies of techno-industrial governments tend to emphasize technological prowess applied to industry. Competent, highly specialized bureaucracies and public agencies in key adjacent areas, such as education and innovation, can support the decisions of techno-industrial governments and provide them with the capacity to effectively carry out long-term strategic plans that support the development of complex, sector-specific technological competencies.

Spain's and Korea's upgrading strategies were shaped by two other factors. The first was the presence of large, prominent local firms with competitive potential. Assuming that firms tend to develop their competitive advantages in their home countries, local firms are more likely to engage with the state compared with foreign-invested firms, which always have an exit option (Porter, 1990). Large firms can also devote more resources to building a relationship with the state and exert greater influence in their favor because of their contribution to the national economy. However, there can be exceptions in those cases where foreign firms contribute resources that are inexistent locally.

The second were the two countries' linkages to more advanced countries. By linkages, I mean interactions with other nations based on geographical, geopolitical, historical, economic, and trade factors. These linkages affected the two country's pathways to upgrading because they influenced public and private preferences, market opportunities, and the likelihood of success of different strategies.

Overall, I find that Spain's strategy of FDI, technological outsourcing, regional integration, and the prioritization of complex services was shaped by the presence of large, established, local firms in complex service sectors, the generalist character of Spanish policy makers, the secondary role of specialist technical agencies, and the country's links to Europe. By contrast, Korea's strategy of technological autonomy, self-sufficiency, and the prioritization of complex manufacturing sectors was shaped by a prevalence of large local firms in manufacturing sectors, the presence of governments with a techno-industrial structure, the existence of world-class higher education and research institutions in technical areas, and the opportunities derived from Korea's close relationships with the US and Japan.

The fourth and last step, is determining why Spain and Korea succeeded where so many other countries failed. The book gauges this by looking at a broader range of socioeconomic and structural elements that strengthened policy consistency, coherence, and sustainability. An important factor behind sustainability is the identification between local business elites and insider industries. Such overlap means that, even when the benefits of upgrading strategies were not equitably distributed, firms in outsider industries were less well organized and therefore less able to articulate a viable counter-strategy. Spain's and Korea's transformations were also animated by broadly shared social aspirations to reach advanced country status combined with an enduring understanding by some elite segments across the political spectrum on the fundamental lines of how to achieve that goal. Finally, upgrading was also made possible by a substantial investment in public goods such as education, innovation, and physical infrastructures, which lowered firms' costs of upgrading, and galvanized social consensus.

1.5 Conclusions and Book Outline

The central argument of this book can now be presented more fully. Spain and Korea reached advanced country status through upgrading. This involved a process by which firms in complex, upstream industries progressively shifted from lower to higher value-added activities within GVCs. Upgrading required deep, sustained coordination between large, local firms in these industries and the state. Coordination took the form of quid pro quo exchanges by which firms gained access to the socially-embedded resources and capabilities they needed to reach the efficiency frontier, and states furthered industry-specific and broader economic objectives of their own.

Within such collaborative frameworks, Spain and Korea were still able to pursue different pathways to upgrading. Spain chose a pathway that was based on FDI, technological outsourcing, and integration with Europe. This approach facilitated upgrading in complex service sectors, such as banking and telecommunications services, but led to a sharp decrease in manufacturing capacity. By contrast, Korea pursued a strategy based on technological autonomy and self-sufficiency. This approach supported upgrading in manufacturing sectors but left many service sectors underdeveloped and underperforming. Spain's and Korea's upgrading strategies enabled both countries to reach advanced country status and allowed firms across multiple (albeit different) industries to become globally competitive.

The rest of this book develops these arguments in detail. Chapter 2 conceptualizes upgrading in the context of late industrializing economies and tells the story of Spain's and Korea's upgrading from the point of view of the book's argument. Chapters 3–5 explain the key aspects of the argument in detail and constitute the empirical core of the book. Chapter 3 concentrates on the banking industry. This chapter connects Spain's and Korea's pathways to upgrading with two different perceptions of the role of the banking industry. The first considers banking as an industry on its own right with high potential for upgrading. The second regards the banking sector as an instrument for the provision of patient capital to manufacturing. The chapter argues that these perceptions not only conditioned strategies for the transformation of the banking sector in the two countries, but given the role of capital as an input for production, they also had a major effect on the two countries' broader upgrading strategies.

Chapter 4 focuses on the ICT industry. ICT's combination of services and manufacturing, and Spain's and Korea's specializations within it, showcase the impact of the two countries' different strategies on their national production structures. The discussion focuses on two institutional elements that shaped Spain's and Korea's strategies: the techno-industrial and generalist organization of each country's government and national differences in their preexisting industrial structure.

Chapter 5 is dedicated to the automotive industry. The chapter explores the role of external linkages in upgrading. The chapter shows that Spain's strong desire to be accepted in the international community motivated the creation of a large, export-oriented industry involving foreign assemblers and a number of globally competitive, local, turnkey suppliers. By contrast, Korea's long-standing history of foreign interference inspired a desire for self-sufficiency that led the country to pursue the development of a local automaker that also controls a large, local supplier industry.

Chapters 6 and 7 reflect and expand on the empirical analysis. Chapter 6 uses short examples of a broad range of industries in complex services and high value-added manufacturing sectors to present a more general position about the Spanish and Korean models. The second portion of the chapter contrasts Spain's and Korea's successful upgrading with Brazil's less successful trajectory to tease out the contribution of a broader range of socioeconomic and structural factors to upgrading. Chapter 7 pulls together the threats of the argument, explores its implications beyond Spain and Korea, and briefly discusses the two countries' main post-upgrading challenges.

2

Rethinking Spain and Korea through a State–Firm Coordination Perspective

2.1 Upgrading and State–Firm Coordination

The liberal and the DS arguments provide useful tools to understand some specific aspects of Spain's and Korea's transformations. However, neither approach provides a satisfactory explanation of how firms overcame their competitive deficiencies and why Spain and Korea pursued different pathways to become advanced economies.

This is because neither perspective characterizes upgrading as a coordination problem between firms and states. Market dynamics and public policies determine the parameters within which upgrading takes place, but ultimately governments and firms are necessary to bring about upgrading and their actions are inherently interdependent. Firms are responsible for generating the type of wealth and the high-quality jobs that enable national economies to grow for long stretches of time, raising citizen's standards of living. Without competitive firms operating at the efficiency frontier, governments cannot expect to deliver on their strategic objectives to reach advanced country status. Likewise, governments are responsible for building the economic architecture of their nation and for designing and implementing the policies that generate the socially-embedded factors that firms need to develop complex advantages. Therefore, without supportive governments, firms are unlikely to reach the top echelons of their respective industries.

This chapter retells the story of Spain's and Korea's upgrading from the point of view of state–firm coordination. The chapter starts in section 2.2 by taking the perspective of Spanish and Korean firms and the competitive limitations they faced within their respective industries. Section 2.3 reframes upgrading as a coordination problem and examines why coordination was likely to take place through quid pro quo exchanges between states and firms. Section 2.4 then discusses what factors led Spain and Korea to adopt different upgrading strategies. The section focuses on three factors: the identities and capabilities of Spanish and Korean governments, the role of

State-Firm Coordination and Upgrading: Reaching the Efficiency Frontier in Skill-, Capital-, and Knowledge-Intensive Industries in Spain and South Korea. Angela Garcia Calvo, Oxford University Press. © Angela Garcia Calvo 2021. DOI: 10.1093/oso/9780198864561.003.0002

pre-existing production structures, and external linkages with more advanced economies. Section five evaluates Spain's and Korea's upgrading strategies and their long-term outcomes. Finally, section 2.5 summarizes and sets the stage for the empirical portion of the book.

2.2 Situating Spain's and Korea's Firms

In the first half of the 1980s, large Spanish and Korean firms operating in complex industries had important limitations in terms of technology, product development capabilities, processes and skills, experience with competition, scale efficiencies, organizational and management capabilities, and infrastructures. Furthermore, firms operated on the basis of low costs and mid-quality products that were not always competitive outside national borders.

Spanish and Korean firms had significant technology, product development, process, and skills deficiencies. These limitations forced firms in complex industries, especially in manufacturing, to develop tie-ins with foreign firms. For instance, Spain's two largest automotive manufacturers produced under foreign license (García Ruíz, 2001), and three of the four largest Spanish electronics manufacturers were also joint ventures (Adanero, 2006). Similarly, the three largest Korean automakers produced through joint ventures (Guillén, 2010). The third, the Hyundai Motor Company (HMC), outsourced all or most elements in its earliest models to other companies (Back, 1990; Amsden and Kang, 1995). In the early 1990s, the two largest Korean electronics firms also relied on foreign machinery and equipment, imported or sourced basic components, and other raw materials for production (Bloom, 1992).

Spanish and Korean firms had relatively little exposure to foreign competition or external markets. Until Spain's accession to the EU in 1986, automotive suppliers were protected by local content rules of around 50–55 percent of the value of the car (García Ruíz, 2001). Most Spanish suppliers had no export-oriented strategy or a relevant international presence (Lagendijk, 1995). Similarly, in 1983, Spanish ICT manufacturers produced primarily for the local market and exported only 15 percent of their production (Adanero, 2006). Korea shifted to export promotion in the first half of the 1980s (Korea Institute for Industrial Economics and Trade [KIET], 2014). Until 1984, Korean automakers focused exclusively on the local market, where they operated unencumbered thanks to high tariff barriers for imported vehicles (KIET, 2014). Korean producers of electronics increased their exports rapidly in the first half of the 1980s, primarily as original equipment manufacturers specialized in consumer products such as microwave ovens (Bloom, 1992).

Given Spain's and Korea's relative economic development, a focus on internal markets meant that Spanish and Korean manufacturing firms had difficulties reaching scale efficiencies. For instance, in 1980 the entire production of the Korean auto industry was only 123,000 vehicles (Hyun, 2018).

Spanish and Korean firms in complex manufacturing competed on labor costs. In 1988, the hourly compensation for Spanish automotive workers was 23 percent lower than France's, 53 percent lower than Germany's, 20 percent lower than Italy's, and 12 percent lower than the UK's (Pallarés-Barberá, 1998). Until 1987, low wages and long working hours were a critical component of Korean firms' competitive strategy (Yang, 2018) and government-imposed labor repression was systematic (Kim, 2003; Kim, 1997). After Korea's democratization, industrial wage increases became a central point of a militant labor movement leading to wage increases of 133 percent between 1987 and 1999 alone (Steers, 1999).

Spain's and Korea's manufacturers produced bare-bones, moderately priced products that served the needs of "low income, unsophisticated consumers prevalent in underdeveloped countries" (Bueno Lastra y Ramos Pérez, 1986, p. 83). Outputs suffered from deficiencies in terms of precision, durability, functional versatility, and finish. (KIET, 1989; Garcia Ruiz 2001; Green, 1992).

Due to the nature of their businesses and widespread protectionism, firms in complex services faced more intense limitations in terms of organizational efficiencies, advanced skills, size, and experience with competition. These constraints were not unique to Spain and Korea but they were more intense than those experienced by firms in more advanced economies. Network industries such as telecommunications services also lagged behind their peers in more advanced countries with regard to network coverage, equipment, and quality of service (Garcia Calvo, 2021). In addition, banks had limited experience with credit risk evaluation, due to the legacies of state-directed investment in the two countries (Pérez, 1997; Garcia Calvo, 2016; Haggard, Lim and Kim, 2003).

2.3 Upgrading as a Coordination Problem

If Spain and Korea were to become advanced countries, their firms needed to overcome these limitations and shift from competing on the basis of costs and privileged access to markets, to competing on the basis of complex advantages based on processes, organizational efficiencies, and advanced product features (Porter, Sachs, and McArthur, 2002). To do so, firms needed to expand their stock of capabilities and resources and integrate and reconfigure internal and external resources, organizational skills, and functional competences (Barney, 1991; Teece, 2007).

Generally speaking, manufacturing firms needed to develop research and product development capabilities, engage specialized, experienced talent, raise patient capital for the development of new and complex products, and secure stable demand. Many firms also needed to downsize and upskill their workforce, expand their range of outputs and geographical reach, develop a competitive culture, and modernize and make more efficient use of technological advancements. In addition, service firms operating in network industries needed to expand and modernize their infrastructure, which involved raising massive amounts of capital, obtaining the necessary permits, and buy licenses to expand their range of services.

Firm level features such as size and internal organization were important in enabling Spanish and Korean firms to build their stocks of capabilities and resources. The diversified structure of the chaebol was a positive advantage, because it provided firms access general resources such as patient capital and talent with general managerial skills (Leff, 1978; Khanna and Yafeh, 2007). The bold, can-do attitude of Korean leaders (Steers, 1999; Chang, 2008) and the innovative, discreet, diplomatic, and decisive leadership style of their Spanish counterparts (Guillén and Tschoegl, 2008) provided the necessary impulse for the transformation of some of the most successful firms.

However, firm-level features were insufficient to foster upgrading. While business groups operating across many sectors can pool general resources, they are less effective at bridging gaps related to the acquisition of industry-specific advanced knowledge, sophisticated skills (Berger, 2013; Mazzucato, 2013), and highly specialized international knowledge networks (Kim, 2012). Yet, these factors are indispensable to build up the research and product development capabilities necessary to develop more complex outputs. In addition, while good leadership is necessary to chart the direction in which a firm strategy evolves, it is not sufficient to ensure that strategies are successfully executed.

Many of the capabilities and resources firms needed were beyond the reach of individual firms because they relied on socially embedded factors. In turn, the availability of these factors depended on coordination between firms and other external actors that operated at the national level (Hall and Soskice, 2001; Berger, 2013; Barney, 1991; Teece and Pisano, 1998; Teece, 2007, 2014, 2018). Hall and Soskice identify five spheres of coordination: industrial relations, education, corporate governance, interfirm relations, and employees. To these, in the case of late industrializing economies, we may also add others such as national innovation systems and trade regimes.

2.3.1 Upgrading and Coordination

The relational character of resources and capabilities reframes upgrading as a coordination problem. In principle, coordination between Spanish and Korean firms and other economic actors could take place through either markets (market coordination) or extensive relational links (strategic coordination) (Hall and Soskice, 2001). In the Spanish and Korean context, market coordination was unlikely to provide adequate support for upgrading. The types of resources and capabilities firms needed to move up from competing on costs to competing on the basis of complex advantages were by nature rare and imperfectly imitable (Teece, 1997). Therefore, it was virtually impossible to purchase them directly through markets. In addition, Spain and Korea still suffered from what Khana and Palepu (2000) call "institutional voids," which made it very difficult for firms to obtain the resources they need from their local ecosystems. Spain and Korea suffered gaps in at least two areas: industrial relations and innovation systems. The gap in industrial relationship derived from the two countries' dictatorial regimes, which had all but forbidden the development of free union movements (Yang, 2018). Gaps in national innovation systems derived from the nature of late industrialization, which relied on absorbing, rather than generating innovation (Amsden, 1989).

Finally, as Spain and Korea sought to join the global economy, the characteristics of global markets organized around GVCs unchained forces that discouraged firms in complex, capital intensive sectors from pursuing upgrading. Firms operating in the context of GVCs could maximize and sustain their profits through capacity expansion rather than through costly qualitative process changes, skill improvements, or investment in the latest-generation equipment, a dependency strategy known as the "maquiladora syndrome" (Smith, 1998). As Spain joined the EU in 1986, becoming the Mexico of Europe was a plausible option given the country's relatively low labor costs and advantageous geographical position relative to Western Europe. Similarly, as US manufacturers started to offshore production, Korean firms could have consolidated their status as original equipment manufacturers. Instead of upgrading, Spanish and Korean firms could also sell their interests to more sophisticated rivals in more advanced economies. This option was encouraged by orthodox economists and was particularly attractive for firms operating in complex industries for which the costs of upgrading were very high, but the changes of succeeding against well-established rivals from more advanced economies were slim.

If markets were unlikely to support upgrading, then upgrading would necessarily need to rely on strategic coordination. The only actor capable of orchestrating coordination effectively in Spain and Korea was the state. States are by nature responsible for building and maintaining the economic architecture of their nations and they have a unique responsibility towards the common welfare (Levy, 2006). They also have significant resources at their disposal to help firms develop socially embedded resources and capabilities because they are responsible for designing and implementing policies in areas such as industrial development, research, infrastructure, labor markets, education, and other public goods (Beramendi, 2015) which Spanish and Korean firms needed to develop complex advantages.

In addition, the Spanish and Korean governments had intrinsic, long-term motivations to change their country's standing in the world (Thurbon, 2016) and had publicly stated their desire to direct and coordinate the process (PSOE, 1982; EPB, 1981). Such public statements were more than a mere declaration of intensions because they responded to broadly-shared social aspirations in the two countries (Pérez-Diaz, 1993; Chang, 2015). Furthermore, by the second half of the 1980s, and for the first time in decades, Spanish and Korean citizens were in a position to hold their governments accountable through democratic processes.

Finally, the Spanish and Korean states had the necessary infrastructure to coordinate and implement upgrading. Such infrastructure consisted of two main components: coherent, competent, bureaucracies that shared a common background (Breznitz, 2007; Hancke, 2001), had well-defined career prospects, and appropriate linkages to business (Johnson, 1982; Evans, 1995; Wade, 1990); and supportive agencies in adjacent areas (Weiss, 1998; Hall and Soskice, 2001). The technical competence of Spanish and Korean civil servants is hardly in question. Without competent civil servants with close ties to business and politics, neither country would have successfully industrialized. Spain's High Corps of State Economists and Trade Experts had been responsible for the 1959 Stabilization Plan that led to Spain's membership in the Breton Woods institutions, the developmental plans of the 1960s and 1970s, and the implementation of the Moncloa Pacts (1977). From the 1970s, members of this group had also nurtured a cohesive network of young, orthodox economists that came to occupy top policy-making positions in the early 1980s (Termes, 1991; Garcia Calvo, 2016). Similarly, Korea's EPB had been responsible for developing and overseeing the implementation of

Korea's multiannual development plans since the 1960s and continued to support the country's transformation until its disbandment in 1994 (Wade, 1998). In addition, Korea counted on a cohesive, high-caliber, specialized civil service, many of whose members had been educated and gained practical experience in the US (Kim, 2012). These civil servants were further supported by a tight-knit network of think tanks, public research institutions, and world-class higher education institutions (Kim and Leslie, 1998).

2.3.2 Coordination and Public–Private Interdependencies

The need for state coordination did not mean a return to the hierarchically structured, state-directed models through which Spain and Korea had industrialized in the 1960s and 1970s. Those models, which had been based on state dominance over firms (Wade, 1990; Haggard, 1990) were no longer fit for purpose. Ongoing processes of market liberalization, privatization, and globalization were in the process of eliminating traditional sources of state power such as coordination of investment decisions, control over cross-border financial flows, and wage repression, which had been central to the success of Spain's and Korea's former developmental models (Shin and Chang, 2003). In addition, Spanish and Korean firms had gained power as a result of their sheer size, newfound financial independence, deep knowledge of technically complex products and services and rapidly changing competitive environments (Coe and Yeung, 2015; Garcia Calvo, 2021).

Upgrading was also unlikely to stem from a coordination model in which firms captured the state and controlled the policy-making process because such models are typically associated with low levels of innovation and competitiveness (Hellman and Kaufmann, 2001) that are incompatible with the types of outcomes we observe in Spain and Korea.

Instead, this book shows that coordination in the Spanish and Korean models was based on quid pro quo exchanges and interdependencies between states and firms (Weiss, 1998). In these interdependent models, national governments and firms exercised control over their decisions and came to develop a set of mutually agreed-upon working rules that enabled both parties to reach beneficial outcomes. Insider firms participating in these agreements developed new sources of competitive advantage, avoided unwanted acquisitions, became technologically autonomous, and generated profits. Governments achieved objectives related to international recognition, autonomy from foreign interference, macroeconomic stability, infrastructure development, long-term growth, and employment generation while also delivering on overarching goals related to higher standards of living and national status in the world arena.

The interdependent nature of state–firm interactions opened the door to national institutional variation since firms and governments in the two countries could reach different agreements to govern their relationship. In turn, Institutional variation opened the door to diverse policies, enabling Spain and Korea to pursue different pathways to upgrading.

2.4 Diverse Coordination and Alternative Pathways to Upgrading

As detailed in Chapter 1, Spain's pathway to upgrading was based on an "integrational" strategy based on attracting FDI, outsourcing technological development, and joining EU-wide value chains. Korea's pathway consisted instead of a "techno–industrial" approach that emphasized self-sufficiency and the development of local technological capabilities. These pathways enabled firms in insider industries to gain access to the resources they needed to overcome their competitive limitations, but in doing so, they constraint the ability of firms in other industries to access other types of resources they needed to achieve comparable outcomes, resulting in characteristic patterns of production specialization in complex services and manufacturing.

Spain's and Korea's choices of strategy were based on a combination of two logics. The first was the "logic of appropriateness" (March and Olsen, 1989), which is a sense of what is suitable and feasible according to the characteristics, identities, and capabilities of states and large firms. Building on Akamatsu's (1962) flying geese framework, I call the second the "logic of socialization", or the tendency to follow a strategy that is at least compatible with if not similar to those of the more advanced economies with which the late industrializing economies have particularly tight geographical, geopolitical, historical, economic, or commercial relationships.

In Spain and Korea, these two logics operated through three mechanisms: the identities and capabilities of policy decision makers, the characteristic of pre-existing production structures, and linkages with more advanced economies. These mechanisms defined the types of firms and industries that became insiders to the system, the choice between integration and self-sufficiency, and each country's approach to technological development.

2.4.1 Identity and Capabilities of Public Decision Makers

For the most part, Spain and Korea prioritized industries whose needs were directly aligned with the background, training, and expertise of policy decision makers, the structure of the civil service, and that of adjacent institutions. This is because the state's ability to provide direction and coordination for economic policy depends on the organizational capabilities, knowledge, and skills of policy decision makers and civil servants (Rueschemeyer and Evans, 1985; Kaufmann, Kraay and Zoido-Lobaton, 1999; Evans, 1995; Lim, Haggard, and Kim, 2003). State activism also depends on the existence of tight inner circles of professionals across the high spheres of the civil service, business, and politics (Hancké, 2001, Loriaux, 2003; Jones and Sakong, 1980).

While Spain and Korea had competent policy makers and bureaucratic structures, there remained important differences in the structure of their national governments, the formal competences of policy makers, and the presence and quality of supportive adjacent agencies. These differences shaped perceived policy priorities, affected governments' ability to design and implement different types of upgrading strategies, and helped create different networks of relationships between public and private sector individuals.

By the structure of governments, this book refers to the denominations, the powers, and the status of ministries with economics functions within the country's cabinet of ministries. By the competences of policy makers, we refer primarily the educational backgrounds of ministers. Based on these two features, the book distinguishes between two types of governments: generalists and techno-industrial.

2.4.1.1 Spain's Generalist Governments

Since the first democratic government in 1976, Spanish cabinets have featured high-profile ministries of economics and industry with broad responsibilities in the areas of macroeconomics, finance, trade, energy, transportation, innovation, competitiveness, communications, and energy. The ministry of economics occupies a preeminent role within Spanish cabinets. Some legislatures have recognized this status by creating the post of deputy prime-minister for the minister of economics. Spanish ministries of economics and industry are typically headed by individuals with a generalist background in economics or law: 11 of the 12 individuals who held the post of minister of industry between 1977 and 2020, and 7 of the 8 people who held the post of minister of economics during the same period had degrees in economics, law, or both. Furthermore, five ministers, shared experiences or an educational background linked to the central bank, while seven were also civil servants at one of Spain's elite civil service corps.

The broad structure of Spanish economic ministries and the ministers' specialization in economics and law prepared them well to identify issues such as the public deficit or the severe banking crisis that started in the late 1970s and to tackle them effectively (Giokas and Pentzaropoulos, 2008; Termes, 1991). The experiences of some of Spain's ministers at the central bank also prepared them well to understand the needs of complex services sectors, especially those of the banking sector, enabled them to see banking as an industry with high potential for upgrading, and to grasp the broader, long-term implications of potentially weak or uncompetitive banks. In addition, the experiences of several ministers at the central bank involved close proximity to large banks and provided the basis for close relationships with private bankers. Furthermore, the affinity between the ministers and the members of the High Corps of State Economists and Trade Experts facilitated plan implementation.

On the other hand, Spanish economic ministers' lack of technical knowledge in fields such as engineering prepared Spanish economic decision makers less well to understand the needs and upgrading potential of complex manufacturing industries. Furthermore, the economic orthodoxy shared by most economists made them less likely to support strategies that resembled classic industrial policy plans. A generalist background in law or economics also provided insufficient training to design and implement the type of long-term, industry-specific plans that manufacturing industries needed to overcome their limitations in research and product development successfully. These weaknesses were underscored by the tendency of Spanish elite civil service corps toward insularity, the lower profile of civil servants with technical profiles in the Spanish hierarchy, and the underdevelopment of supportive institutions in key adjacent areas such as higher education and research (Rico, 2006).

Taken together, these features of Spanish governments tilted the balanced in favor of a strategy that favored upgrading in complex service sectors. Such prioritization, and especially the government's view of pivotal sectors such as banking, had important implications for upgrading in manufacturing sectors. When the needs of banks to divest from long-term investments in industry clashed with those of manufacturing firms to secure patient capital for the development of complex products, the government chose to enable the banks to divest their industrial portfolios, making it difficult for manufacturing firms to raise the capital they needed to upgrade. Over the long term, such choices had a marked effect on Spain' production structure, resulting in a distinctive pattern of upgrading in services with a sharp decline in manufacturing capacity.

2.4.1.2 Korea's Techno-Industrial Governments

Until 1994, the EPB, the super-ministry that had devised and coordinated Korea's industrial strategies in the 1960s and 1970s, concentrated most economic policy-making powers (Oh and Larson, 2011). Thereon, many of the EPB's functions were distributed across several ministries, including the ministries of economics and finance. The purpose of such distribution was to avoid an over concentration of economic powers, with the result that each of these ministries remained relatively weak and there was considerable in-fighting between them (Thurbon, 2016). The power vacuum was filled by the rise of the ministry of information and communication (MIC), know in 2021 as the ministry of science and ICT, a large ministry with responsibilities for economic policy planning, ICT policy, science, technology, and innovation. The power shift from the EPB to the MIC can be traced back to the early 1980s, when Korea abandoned its HCI effort and established a direct and privileged line of communication between the MIC minister and the president (Oh and Larson, 2011).

The positions of minister and vice minister of the MIC have since consistently been attributed to trained engineers (Garcia Calvo, 2021). The technical knowledge of the ministers, together with the power associated with an open line of communication to the president, prepared Korean decision makers well to understand the needs of firms operating in complex manufacturing industries, to design detailed, multi-year strategies that helped firms overcome limitation in the areas of research and product development, and to build working relationships with local manufacturing firms based on a common educational background.

By contrast, the ascendancy and technical background of appointed officials at the MIC, together with weakness and in-fighting between economic ministries, left Korean policy makers less well prepared to develop a framework that would ensure the growth of autonomous financial institutions. It also made them more prone to perceive upstream service sectors such as telecommunications and banking as providers of critical inputs for manufacturing rather than autonomous sectors, a feature common across Asian developmental models (Thurbon, 2016).

Since the 1980s, the capabilities of the MIC's appointed officials have been supported by a cohesive, high-caliber, civil service with additional technical skills, many of whose members have been educated in some of the US's top schools and gained practical experience in places such as Bell Labs

(Kim, 2012), the prestigious research lab network linked to AT&T. The strategic capabilities of the MIC have also been reinforced by a tight-knit network of public agencies such as the Industrial Advancement Administration, a government agency tasked with coordination, quality management, technical assistance, and standardization that played a central role in technology diffusion (Lim, 1998), ministry affiliated think tanks such as the Korea Development Institute (KDI), public research institutions such as the Electronics and Telecommunications Research Institute (ETRI), and a world-class technical school, the Korean Advanced Institute of Science and Technology (KAIST) (Kim and Leslie, 1998).

These factors tilted the balance in favor of an upgrading strategy that prioritized the interests of firms in complex manufacturing sectors such as electronics and automotive over those of complex services. As was the case in Spain, this preference meant that, when the needs of manufacturing firms clashed with those of firms in complex services, the priorities of manufacturing firms for inputs such as patient capital and stable demand were tended to first, often to the detriment of firms in services that would have preferred to invest in activities that offered more immediate prospects of profit. The result was a distinctive pattern of upgrading in which manufacturing sectors surged, while firms in complex services found it difficult to undertake a comparable transformation.

Although the identity and characteristics of governments played a determinant role in shaping Spain's and Korea's strategies, two additional factors also had significant influence: the characteristics of pre-existing production structures and the two countries' external linkages with more advanced economies.

2.4.2 Characteristics of Pre-existing Production Structures

Spain and Korea prioritized upgrading in industries or segments of industries in which there were already local, large firms. State activism is underpinned explicitly or implicitly by nationalist impulses (de Bolle and Zettlemeyer, 2019; Brazys and Regan, 2016), which makes local firms more likely to be on the receiving end of state activism. Most firms develop their competitive advantages in their home markets (Porter, 1990), making transformational strategies that support local firms more likely to be effective. Finally, large firms can devote more resources to building a relationship with the state and exert greater influence in their favor than smaller firms due to their contribution to the national economy.

In Spain, the preference for local, large firms meant prioritizing telecommunications services, where the incumbent operator was the country's largest, locally-owned firm (Amado Calvo, 2010), over producers of telecommunications equipment, which were joint ventures (Adanero, 2006). Local ownership also tilted the balance in favor of prioritizing Spanish large banks, which were locally owned, over most manufacturing industries, which depended on foreign technical assistance, equipment, and capital. Local preference also discouraged the prioritization Spanish automakers, all of which operated on the basis of technological partnerships with foreign firms.

Korea's preference for local, large firms was, if anything, more obvious than Spain's. Korea prioritized local firms even when they still depended heavily on foreign technology, raw materials and components, operated as joint ventures with foreign firms, or were not yet able to produce state-of-the-art outputs (Bloom, 1992; KIET, 2014; Steers, 1999). This is in great part due to two reasons. First, because at the time the limitations of Korean firms in complex manufacturing sectors made technological dependence unavoidable. Second, because Korean firms viewed technological partnerships as a stepping stone in the pathway to the development of local technological capabilities.

2.4.3 External Linkages with Advanced Industrialized Countries

Finally, Spain and Korea designed upgrading strategies that were consistent with the market opportunities derived from their relationships with advanced countries with which they had the closest linkages. This is because economic, historical, and social linkages influence public and private preferences, market opportunities, and the likelihood of success of different strategies.

Specifically, Spain's integrational strategy was heavily influenced by the country's desire for international recognition and integration into the EU. In addition, Korea's techno-industrial strategy was inspired by the country's relationships with the US and Japan.

Spain became a member of the EU in 1986, hardly two months before the signature of the Single European Act that pledged to establish a single market by 1993. The prospect of Spain's accession to the EU, together with comparatively low labor costs, a pre-existing industrial base, expectations of a growing local market, and a suitable geographical location to serve surrounding Western European markets, made a strategy based on attracting

FDI and exporting to surrounding European markets feasible. Spain took this route by introducing legislation that enabled foreign investors to operate in most manufacturing sectors under the same conditions as resident Spaniards. Foreign investors responded favorably: by 1992, the country's share of world FDI represented about 5–6 percent, a much higher share than Spain's 1 percent share of global GDP (United Nations Conference on Trade and Development [UNCTAD] Data Center, 2020).

The majority of foreign investment took the form of acquisitions, involved heavy downsizing, and did not necessarily serve as a platform for innovation and technological spillovers. In the electronics sector, for instance, Alcatel's acquisition of Standard Electrica involved downsizing from 23,000 to 5,000 employees (Cubero Postillo, 1992). Other investors closed the manufacturing operations of their acquired companies or transferred them abroad and used their Spanish bases instead for wholesaling and service provision. The result was a sharp decrease in manufacturing capacity: Between 1979 and 1993, Spain lost one third of its manufacturing capacity, a steeper drop than that of any other Western European economy (EU KLEMS, 2009).

Spain also had strong institutional, linguistic, and cultural linkages with its former colonies in Latin America. There is no doubt that these linkages played an important role in facilitating the international expansion of Spanish firms (Guillén and Tschoegl, 2008; Vives, 2010), but they had a limited impact on upgrading. Unlike mere increases in scale, upgrading involves the development of complex advantages, which in turn requires exposure to cutting edge technologies and organizational models. Spanish firms were unlikely to gain exposure to these factors through their expansion to less advanced countries in Latin America. In addition, size was neither a necessary nor a sufficient condition for reaching the efficiency frontier in complex services, as evidenced by the underwhelming international experiences of the British, French, and Portuguese incumbent telecommunications operators, and the rise of newer operators from countries such as Mexico (OECD *Communications Outlook*, 2013).

Korea's commitment to technological self-sufficiency and manufacturing upgrading needs to be understood in the context of the country's relationships with Japan and the US, which were Korea's largest providers of technology, components, and skill formation as well as Korea's largest export markets until the 2000s. Korea's commitment to technological self-sufficiency is also tied directly to the ebbs and flows of America's defense and trade relationship and to Korean's reverence for US higher education. President Eisenhower's "Atoms for Peace" speech, in 1953, opened up nuclear research for civilian purposes to countries that did not previously have nuclear technology and inspired Korea to develop its own nuclear energy program (Andrews-Speed, 2020). President Nixon's 1970's announcement that allies of the US were to assume the primary responsibility for their defense, and the US's subsequent unilateral reduction of troops in Korea, was also an important factor behind Korea's emphasis on dual-purpose industries such as electronics and motor-vehicles from the 1970s (Sakong, 1993; Lee and Markusen, 2003; Pai, 2004).

Furthermore, by the mid-1980s, economic developments in the US played a major role in creating market opportunities that Korean firms in manufacturing industries could hardly ignore. The US's incipient offshoring of electronics (Bloom, 1992), an industry in which American firms controlled approximately 80 percent of the market (Adanero, 2006), created a major opportunity for Korean electronics manufacturers, provided they were able to shift from consumer to much more complex professional electronics outputs. In addition, from the mid-1980s, the US's increasing protectionism in the automotive industry, in conjunction with Japanese voluntary export restrictions and high oil prices, created a market opportunity for the type of compact, fuel-efficient autos that Korean manufacturers specialized in (Green, 1992).

Key to taking advantage of opportunities in the US were human skills. Korea's emphasis on education at all levels, and the prestige associated with obtaining a US's higher education institutions became invaluable assets that Korea capitalized on by using economic incentives to induce the return of US-educated Koreans (Oh and Larson, 2011; Song, 1997).

At least three factors related to Korea's complex relationship with Japan also influenced Korea's stance on upgrading. The first was the desire to "beat Japan" a spirit rooted in the complex historical relationship between the two countries and passed on to the younger generations through the education system (Forbes and Wield, 2002). The second was Japanese technology. After the normalization of relationships between Korea and Japan in 1965, Japan became Korea's largest trading partner, investor, and technology licensor (Kim and Leslie, 1998), enabling Korea to improve the quality of manufacturing outputs. From the early 1980s, increasing Japanese reluctance to share technology with Korean firms (Bloom, 1992) also had a major influence on Korea's approach to industry, forcing firms to develop their own technology and product development capacity (Kim, 1997).

2.5 Assessing Spain's and Korea's Upgrading

Spain's and Korea's strategies enabled local firms in complex industries to overcome their limitations and become globally competitive across a number of complex industries including telecommunications services, electronics, retail banking, and automotive. In 2020, Spanish and Korean firms in these industries were amongst the world's most competitive, exercised a degree of market power, and had recognizable brand names. Wealth generated from these firms stimulated growth in adjacent economic areas, fueled long periods of growth, and enabled Spaniards and Koreans to enjoy higher standards of living than at any previous point in the two countries' modern histories. As a result, as of 2020, the economies of the two countries had similar sizes, and their citizens had attained strikingly similar levels of income per capita (Table 2.1).

But the purpose of upgrading is not to reach a predetermined end line at a given point in time. It is to ensure that the two countries generate sustainable growth, maintain or reduce the gap with the most advanced countries, and enable people to have better opportunities in life. This section evaluates Spain's and Korea's integrational and techno-industrial strategies against these goals using three criteria: the vulnerability of the two countries to external shocks, the capacity to foster sustained competitiveness, and the ability to generate stable employment.

2.5.1 Vulnerability to External Shocks

Despite important differences in Spain's and Korea's strategies, the two countries remain highly vulnerable to external shocks and sharp contractions in global demand. Spain and Korea were amongst the countries most afflicted

Table 2.1 Gross national income and population

	GNI(US$ billion)	GNI per capita (US$)	PPP GNI per capita (US$)	Population
United States	18,980	58,270	60,200	325,719,178
China	12,043	8,690	16,760	1,386,395,000
Japan	4,888	38,550	45,470	126,785,797
Germany	3,597	43,490	51,760	82,695,000
United Kingdom	2,676	40,530	43,160	66,022,273
France	2,548	37,970	43,720	67,118,648
India	2,431	1,820	7,060	1,339,180,127
Italy	1,878	31,020	40,030	60,551,416
Brazil	1,796	8,580	15,160	209,288,278
Canada	1,573	42,870	45,750	36,708,083
Korea, Rep.	1,460	27,180	38,260	51,466,201
Russian Federation	1,356	9,230	24,890	144,495,044
Spain	1,266	28,380	38,090	46,572,028

World Bank development indicators data for 2017.

by the 2008 downturn. Between mid-2008 and the end of 2009, Spain's real GDP contracted by 4.6 percent (Bank of Spain, 2017). In response, Spain implemented a battery of macroeconomic measures including fiscal consolidation, macroeconomic stability, and structural reforms (Fatás and Summers, 2016; Orphanides, 2015). The country also requested a line of credit of up to a €100 billion from the European Union to recapitalize financial institutions, of which it used €41 billion (European Commission, 2019). Korea was the Asian country most affected by the 2008 economic crisis (Shin, 2014). In the last quarter of 2008 alone, exports decreased by 40 percent and the Korean Won devaluated by 30 percent. The government responded by launching a stimulus package to soften the blow of the crisis (Alp, Elekdag, and Lall, 2012). It also negotiated a series of emergency debt swaps with the US, Japan, and China, totaling US$90 billion, to stave off a currency exchange crisis (Yoon, 2011; Shin, 2014).

By 2014 Spain and Korea had returned to growth but the crisis showcased the two countries' heavy dependence on the external environment. Spain's integrational strategy entails, by definition, a high degree of dependence on its external environment via FDI and technological outsourcing. Korea's techno-industrial approach aimed to make the country self-sufficient but in practice, the country is still heavily dependent on its relationships with the rest of the world. Exports account for half of Korea's GDP (OECD, 2018b), critical raw materials for major industries such as electronics are imported (Green, 2019), and since the Asian crisis of 1997, many manufacturing jobs have moved abroad.

Although both countries are highly vulnerable to external shocks, Spain's integrational approach confers the country some advantage over Korea's self-sufficiency. Spain's relationship with its main trading partners in the EU is embedded in a thick institutional structure that provides a high degree of trade security and helps create a climate of collaboration–competition. Korea's relationship with major trading partners, China and Japan, lacks a comparable institutional framework. This makes relationships more broadly contingent on variable political factors, as evidenced by the impact of trade disputes with China and Japan in 2019 (Song, 2019; White, 2019). The 2020 Regional Comprehensive Economic Partnership (RCEP) could eventually come to change some of these parameters, but as of 2021 it is still too soon to know.

2.5.2 Sustained Competitiveness

As Spain and Korea upgraded, their main concern was to overcome firms' competitive limitations to create complex advantages that would enable firms to reach the efficiency frontier. The purpose of this process was to enable firms to generate additional wealth with which to raise the standard of living of Spaniards and Koreans. By contrast, as Spain and Korea shift to a post-upgrading context, their goal is to maintain their status as advanced economies and continue closing the gap with the world's most advanced countries. This will depend on the capacity of firms to continue creating value through productivity growth and innovation.

Spain and Korea may continue to create value through increases in productivity. Until recently, Korea's increases in multifactor productivity have been consistently higher than Spain's (Figure 2.1), suggesting that Korea is in a better position than Spain. Nonetheless, these figures need to be taken with caution. Korea's specialization in manufacturing and Spain's specialization in services means that the figures could be overstating Korea's productivity increases, understating Spain's, or both. In addition, despite showing progressive increases, in 2018, Korea's GDP per hour worked was still 25 percent lower than Spain's (OECD, *Level of GDP per Capita and Productivity Statistics*, 2020). In practice, this means that to reach similar levels of output, Koreans work on average 292 hours a year more than Spaniards (OECD, *Labor Force Statistics*, 2020). Many attribute Korea's lower labor productivity to entrenched factors that will be difficult to change. These include antagonistic labor relations (Steers, 1999) and corporate cultures that encourage presentism and compliance (Surdej, 2015). Therefore, it is unclear whether Korea may be able to close the labor productivity gap with Spain in the short term.

The second way Spain and Korea may generate additional value is by creating knowledge that is new to the world. Spain's integration strategy encouraged firms to outsource technological development and focus on applied innovation. By contrast, Korea's techno-industrial approach, emphasized technological self-sufficiency through a deliberate emphasis

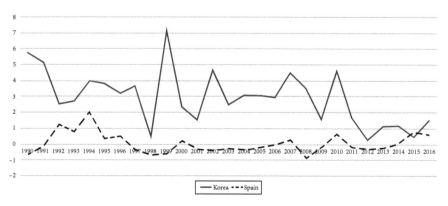

Figure 2.1 Multifactor productivity (1990–2016).

Source: OECD, Growth in GDP per capita, productivity and ULC Dataset.

on the development of innovation institutions, centrally coordinated R&D programs, and high levels of private R&D investment. This means that, in principle, Korea should outperform Spain in terms of innovation.

Korea's and Spain's figures on innovation support this interpretation. In 2018, Korea's gross domestic investment in R&D relative to GDP was 4.5 percent of its GDP, the world's second highest level after Israel (OECD, *Main Science and Technology Indicators*, 2020). By contrast, Spain's investment in R&D was only 1.2 percent of its GDP, or half the OECD average (OECD, *Main Science and Technology Indicators*, 2020). Korea also has a sophisticated innovation infrastructure to support firm's capacity to generate new knowledge.

Despite these indicators, it cannot be assumed that Spanish firms will necessarily underperform. Chapter 5 shows that while dependence on foreign-owned lead firms is a clear vulnerability, especially in times of production scale back, Spain's integration into European modular value chains creates significant opportunities for cost-efficient innovation for large Spanish suppliers with well-established reputations and pre-existing relationships to multiple lead firms. On the other hand, despite Korea's sophisticated innovation infrastructure and high investment in R&D, it is not given that Korean firms in iconic sectors such as the automotive may respond effectively to ongoing changes in their competitive environment. In fact, since 2016, slow entry into the emerging market for electric vehicles has strained HMC's profitability and sent SsangYong, a smaller automotive producer, into bankruptcy. The hierarchical, self-sufficient structure of Korean manufacturing value chains amplifies the impact of lead firm's slow responses to change because the travails of lead firms are quickly transmitted to their vast networks of suppliers, threatening the survival of the whole industry. Furthermore, the dominant position of the chaebol in the Korean economy, and their ability to recruit the best talent, crowds out innovation by smaller firms (OECD, 2009, 2014). Finally, Korea's R&D investment is highly concentrated. In 2015, the last year for which data is available, the electronics industry single-handedly accounted for 50 percent of Korea's R&D investment (OECD, *Main Science and Technology Indicators*, 2020). Such concentration raises questions about the innovation capacity of firms in other Korean industries.

2.5.3 High Quality Jobs and Welfare Standards

Spain's and Korea's upgrading strategies have certainly improved people's chances in life relative to previous generations. However, the two countries' relatively narrow specializations in a few sectors have resulted in two-headed productive structures that constrain Spain's and Korea's ability to generate stable, career-track employment. This situation calls into question the two countries capacity to continue increasing the chances of their citizens through future rounds of upgrading.

Spain's specialization in services and the country's sharp decrease in manufacturing capacity have translated into a low demand for professionals with technical skills and few incentives for the unskilled to further their training. As of 2018, 40 percent of those aged 25–64 had capped their education below upper secondary education (below high school level) (OECD, *Education at a Glance*, 2019) and only 23 percent had upper secondary or post-secondary non-tertiary education. Not only do many unskilled Spaniards find it difficult to find employment, but a bottom-heavy labor force compromises Spain's future economic growth because unskilled workers are difficult to redeploy to new and more complex functions.

On the other hand, university education has expanded rapidly in Spain since the late 1980s. In 2018, 37 percent of those aged 25–64 had attained some level of tertiary education, a percentage that is in line with the OECD's average (OECD, *Education at a Glance*, 2019). However, the concentration of career-track jobs in only a few industries means that there is more supply than demand for qualified employment. The results are underemployment and precariousness. In 2018, 37.6 percent of those that had tertiary education were employed in roles that did not require such qualification, the highest rate of underemployed in the EU (CYD report, 2018). The mismatch between supply and demand of qualified employment contributes to Spain's high rates of temporary contracts. As of 2018, 27 percent of those employed had temporary contracts, the second highest rate in the OECD (OECD, *Labor Force Statistics*, 2020).

High rates of underemployment and precarious employment compromise the sustainability of the Spanish model. A strong set of highly educated individuals is a precondition for growth in advanced economies, but unused, skills stagnate and devaluate. An additional concern is that young university-educated individuals tend to be mobile, which means that Spain may end up exporting its most valuable resource. Furthermore, high rates of temporary employment discourage capital and labor investment in firm- and sector-specific skills, with negative effects on productivity. Finally, underemployment and precarious employment prevent many from taking important life decisions such as starting a family. In 2018, Spain's fertility rate was only 1.31 children per woman, well below the 2.1 replacement rate, and the second lowest in the OECD, immediately after Korea's (OECD, *Family Database*, 2020). Rapid immigration during the boom years in the late 1990s and early

2000s has so far enabled Spain to compensate for a rapidly aging population. The expansion of public welfare provisions since the 1980s, and the prevalence of strong intergenerational family ties has also enabled Spaniards to maintain their economic standing. However, this situation does not bode well for the future and wellbeing levels could very well decrease, especially as Covid-19 stimuli packages fade and the full extent of the crisis sets in.

Korea's specialization in manufacturing, together with a heavy emphasis on education, have led to high rates of education among the Korean workforce. Unlike in Spain, only 11.8 percent of those aged 25–64 in Korea have capped their education below upper secondary levels, and an additional 39 percent have attained upper secondary or post-secondary non-tertiary education (OECD, *Education at a Glance*, 2019). A better trained labor force enhances Korea's future prospects for upgrading because well-educated workers can shift more easily to new positions. Korea's emphasis in education also translates into high rates of tertiary education. In 2018, 49 percent of those aged 25–64 had attained some level of tertiary education, one of the highest rates in the advanced world (OECD, *Educational at a Glance*, 2019).

However, as in Spain, the concentration of Korea's economic activity in a handful of sectors and the substitution of permanent with non-permanent employees after the 1997 Asian crisis mean that the supply of career-track jobs has declined sharply. In 2018, 21 percent of those employed worked on the basis of temporary contracts. Although the rate is lower than Spain's it is still one of the highest rates in the OECD (OECD, *Labor Force Statistics*, 2020). In addition, Korea's specialization in manufacturing industries no longer guarantees a steady supply of stable jobs. Although manufacturing accounts for 29 percent of Korea's GDP (OECD, *National Accounts Dataset*, 2020), in 2018 it only employed 16 percent of the Korean workforce (vs. 13 percent in Spain) (OECD, *Labor Force Statistics*, 2020).

As in Spain, precarious employment compromises the sustainability of the Korean model and has a negative impact on wellbeing. Many of Korea's non-regular workers are employed in the atomized retail sector, which tends to offer few prospects of career advancement, lower salaries, and few, if any, benefits. Chaebol have continued to be the largest providers of permanent, career-track jobs in Korea, but as opportunities have declined, competition has increased. To succeed in the chaebol's rigid hiring system, one must have graduated from one of Korea's three elite universities (Seoul National, Korea University, and Yonsei University). Preparation for acceptance to an elite Korean university is costly and starts early in life. The financial costs associated with providing children with the standard of education necessary to gain acceptance to an elite university are a key factor behind Korea's low fertility rates (1.05 children per woman) (OECD, *Family Database*, 2020) and high levels of household debt (184 percent of disposable income in 2018 compared to 107 percent in Spain) (OECD, *National Accounts Dataset*, 2020). Social pressure to perform academically is also a leading cause of teen suicide (Yonhap, 2019).

Furthermore, limited availability of regular jobs contributes to sustain employment practices that have a strong negative effect on Koreans' wellbeing. One of them is Korea's long-standing male breadwinner model, which tends to exclude women with tertiary education from career-track jobs. In 2018, Korea was the most gender-segregated market among OECD countries, with only 1.5 women employed in positions involving managerial responsibilities for every 10 men (OECD, *Employment Dataset*, 2020). In Spain, the equivalent relationship was 3.5 women for every 10 men (OECD, *Employment Dataset*, 2020). A limited supply of regular jobs, together with the long-standing custom of regular salary increases based on seniority rather than performance, also incentivizes large firms to compel their regular employees to retire in their early 50s to contain labor costs. Presented with meager pensions, and in a context defined by a small welfare state and weakened family ties (Yang, 2018), many retirees face a choice between poverty and creating their own opportunities in the retail sector. The stigma associated with poverty and male unemployment pushes many to extreme measures including suicide, a statistic in which Korea outnumbers every other developed nation (OECD, *Health Statistics*, 2020).

On the whole, this cursory, and necessarily incomplete evaluation of Spain's and Korea's outcomes indicates that although their upgrading strategies enabled the two countries to become advanced economies, both models have lingering weaknesses. Spain's strategy of FDI and technological outsourcing enabled firms in complex services to become globally competitive but at the expense of declining manufacturing capacity, a dependence on lead firms located abroad, and a decrease in the country's ability to determine the direction of innovation. Integration in EU-wide value chains generates significant opportunities for cost-efficient innovation by large firms with established reputations, but small and medium enterprises are less likely to have the financial resources and the networks necessary to take advantage of these opportunities. A narrow specialization in complex services limits the country's capacity to generate career track jobs, which in turn has effects on the quality of human capital and wellbeing.

Korea's strategy of technological sufficiency, together with an emphasis in education laid the necessary infrastructure to enable firms in a few manufacturing industries to become globally competitive and generate knowledge that is new to the world. However, organizational rigidities decrease both the potential for higher productivity and innovation. The quest for technological self-sufficiency is a hallmark of Korea's model, yet the country is simultaneously dependent on exports, which are contingent on relationships with major trading partners. This makes Korea vulnerable to external shocks, and to the vagaries of political relationships with close trading partners and neighbors such as China, which have conflicting agendas. Finally, Korea's highly educated workforce bodes well for the country's economy, but the combination of hyper-competition for entry-level career-track jobs, high rates of non-permanent employment, early retirement, and systematic exclusion of women from qualified employment limits those positive effects and has a major impact on wellbeing.

2.6 Conclusions

This chapter has developed the basic argument of the book in detail. In the early 1980s, Spain and Korea were industrialized economies but there was still a significant gap between them and the world's most advanced economies. The competitive limitations of Spanish and Korean firms were at the center of that gap. Firms had significant shortcomings in terms of technology, product development capabilities, experience with internal and external competition, organizational and managerial capabilities, and infrastructures. Due to these limitations, Spanish and Korean firms competed primarily on the basis of costs and produced mid-quality, moderately priced outputs. To overcome their limitations, firms needed socially-embedded resources and capabilities that were contingent on coordination with external economic actors that operate at national level. In late industrializing economies of the characteristics of Spain and Korea, such coordination was unlikely to take place through markets. The resources and capabilities firms needed were by nature rare, imperfectly imitable, and therefore unavailable for direct purchase through markets. Furthermore, the presence of institutional voids made it difficult for Spanish and Korean firms to find the resources they needed within their national ecosystems. Additionally, global markets organized around GVCs unchained forces that discouraged firms in complex sectors from undertaking upgrading. In such a context, the only agent capable of orchestrating the type of coordination that could foster upgrading was the state. The Spanish and Korean states were both willing and able to support upgrading. However, differences in the characteristics of Spain's and Korea's production structures, the identities and characteristics of their public decision makers, and their external linkages with more advanced countries led the two countries to pursue different upgrading strategies. Spain pursued an integrational strategy based on attracting FDI, outsourcing technological innovation, and integrating within the EU. By contrast, Korea pursued a techno-industrial approach based on achieving technological self-sufficiency in manufacturing industries and treating complex services as providers of necessary inputs to manufacturing. Both strategies enabled some Spanish and Korean firms in complex sectors to become globally competitive, Spain and Korea to join the ranks of advanced economies, and the citizens of both countries to enjoy much higher standards of living. Nonetheless, the two countries remain highly vulnerable to external shocks, have limited capabilities to generate new knowledge, and suffer from important social disequilibria that threaten the sustainability of their models and curtail people's wellbeing. To continue closing the gap with the world's most advanced economies, Spain and Korea need to address these factors.

The next three chapters present detailed empirical material on processes of upgrading in three key sectors: ICT, banking, and the automotive industry. In addition, Chapter 6 uses additional mini-cases and a brief counterfactual comparison with Brazil to provide a more general view of Spain's and Korea's strategies and the broader socioeconomic and structural factors that enabled the two countries to upgrade while other late industrializing economies were unable to. Chapter 7 draws general conclusions from the book's argument and uses them to discuss the most significant challenges Spain and Korea face in the 2020s.

3

Industry or Instrument?

Two Ways of Interpreting the Banking Sector and Their Impact on Bank Upgrading

3.1 The Banking Sector and Upgrading

In the 1980s, the banking sector was in the midst of a major transformation. Corporate demand for new types of financial products and operations, the progressive liberalization of capital markets, state retrenchment from economic activities, and the financial impact of the oil crises triggered a shift from developmental credit systems to profit-oriented financial sectors.

Spanish and Korean large or systemic banks (banks that due to their size have the potential to destabilize the economy if they fail) faced these challenges from a position of disadvantage. Spain's and Korea's late, inward-looking industrializations, the size of the two countries' economies, and the lack of Spanish and Korean firms with a significant international presence meant that Spanish and Korean banks were smaller, had limited international experience, and were less exposed to competition than their counterparts in more advanced economies.

Spanish and Korean large banks also faced obstacles to transformation derived from the specificities of their countries' institutional structures and the distribution of power between states, banks, and manufacturers. In Spain, where large banks occupied a position of power relative to manufacturers, the largest banks lacked incentives to transform a system that had made them profitable, whereas a set of smaller, progressive banks lacked the resources to overcome institutional inertia and the opposition of the bigger, more traditional banks. In Korea, where large banks were instruments of the state's industrial policy, the banks did not have the autonomy or the incentives necessary to overcome unsafe practices and undertake internal restructuring.

By the 2010s, Spanish large banks were some of the world's most efficient, profitable, and best-run (Table 3.1). In 2015, Santander was the world's tenth largest bank, measured by a composite score of revenue, profit, assets, and

State-Firm Coordination and Upgrading: Reaching the Efficiency Frontier in Skill-, Capital-, and Knowledge-Intensive Industries in Spain and South Korea. Angela Garcia Calvo, Oxford University Press. © Angela Garcia Calvo 2021. DOI: 10.1093/oso/9780198864561.003.0003

Table 3.1 Main bank ratios (2009)

	Spain	Switzerland	US	Sweden	Germany	Italy	Netherlands	France
Net income/assets	0.023	0.021	0.051	0.020	0.017	0.022	0.016	0.015
Net non-interest income/total income	0.308	0.638	0.402	0.477	0.204	0.363	0.307	0.580
Operating expenses/net income	0.372	0.774	0.589	0.574	0.756	0.632	0.691	0.624
Operating expenses as % of assets	0.009	0.016	0.030	0.011	0.013	0.014	0.011	0.009
Tier 1 and Tier 2 capital as % of assets	0.086	0.064	0.112	0.082	na	0.065	0.055	na
Institutions	153	207	6905	59	1774	768	93	325
Branches per 1,000 inhabitants	0.323	0.213	0.268	0.205	0.455	0.564	0.190	0.609
Employees per branch	7.4	53.8	23.2	22.0	17.0	9.7	35.1	11.1
Inwards FDI positions (US$ million)	27,812	319,729	254,411	256,694	53,654	91,957	91,870	111,109
Outwards FDI position (US$ million)	157,633	344,217	733,245	420,433	194,384	312,116	175,864	237,307

Source: OECD Banking statistics, Factbook statistics (population) and International Direct Investment Statistics (FDI positions). Own elaboration.

FDI positions exclude insurance and pension funding activities.

market value (Chen, 2015). Korean banks were not as successful. In 2020, Korea's largest bank was less than a third the size of Santander in terms of sales, assets, and market value (Forbes Global 2000 list, 2020). In addition, some Korean banks had internal problems. For instance, in 2015, Woori, a bank that had been nationalized immediately after the 1997 crisis, put on hold its fifth privatization attempt (Ho, 2014; Son, 2019).

This chapter contrasts the successful transformation of Spain's large banks with the modest trajectory of their Korean counterparts. The analysis becomes a vehicle to characterize two different patterns of state–firm coordination and their impact on upgrading. In the first, banks are insiders and agents of a quid pro quo structure between the banks and the state, and the state prioritizes financial stability over the growth of manufacturing. In the second, banks are instruments at the service of a tight relationship between the state and manufacturing firms and the state prioritizes the needs of productive industry over those of the banks.

To situate this analysis, the chapter starts with an overview of the characteristics and changing structure of national credit markets. The following two sections present evidence of Spain's and Korea's coordination structures, the role of banks within them, and their impact on upgrading. The detailed case analyses of the two countries follow a parallel structure. They start by characterizing the structure of the banking sector, then connect the pattern of coordination in each country with the transformation and performance of large banks and manufacturing. The final section summarizes the findings, discusses their implications, and sets the scene for the following chapter.

3.2 The Structure and Transformation of the Banking Industry

In the early 1980s, the structure of the financial sector varied greatly from country to country. Countries that had industrialized in the late 1800s or afterward, such as Germany, France, and Japan, had relatively underdeveloped capital markets and relied strongly on credit markets to provide patient capital for industrial development (Gerschenkron, 1962; Zysman, 1983).

The developmental nature of credit-based systems in late industrializing economies meant that in addition to supervising the stability and efficiency of the banking sector, the state also influenced credit allocation. However, the institutional structure of banking systems among late industrializers varied across countries. This variation stemmed primarily from differences in the distribution of power between the state and large banks.

For example, in France, where the state owned the three largest commercial banks, the state was directly responsible for credit allocation decisions and banks had relatively few incentives to develop proper credit evaluation and risk assessment mechanisms (Zysman, 1983). In contrast, in Japan, where commercial banks were privately owned, the banks were directly responsible for credit allocation decisions and had a keen interest in evaluating credit risk; nonetheless, the state enticed the banks to extend credit to preferential industries by issuing certain amounts of low-interest loans implicitly guaranteed by the state (Hoshi, 1995; Zysman, 1983).

By the 1970s, developmental banking systems were under strain. Rapid worldwide economic growth in the 1960s generated liquidity and fostered corporate demand for new types of financial products and operations. Credit institutions responded by developing innovative products, such as the Euromarkets. In addition, in 1973 the US abandoned the system of fixed exchange rates. These two developments decreased the efficacy of capital controls and eliminated their main purpose, fueling a wave of capital market liberalization across industrialized economies (Caves, Frankel, and Jones, 2007). The outcome were deeper capital markets that enabled large firms, even those based in credit-based late industrializing economies, to rely more on financial markets to meet their needs.

While these changes were happening, the 1970s oil crises laid bare the limitations of classic industrial policies. States responded by retrenching not only from productive activities, but from the credit allocation systems that underpinned them. Across the board, countries adopted measures intended to privatize banks and introduce a degree of competition. However, national credit systems did not converge toward a single institutional model across countries. Key aspects, such as bank supervision and, therefore, the solvency and risk management of the system, remained the responsibility of national central banks. In addition, liberalization did not result in the emergence of a globally competitive environment. Instead, local banks continued to handle the overwhelming majority of commercial banking operations in most markets (Epstein, 2017). Finally, despite common trends such as securitization and an increase in banks' fee-based activities, the balance of forces among states, banks, and manufacturing that underpinned national credit systems, did not change uniformly across countries.

Spain's and Korea's responses to these trends were different. I argue that their strategies derived from variations in the two countries' pre-existing patterns of coordination among the state, banks, and manufacturing firms. Spain's pattern of coordination was based on a close relationship between the state and large banks, with manufacturers occupying a secondary position.

From the late 1970s, the relationship between the state and the banks evolved into a cooperative, quid pro quo arrangement, through which the banks helped the state modernize its outdated financial system and ensure its stability while the state provided steady support for progressive large banks to break the old banking cartel, achieve a competitive transformation, and upgrade.

Korea's pattern of coordination was based on the state's support for the development of manufacturing capacity. Banks were state instruments used to provide a steady provision of low-cost capital to manufacturers. This relationship not only deprived banks of the autonomy and incentives they needed to restructure and become globally competitive, but also caused a major financial crisis and prevented Korea from becoming a global financial hub. The next two sections examine in detail Spain's and Korea's strategies and develop the argument.

3.3 State–Bank Coordination and Upgrading in the Spanish Banking Sector

This section analyzes the transformation of Spain's large banks. The first subsection characterizes the pre-existing relationship between large banks and the state and outlines the banks' competitive limitations. The second subsection shows how the relationship between the state and the banks evolved into a quid pro quo exchange though which banks enabled the state to modernize the Spanish financial industry and ensure financial stability in exchange for support for the transformation and upgrading of the banks. The third subsection shows how the prioritization of financial stability and the banks' interests exposed manufacturers to market rigors they were not ready to withstand. The combination of bank prioritization and rapid market exposure of manufacturers led to a large decline in manufacturing capacity and shaped Spain's overall specialization in complex services.

3.3.1 The Spanish Banking Elite

In 1985, the Big Seven, Spain's group of large banks (Central, Hispano-Americano, Banesto, Santander, Bilbao, Vizcaya, and Popular) was Spain's most powerful business elite. The banks, created with local capital, were privately owned and publicly listed. Unlike firms in other critical industries, such as telecommunications services, railways, or automotive, the Big Seven had avoided nationalization because they supported Franco during the civil war (Tortella and García Ruiz, 2003).

During the Francoist period (1939–75), the banks consolidated their political and economic influence and operated as a loosely organized cartel (Rivases, 1988). Banks gained political influence by lending their expertise to the government. Between 1945 and 1975, bankers occupied 213 positions in different government bodies (Pérez, 1997). The banks' economic power derived from their dominant role in the Spanish financial system: large banks provided the largest share of capital for industrialization in the 1960s. However, unlike classic developmental systems, in which the state established interest rate ceilings to provide cheap credit to manufacturers, in the Spanish model, the banks established interest rate *floors* for their own benefit (Pérez, 1997). This system enabled the banks to multiply their profits sixfold (Torrero, 2001) and likely harmed local manufacturers. In 1985, the banks' profits, measured in terms of net income over assets, were some of the highest among western economies (Garcia Calvo, 2016).

Two features of the Spanish institutional environment enabled the banks to exercise this much power. First, the banks were effectively self-governed because the bankers occupied a number of decision-making positions both within the government and the Bank of Spain (BoS) (Pérez, 1997). Second, the Big Seven faced little competition from other credit institutions. The Banking Act of 1946 had prohibited the foundation of new banks and heavily constrained competition from savings banks. In addition, the stock market was narrow and inefficient until its reform in 1988 (Pellicer, 1992). Moreover, large banks dominated investments in the stock market because most licensed brokers worked for the banks (Guillén and Tschoegl, 2008).

Despite their powerful position within Spain and their strong for-profit orientation, the Big Seven faced competitive deficiencies relative to systemic banks in more advanced countries. Specifically, Spanish large banks were relatively small and had limited international exposure, little experience with competition, and high operational costs.

Many large banks from more advanced countries such as the UK, France, and Germany, had been conceived as international banks and had extensive experience with trade and international investment operations. For example, Deutsche Bank's purpose at the time it was established was "the promotion and easing of trade relations between Germany, the other European countries, and overseas markets" (Deutsche Bank, 2020, p. 4). Spain's rapid colonial decline in the 1800s, the country's inward-looking stance during most of the twentieth century, and its limited industrial development prior to the 1960s meant that, unlike their European counterparts, Spanish banks had been created for and operated almost exclusively within the domestic market. Spanish banks' lack of international exposure persisted well into the 1990s. In 1996, the volume of Spanish banks' cross-border assets was only US$10.7

million compared to US$79.9 million for Germany and US$73 million for France (White, 1998).

Large Spanish banks were also small by international comparison. The largest, Banco Central, ranked only 100th in the world and was about one-fifth the size of Banque Nationale de Paris and one-fourth the size of Barclays and Deutsche Bank (Guillén and Tschoegl, 2008). In addition to the banks' insignificant international presence, the banks' size was the combined result of two factors. First, they operated within a small domestic economy, and second, Spain had a relatively high number or large banks. In 1985, Spain's volume of domestic credit operations was approximately one-fifth of the equivalent measure in Germany and one-third of that in Italy (OECD, *Banking Income Statement and Balance Sheet Statistics dataset*, 2020). These figures were in line with the size of the Spanish economy, which was 25 percent of Germany's and 40 percent of Italy's at the time (World Bank Development Indicators, 2020). The impact of Spain's smaller economy on the size of its banks was exacerbated by Spain having seven large banks, whereas larger credit-based economies, such as Germany and France, had only four. The large number of Spanish large banks can be traced back to Francoism and to the dictator's refusal to allow the mergers of large banks to prevent them from potentially challenging his power (Rivases, 1988).

Large Spanish banks also had limited experience with both foreign and domestic competition. The presence of foreign banks in Europe had grown steadily. Between 1970 and 1985; the number of foreign banks operating in France rose from 58 to 147, in Germany from 77 to 287, and in Italy from 4 to 40 (White, 1998). In contrast, in 1980 only four foreign credit institutions operated in Spain, all through exceptional individual concessions issued by Franco (Consejo Superior Bancario Annual Statistics, 1985). Spanish banks also faced very limited domestic competition. Until their consolidation in 1988 (Law 24/1988 of July 28), Spain's wholesale markets were "narrow and archaic" (Pérez, 1997, p. 22), and until 1989, savings banks were subject to strict operational and geographical constraints that limited their ability to compete for commercial operations (Law 13/1989 of May 26).

Finally, large Spanish banks were significantly less productive than their counterparts in Germany, France, and Italy (Table 3.1) and had relatively high operational costs. These higher operational costs not only indicated the presence of operational deficiencies, but were also the result of a rapid expansion in the number of branches that led to high increases in fixed costs: between 1973 and 1983, the number of bank branches in Spain more than trebled, from 5,437 to 16,046 (Fainé Casas, 2005).

3.3.2 State–Bank Coordination, Economic Modernization, and Bank Upgrading

Spain's first democratic government saw economic transformation as a fundamental part of the country's transition to democracy. To this effect, representatives of all parliamentary forces passed a broad agreement, known as the Moncloa Pacts (1977), which defined the main lines of Spain's transformation into a democracy and an open economy. Initial policy measures derived from the pacts focused on strengthening financial stability through three specific objectives: reinforcing the powers of the BoS to conduct monetary policy, developing effective bank supervision mechanisms, and setting the basis for a competitive financial system (Fuentes Quintana, 1985).

To implement these goals, the government and the BoS relied on close cooperation with the large banks on the basis of quid pro quo exchanges that enabled both the state and the large banks to overcome their respective limitations and further their objectives.

The basis for cooperation was the inherent interdependence between the state and the banks. The government and the BoS could not fulfill their objectives without cooperation from the large banks. A central bank can exercise monetary policy through two alternative mechanisms: variation in interest rates or control of the monetary base growth. The first mechanism requires the existence of an active interbank lending market, but in the late 1970s, Spain only had a rudimentary interbank lending market, which was insufficient for the BoS to exercise monetary policy (Pérez, 1997; J. Pérez, 2012). The second mechanism, the one Spain pursued, requires synchronization with the banking system, typically via large banks, because banks expand the monetary base through their ordinary credit operations.

To fulfill the government's reform objectives, the Big Seven also needed to agree to a more powerful BoS and accept the principle of economic liberalization. The banks were expected to oppose these reforms because the BoS could only become more powerful at the expense of the large banks, and because liberalization was likely to drive interest rates down, reduce large banks' margins, and threaten their control of the market. Such agreement was possible because by the late 1970s, a minority of progressive bankers supported a degree of change. These bankers advocated the elimination of mandatory investment coefficients in preferential sectors and increases in the interest rates at which firms in such industries could borrow. This is because with the ongoing crises, such investments had become unprofitable and harmed banks' earnings (Pérez, 1997). Some bankers also saw the advantages of introducing a rigorous supervisory system to keep in check dubious banking practices and help prevent crises that could disrupt businesses and stain banks' reputations (Pérez, 1997). Nonetheless, the Big Seven opposed market competition with foreign and domestic rivals, which would have directly affected their bottom lines (Termes, 1991).

Ultimately, the situation was addressed through a quid pro quo arrangement that reflected the concerns of progressive bankers regarding mandatory investment in manufacturing sectors and competition while also fulfilling the government's objectives of strengthening the role of the central bank and ensuring financial stability. Royal Decree 1,839/1977 established the progressive reduction of mandatory coefficients and brought interest rates for preferential industries close to market rates. Royal Decree 1,839/1977 enabled savings banks to offer the same types of products as banks, but it maintained geographical restrictions, thereby limiting their ability to compete directly with the Big Seven. In addition, Royal Decree 1,388/1978 authorized the installation of foreign banks in Spain, but it imposed such heavy constraints on their operations that their presence remained testimonial. These reforms were followed by a set of measures that strengthened the powers of the BoS, set the basis for a more autonomous monetary policy, and established a rigorous bank supervision mechanism. Law 30/1980 dismissed professional bankers from decision-making roles at the BoS, substituting them with public employees, and established a system of incompatibilities between public and private employment in the banking sector. In 1976, the BoS introduced a telephony-based interbank exchange system, the first step toward creating a fully-fledged, real-time payment system that could enable the central bank to conduct an active monetary policy with greater autonomy (Pérez, 2012). Finally, the BoS introduced a rigorous and intrusive mechanism of micro prudential supervision based on the constant supervision of large banks through a team of inspectors that worked full-time at the supervised banks (Bank of Spain, 2009). The BoS complemented this system with other indirect control measures over banks, including the ability to veto candidates to board-level positions.

A major episode of this period, the resolution of the 1977–85 banking crisis, strengthened the relationship between the state and the large banks, showcased the quid pro quo nature of the system, and confirmed the active role of the banks in the relationship. Between 1977 and 1985, 51 banks out of the existing 110 banks, which accounted for 20 percent of the country's deposits, required rescuing (Dziobek and Pazarbasioglu, 1998). There were two possible options to rescue and turn around the ailing banks: nationalization or private-sector turnarounds. The BoS opted for the second. It created the Deposit Guarantee Fund (Royal Decree 3,048/1977 of November 11, Royal Decree 54/1978 of January 16, and Royal Decree-Law 4/1980 of March 28), funded through contributions from the banks. The fund bought the majority of an ailing bank's stock at a symbolic price, restructured the bank using talent from other banks, and then sold it off via public auction (Dziobek and Pazarbasioglu, 1998; Martín Aceña, 2005). From the point of view of Spain's orthodox policymakers, this approach had two benefits: it was in line with its goal of moving toward a competitive banking system and it had a low impact on the public deficit. For the banks, the turnarounds involved substantial costs, but in exchange for their cooperation, large banks were able to expand their national presence by purchasing intervened banks, usually at symbolic prices.

The BoS's able management of the crisis also raised the profile of a cohesive network of young economists formed at the central bank' research department (Malo de Molina, 2012). After the 1982 election, and for well over a decade, members of this emerging elite dominated the ministries of economics and industry and many second-tier policymaking positions (Estefanía, 1986), consolidating and providing continuity to state–bank cooperation. This relationship played a significant role in the competitive transformation of large banks from the late 1980s to the 1990s.

From 1986, the year Spain joined the EU, the BoS's priorities shifted toward the competitive transformation of the banking sector. A competitive banking sector in the hands of Spanish bankers was seen as a fundamental tool to prevent speculative attacks that could destabilize the financial system (Pérez, 1997; Guillén and Tschoegl, 2008). Because the Big Seven were fully private firms, the state could incentivize and support their competitive transformation but only the banks could carry it out. Not all large banks were willing to do so. The three largest banks (Banesto, Central, and Hispano-Americano), which were still run by the same bankers who headed them through the Francoist period, defended the traditional cartel-like business model (Rivases, 1988). In contrast, the progressive leaders of the four remaining large banks (Santander, Bilbao, Vizcaya, and Popular) understood that their ways of doing banking were becoming obsolete and saw the EU's single market as a unique business opportunity, provided they could become competitive enough to take advantage of it (Garcia Calvo, 2016).

The progressive banks faced significant obstacles they could not overcome autonomously. Size was a major concern for progressive banks because they were smaller yet better run than the larger, more traditional banks, which made them more attractive targets for potential foreign acquirers. The fastest path to growth was through mergers, but the progressive banks faced several constraints. First, if the sector was immediately liberalized, the banks risked being acquired by foreign investors before having a chance to adjust and grow organically. In addition, mergers and subsequent changes to the banks' boards of directors required approval from the BoS. Finally, mergers needed to be followed by structural reforms to lower fixed costs and increase efficiency. These were likely to involve massive layoffs of employees who were protected by pre-existing lifelong contracts.

As in the previous decade, Spain addressed these challenges through a coordinated approach that reflected the interests of the progressive bankers while furthering the BoS's own goals of protecting financial stability. The government supported a strategy of mergers through generous tax exemptions (Guillén and Tschoegl, 2008). The BoS also gave its approval for several mergers among the banks. In addition, the government temporarily sheltered large banks from foreign competition by exercising tight control over foreign investment. Law 26/1988 of July 29 mandated that anyone taking control of 5 percent of the social capital of a bank needed to inform the BoS. Participations above 15 percent required a specific authorization. The government also intervened to prevent speculative investments. This was, for instance, why Minister Solchaga requested the Kuwait Investment Office to withdraw its stake in Banco Central in 1987 (Congress, intervention by Minister D. Carlos Solchaga Catalán. Daily Session Transcript, Fourth Legislature, Session 48, February 9, 1993). Finally, the government facilitated bank restructuring with generous negotiated packages. Employment at Spanish commercial banks decreased continuously from 1980 to 2004, with a loss of 70,000 jobs (OECD, *Banking Income Statement and Balance Sheet Statistics Dataset*, 2020). Most of the layoffs took the form of voluntary pre-retirement agreements brokered by the state, which contributed approximately half of the ensuing pensions.

These measures substantially lowered the risks and costs of the banks' transformations, and the progressive bankers embraced the opportunity. In 1987, two of the progressive banks launched innovative savings products that unchained a deposit war, signaling the breakup of progressive and traditional bankers and the start of aggressive competition between the two groups. Thereon, the Big Seven embarked on several rounds of bank-led mergers in which the progressive banks ultimately had the upper hand. By 1999, six of the Big Seven had consolidated into two banks: Santander and BBVA (Banco Bilbao Vizcaya Argentaria). Starting in the 1990s, the large banks also expanded internationally, first into Latin America and, from the mid-2000s, into Europe and North America. Along with being a defensive strategy against hostile acquisitions, internationalization enabled the banks to diversify their operational risks and boost their profits. Banks also underwent massive internal restructuring to lower fixed costs. Santander, for instance, went as far as selling its headquarters real estate (Navarro, 2008).

Spain's coordination model subsisted into the 2010s, although coordination became less salient until 2012, when a new financial crisis called for a negotiated solution. At the center of the crisis was the solvency of Bankia, a bank recently formed through the merger of several financially unstable savings banks. Rather than address the problem publicly, a technical solution was found through a private agreement between the government and the systemic banks. Namely, the prime minister called two private meetings with the minister of economics and the CEOs of the country' three systemic banks (Valls, 2019). In the aftermath of these meetings, the president of Bankia was asked to step down and was substituted with a retired BBVA board member.

3.3.3 The Decline of Spanish Manufacturing

Spain's state–bank cooperation supported the competitive transformation of the banks but exposed productive industry to market rigors in a way that contributed to its decline and shaped Spain's specialization in services. Ultimately, this outcome showcases the secondary role of manufacturing in the Spanish model compared to the central role of large banks.

The country's early reform package, which involved a combination of limited banking competition and a decrease in mandatory investment coefficients, negatively affected manufacturing sectors. Because competition remained limited in the banking sector, Spanish banks were able to continue charging double-digit interest rates in the midst of an acute economic crisis. For example, in 1980, the president of the Spanish Banking Association admitted to charging an interest rate of 20 percent (Torrero, 1989). The decrease in subsidized credit, together with high interest rates made it difficult for manufacturers to find affordable, long-term credit to overcome liquidity problems, let alone develop the new, complex products they needed to upgrade. Many manufacturers were forced to downsize, sell their operations to foreign investors, or close down. Between 1977 and 1996, the contribution of manufacturing to Spain's GDP decreased by nine percentage points, which was more than the UK's, the European country that suffered the most significant decline in manufacturing during that period (EU KLEMS, 2009).

These development generated political opposition to the reforms championed by Spain's orthodox economists. In the early 1980s, Spain's vice prime minister advocated an alternative strategy based on public deficits and strong support for industrial employment France's experience using that approach in the early 1980s weakened his arguments (Smith, 1998). The two largest unions also opposed the government's strategy and organized a successful general strike that forced the government to soften some of its restructuring measures after 1988. However, by then, the industrial decline was significant, and the government did not change course, which highlights the secondary role of manufacturing in the Spanish model.

3.4 State–Industry Coordination and the Modest Performance of Korean Banks

This section examines the transformation of the Korean banking sector through an analysis that mirror's the structure of the previous section. It shows that, unlike in Spain, where banks had considerable leverage over the state and the priorities of banks took precedence over those of manufacturers, in Korea, the balance of power between the state and the banks was strongly skewed toward the state, which used the banks to help support the restructuring and competitive transformation of large manufacturing firms in key sectors. The downside of the Spanish model had been the decline of manufacturing sectors. In contrast, the downside of the Korean strategy was that it compromised financial stability, constraint the banks' capacity to upgrade, and frustrated Korea's ambition to become a regional financial hub.

3.4.1 Banks as a State Instrument

In 1979, large (national) Korean banks were the government's most effective instrument of industrial policy (Jones and Sakong, 1980). The Korean national banking system encompassed five commercial banks (Korea First, Seoul Bank, Hanil, Chohung, and Kookmin), four specialized banks, and three development banks (Korea Development Bank [KDB], Export-Import Bank of Korea [KEXIM], and Long-term Credit Bank) (Choi, Hasan, and Waisman, 1994; Kim and Boyer, 1994; Ubide and Baliño, 1999). This chapter focuses primarily on commercial banks.

In the early 1960s, President Park Chun Hee's regime had strengthened its power over the banks and turned them into an instrument to implement its strategy of rapid industrialization through manufacturing. Park nationalized commercial banks and founded specialized and development banks (Gilbert and Wilson, 1998). In addition to owning the banks, the government provided a significant portion of the banks' resources in the form of foreign loans obtained under the state guarantee (Park and Weber, 2006), appointed the heads of the banks, and staffed them with civil servants that measured their performance on the basis of national growth rather than profitability (Thurbon, 2016).

The government used its control over the banks to foster the development of strategic manufacturing industries by issuing policy loans: loans with very low or negative interest rates, long maturities, and non-conditional guarantees. By the end of the 1970s, policy loans accounted for 60 percent of all domestic credit (Yoo, 1994). Bank instrumentalization was an effective policy implementation mechanism because manufacturers had few alternative sources of credit. The stock market was underdeveloped, having been nationalized in the early 1960s (Park and Weber, 2006). The creation of new banks and non-bank financial institutions (NBFIs) was severely constrained (Park, 1994). Foreign banks were allowed to establish themselves in Korea, but their operations were also severely restricted (US Department of the Treasury, 1979). As late as 1997, foreign banks accounted for only 2 percent of total assets (Ubide and Baliño, 1999). Foreign direct investment, had manufacturers been willing to give up control of their firms, was also severely limited.

Korea's late development meant that the banks suffered from the same competitive limitations as their Spanish counterparts in terms of size, international experience, and operational costs. In addition, the banks' subordination to the government meant that commercial banks faced additional competitive weaknesses. Specifically, the government's appointment of banks' presidents and other top-ranked decision makers meant that the banks lacked autonomy to develop their own strategies. The banks' lack of responsibility for credit allocation discouraged the development of effective credit evaluation and risk assessment mechanisms, while the prevalence of policy loans and their low interest rates provided few incentives for banks to increase their operational efficiency or launch new products. Additionally, the highly beneficial conditions of policy loans encouraged manufacturers to make side payments to the banks to increase the amount of credit allocated to them, which bred corruption (Aliber, 1994).

Korea's institutional structure further weakened the banks by failing to provide incentives for them to avoid unsafe business practices. The assumption that the state stood behind the banks meant that little attention was paid to developing an efficient, unified, micro prudential supervision system, establishing adequate accounting standards and auditing and disclosure mechanisms, or instituting good internal liquidity management controls (Ubide and Baliño, 1999). In addition, the practice of designating a "main bank" translated into overexposure (US Department of the Treasury, 1979). As the industry moved toward a market-oriented system, these weaknesses made the banks prone to adopting risky behaviors that threatened not only the stability of individual banks, but also that of the entire financial system.

3.4.2 State–Industry Coordination and Failed Bank Upgrading

In 1980, the Korean government faced a dire political and economic situation. Following President Park's assassination in 1979, and after a brief interregnum, President Chun Doo Hwan (1980–88) seized power through a military coup worthy of an action movie. He set the tone of his presidency by responding violently to a popular pro-democracy rising, leaving hundreds dead in the city of Gwanju (Kim, 2003). Adding to a context of rising political discontent, the 1970s oil crises revealed massive inefficiencies in Korea's strategy of cheap credit allocation (Park, 1994; Eichengreen, Lim, Park, and Perkins, 2015). Against this background, the state could neither continue its past practices nor unravel the system because sudden credit restrictions to manufacturing firms would have resulted in widespread failure among the chaebol and caused a massive rise in unemployment, fueling mass protests that would have ended the regime.

Korea resolved this impasse through a strategy consisting of maintaining its techno-industrial orientation and using financial liberalization to expand the range of financial options available to manufacturing firms. This had the advantage of preventing firms' widespread failure while reducing their reliance on policy loans. Under this approach, banks continued to be an instrument of support for ailing firms rather than an industry in need of a major overhaul. Tellingly, despite the large number of legal reforms launched in the early 1980s and early 1990s, no effort was made to transform the institutional mechanisms governing the stability of the banking system or prevent the banks from engaging in risky practices.

Between 1980 and 1992, the government expanded the range of options available to manufacturers by developing money markets and facilitating access to foreign investment. The government used legal instruments to introduce a series of new financial instruments such as repurchase agreements, commercial paper, certificates of deposit, and commercial paper (Amsden and Euh, 1993). In addition, the government enabled foreigners to purchase shares in Korean firms (Park, 1996) while simultaneously encouraging Korean firms to list in the stock market by giving them preferential tax treatment (Ubide and Baliño, 1999) and requiring them to repay bank loans with funds raised through stocks and bonds (Park, 1994). Finally, the government expanded financial options available to manufacturers by making FDI more easily available. To encourage foreign investment, the 1983 Foreign Investment and Foreign Capital Inducement Act shifted from a list of sectors in which foreigners could invest to a list of sectors in which they could not, simplified administrative requirements, and introduced tax benefits and guarantees on the repatriation of dividends (Park, 1996).

In parallel, the government introduced a series of legal measures to progressively reduce the use of policy loans. In 1982, the state abolished preferential lending rates and unified lending bank rates at 10 percent (Amsden and Euh, 1993), which made policy loans less attractive. In 1984, the state froze the total amount of bank credit available to the chaebol (Park and Kim, 1994). Furthermore, from 1984, financial institutions could set their lending rates within a set of parameters (Park, 1996), and from 1988, the Ministry of Finance was no longer able to set ceilings on interest rates or to allocate credit to special borrowers (Amsden and Euh, 1993).

Finally, between 1980 and 1983, the state sold its shares in the four commercial banks it owned (Kim, Kim, and Boyer, 1994), loosened restrictions on the foundation of new banks, and relaxed the requirements for establishing new NBFIs (Park, 1994; Gilbert and Wilson, 1998).

However, neither the privatization of commercial banks nor the legal limits imposed on policy loans prevented the state from continuing to use commercial banks as instruments to support manufacturers (Amsden and Euh, 1993; Shin and Chang, 2003; Gilbert and Wilson, 1998; Park, 1994, 1996). Although commercial banks were privatized, the government continued to control them indirectly. The government influenced the banks' credit allocation decisions through the appointment of the banks' presidents and other officers (Kim, 2003). The government also used its regulatory powers to indirectly induce banks to keep interest rates low. A bank that did not follow public guidelines could expect retaliation in the form of unexpected inspections, difficulty using the Bank of Korea's discount window, or obstacles obtaining the central bank's approval to increase paid-in capital and reassess its portfolio (Amsden and Euh, 1993).

The continuation of these practices in the absence of sufficient measures to address the banks' shortcomings not only disincentivized bank upgrading but also, in conjunction with more decisive capital market liberalization in the 1990s, encouraged the banks to engage in risky practices without building the necessary capital base to withstand shocks. This made Korea's financial system increasingly vulnerable, and ultimately paved the way for a major financial crisis.

Under President Kim Young Sam (1993–98), controls over capital account transactions were relaxed and eventually eliminated (Park, 2013). Manufacturers took advantage of the availability of credit to undertake major capacity expansions financed primarily through domestic credit institutions: In 1997, 50 percent of manufacturing firms' external financing still came from banks (Ubide and Baliño, 1999). Commercial banks met firms' demand for credit by borrowing on a short-term basis from international wholesale markets (Park, 2013). The massive increase in short-term liabilities relative to national holdings of foreign reserves, the deterioration in the quality of the loans to increasingly leveraged firms, and the maturity mismatch between foreign borrowing and domestic lending made the Korean financial sector vulnerable to a sudden reverse of capital inflows. When capital inflows stopped in 1997, the result was a severe financial crisis that forced Korea to request help from the IMF.

In response, the government orchestrated a restructuring program that consisted of nationalizations, managed exits, and government-led mergers. The government intervened in four of the five large banks. It took a 94 percent stake in Korea First and Seoul Bank, a 95 percent stake in the merger between Hanil and two other banks (renamed as Woori in 2002), an 80 percent stake in Chohung Bank, and a minority stake in Kookmin (Ubide and Baliño, 1999). In addition, in 1998, the government forced five banks to exit the market. Finally, in 1999 the government forced nine banks to merge, forming four successor banks. In 2000, two more were merged to form another successor bank (Ro, 2001).

Bank nationalization was intended to facilitate restructuring and prepare the banks for privatization. However, in practice, the banks' competitive transformation was slow, and operational performance remained below international standards for over a decade. A comparison with Spain is revealing. In 2009, Korea's cost to income ratio, a measure of operational efficiency, was 59 percent, much higher than Spain's 45 percent. Return on assets and return on equity, both of which are measures of profitability, were 0.2 and 5.9 percent respectively, much lower than Spain's respective 0.8 and 11.1 percent figures (World Bank Global Financial Development Indicators Dataset, 2019). In addition, banks were slow to introduce reforms to traditional practices such as seniority pay structures. Spain introduced performance-based pay in the 1980s, but it took until the 2010s for Korean banks to do so, and when they did, they were met with considerable resistance. In 2011, employees at

Korea First (which had been acquired by Standard Chartered in 2005) staged Korea's longest-ever banking industry strike in an attempt to prevent the bank from substituting the bank's seniority pay structure with performance-based pay (Song, 2011).

Tellingly, but despite the severity of the crisis and its long-term impact on the banks, Korea continued to see the banking system "as a quasi-public utility that should help the growth of the manufacturing sector rather than an industry that stands alone and that should make profits, reinvest and grow" (Mundi, 2013). For instance, the state did not voluntarily abandon the practice of inducing banks to provide financial assistance to ailing Korean firms. Hynix is a case in point. In 2001, Hynix, which at the time was the world's third largest semiconductor manufacturer, had debts exceeding ₩10 trillion. Despite a first, failed bailout, bank creditors converted loans totaling ₩4 trillion into equity, rolled over bonds worth ₩2.5 trillion, and extended an additional ₩650 billion for new investments. Through these measures, Korea's large nationalized commercial banks came to own 50 percent of Hynix (Oxford Analytica Daily Brief, 2001). However, by the early 2000s, international views on such kind of public activism had changed and the governments of the US and Japan contested Korea's approach before the World Trade Organization (WTO). They argued that the Korean government had directed large banks to rescue Hynix and that the bailout amounted to a subsidy (WTO, 2007). Accordingly, the US and Japan imposed countervailing duties which were later reviewed by the WTO Appellate Body (WTO, 2005, 2008; Andersen, 2009).

Privatization processes and, especially, the entry of foreign capital into the banking industry were expected to help eliminate soft lending and stimulate bank restructuring. However, the government was reluctant to accept foreign control of large banks and privatizations have failed to live up to expectations. In fact, after an initial surge in foreign presence, foreign financial institutions have scaled back or exited Korea. Under the terms of the IMF agreement, Korea First and Seoul Bank were intended for foreign purchase but ultimately only Korea First was acquired by a foreign banking institution (Bonin and Imai, 2007). HSBC's offer for Seoul Bank fell through in 2008 after a nine-year delay caused by regulatory obstacles (Segal and Kirk, 1999; Kim Yeon-hee and Rhee So-eui, 2008). As of 2020, a third bank, Woori, has been through five unsuccessful privatization attempts owing to a combination of regulatory obstacles, poor business outcomes, and a lack of interest from potential purchasers (Financial Times, 2013; Kim and Cho, 2020; Global Capital, 2011).

More generally, the presence of foreign investors never reached significant levels, and has declined since the 2010s. The percentage of bank assets held by foreign firms reached 12 percent in 2009, but by 2013, the last year for which data is available, it had declined to 7 percent (World Bank Global Financial Development Indicators Dataset). By 2020, six additional foreign banks had exited or reduced their presence in Korea (Reuters, 2013; Yoon, 2019; Mundi, 2013; Kim, 2019; Morris, 2020). The difficulties faced by foreign financial institutions in Korea have frustrated Korea's aspirations to turn Seoul into a regional financial hub. In 2020, Seoul ranked only 33rd worldwide and 11th in the Asia–Pacific region in the Global Financial Centers' Index (GFCI, 2020).

3.4.3 The Impact of Korea's Strategy beyond Banking

Korea's strategy was based first and foremost on supporting manufacturing firms by using large banks as providers of soft, long-term loans. This strategy prevented the banks from receiving the support they needed to overcome their competitive limitations and encouraged risky practices that led to a major financial crisis. However, Korea's model provided manufacturers access to the liquidity they needed to overcome episodes of crisis and the patient capital necessary to develop new and complex products to upgrade.

Despite the depth and breadth of the 1997 crisis, Korea did not abandon its techno-industrial approach. Instead, it modified the types of instruments it used to provide patient capital to strategically important sectors and firms. Although there were a few high-profile cases, such as the rescue of Hynix in the 2000s, direct government pressure on large commercial banks to support ailing firms decreased. In fact, several large banks have changed their business models and shifted from corporate to consumer credit (Oxford Analytica Daily Brief, 2001; Choi and Fairclough, 2004). Instead, since the 2000s the government has increased its reliance on public development banks and the National Pension Service (NPS), Korea's large, sovereign wealth fund, to usher Korea into a fourth industrial revolution (KDB, 2018). In 2016, state-owned policy banks, such as the KDB and KEXIM, accounted for 25 percent of all loans in Korea (Thurbon, 2016). Since then, the role of state-owned banks has continued to increase: Between 2016 and 2018, KDB's volume of investment rose by 75 percent (KDB, 2018). The NPS also plays a fundamental role in the provision of patient capital to large firms. In 2019, the NPS owned 7 percent of Korea's outstanding stocks and 18 percent of its bonds. In 2020, 16 percent of the NPS (approximately US$110 billion) was invested in domestic equity. This included sizeable shares in strategic Korean firms such as Samsung Electronics, HMC, and LG Chem (NPS, 2019).

3.5 Conclusions: Banking as an Industry or Banking as an Input

This chapter studied the diverging trajectories of large Spanish and Korean banks since the 1980s through an institutional perspective. At the beginning of the 1980s, Spain and Korea had bank-based financial systems. Large banks in both countries shared competitive limitations in terms of size, international experience, and exposure to competition that can be linked to late development.

As the global financial industry evolved, national differences in the balance of power between banks and the state and between banks and productive industry led Spain and Korea to pursue very different transformational strategies. In Spain, where large banks were the country's most powerful economic group, policy decision makers adopted a strategy that saw an active macroeconomic policy and financial stability as the keystone to transform the country's economy. Accordingly, the state and the large banks engaged in a series of quid pro quo exchanges through which the state obtained cooperation from large banks to further its objectives and the banks benefited from asymmetric regulation (regulation that benefited a certain type of actor or industry player more than the rest) that enabled a subset of progressive bankers to break down the pre-existing cartelistic structure, overcome their competitive limitations, and become globally competitive. By contrast, in Korea, where large banks were the government's most effective instrument to support the productive industry, the state continued to use the banking sector to channel credit to manufacturers while the banks failed to gain real strategic autonomy, overcome their competitive deficiencies, and receive the institutional support necessary to strengthen their practices, ultimately putting the whole financial system at risk.

These strategies had a significant impact beyond the banking sector. In Spain, banks received dedicated support for upgrading but manufacturing firms were deprived of the liquidity they needed to overcome a complex crisis and the stable capital required to generate and market new and complex outputs. The result was a steep decline in manufacturing capacity. By contrast, in Korea, manufacturers received access to the capital resources they needed, initially from the banks, and later from a broader range of financial institutions including government-owned banks and the NPS. However, this strategy deprived the banks of the direction, incentives, and support they needed to overcome their competitive limitations, introduce new practices, and limit risky practices, leading to a major financial crisis with a long aftermath.

The following chapter examines Spain's and Korea's upgrading from the perspective of the ICT industry. The chapter serves as a conduit to characterize the two countries' governments and discuss how policy makers' backgrounds and specializations shaped Spain's and Korea's choice of upgrading strategies. The chapter also shows how Spain's and Korea's views of complex services and manufacturing were part of a broader strategy in which these types of industries played well-defined roles in facilitating industrial transformation and upgrading.

4

Services vs. Hardware?

The Role of Government Identities
and Preferences in ICT Upgrading

4.1 Introduction

By the mid-1980s, the worldwide ICT industry, defined as telecommunications services (voice and data transmission over fixed and mobile networks) and telecommunications equipment (network and user equipment), was going through a revolution. Technological advances were transforming a mature, stable, utility sector into two of the world's most dynamic, complex, competitive, and lucrative industries: telecommunications services and electronics manufacturing.

Spanish and Korean ICT firms faced their industry's transformation from a disadvantaged position. National telecommunications operators suffered from organizational deficiencies, physical infrastructures were inadequate, and quality of service was low. Electronics manufacturers lacked the technological capacity to produce state-of-the-art equipment, depended on incumbent telecommunications operators, and were generally no match for emerging, mostly US firms, that were poised to dominate global markets.

Astonishingly, by the 2010s, Spain and Korea boasted globally competitive ICT industries. By 2011, Telefonica, Spain's former monopoly operator, was the OECD's fourth largest integrated telecommunications operator (OECD, *Communications Outlook* 2013) and had become one of the most efficient and best managed integrated operators (Giokas and Pentzaropoulos, 2008). Similarly, by 2013 Samsung had become the world's second largest producer of semiconductors, a critical component of electronic products, including smartphones (Matthew, 2014). By 2016, Samsung was also one of only two profitable producers of smartphones (Reisinger, 2016).

These positive outcomes were not without tradeoffs. Spanish manufacturing declined significantly: By 2016, electronics represented only 18 percent of the Spanish ICT sector (AMETIC, 2018) and none of the local firms had the scale or the resources necessary to lead the industry. Similarly, Korea's incumbent

State-Firm Coordination and Upgrading: Reaching the Efficiency Frontier in Skill-, Capital-, and Knowledge-Intensive Industries in Spain and South Korea. Angela Garcia Calvo, Oxford University Press. © Angela Garcia Calvo 2021.
DOI: 10.1093/oso/9780198864561.003.0004

operator, Korea Telecom (KT) missed opportunities to carve a leading position in the mobile segment, saw its market share decline significantly, and suffered through three consecutive high-level corruption scandals that mired the company's performance (Reuters, 2008, Kim, 2013, The Investor, 2018, Yonhap, 2018).

This chapter explains how Spain's and Korea's ICT industries reached the efficiency frontier by specializing in telecommunications services and electronics equipment manufacturing respectively and explores the impact of their choices on other segments of the industry. The analysis serves as a vehicle to establish a relationship between the structure of Spain's and Korea's governments, and the two countries' preference for upgrading in complex services and manufacturing.

The chapter's structure is similar to that of the previous chapter. Section 4.2 reviews the transformation of the industry. Sections 4.3 and 4.4 present detailed material on the Spanish and Korean ICT sectors. Each of these two sections is divided into three subsections. The first characterizes the country's production structure, the second explores state-firm coordination mechanisms, and the third connects them to outcomes in manufacturing and services. The final section of the chapter summarizes, concludes, and makes the bridge to the next chapter.

4.2 The Transformation of the ICT Industry

Until the mid-1980s, the structure of the ICT industry in most countries followed the PTT (public telephone and telegraph) model. The model was based on the natural monopoly paradigm (Thatcher, 2004, 2007), which relied on the assumption that competition by multiple operators would hinder service expansion, especially in low-profitability (mostly rural) areas. The model enshrined a hierarchical structure in which a public, or publicly-controlled, telecommunications operator (PTO) depended on short-term political decisions about annual budgets and increases in service tariffs to make decisions regarding long-term investments in infrastructures and service provision. Manufacturers of network equipment depended on demand from the national PTO. In most countries, operators purchased equipment produced by vertically integrated local manufacturers under schemes that aimed to foster national industrial development.

Until the late 1970s, telecommunications networks transmitted voice signals through electrical impulses over copper wire. The transition to digital signal transmission systems put the PTT model under strain. Digital signal transmission enabled alternative service providers, such as cable operators, to use their existing infrastructures to provide telephony services, eroding the basis for a single national telecommunications operator. In addition, digital transmission systems expanded the range of possible communication services, including data transmission and mobile telephony. This generated demand from major corporate users, who pressured their governments to modernize public networks. However, digital network equipment was significantly more complex and much more costly to develop than analog systems. Starting in the 1950s, the development of the first electronic switching systems had taken two AT&T subsidiaries over a decade of collaborative research between large teams of physicists, computer scientists, and engineers. The development of full-scale commercial switching systems took an additional decade (Millman and the AT&T staff, 1983). Sustaining the research and development process throughout both phases required massive amounts of patient capital, access to AT&T networks to test, debug, and scale up models for commercial operators, and sufficient guarantee of commercialization from the PTO (Millman and the AT&T staff, 1983). The cost and complexity of digital network equipment meant that vertical integration between local manufacturers and PTOs became an obstacle. Manufacturers, especially those based in small and middle-sized countries, were unable to fund, let alone recoup, the steep research and development costs of electronic switches by relying only on demand from the national PTO. Furthermore, the technological complexity of digital equipment meant that while local manufacturers strived to develop new equipment, PTOs were forced to sit through long delays in equipment delivery and to pay a high price premium. In Europe, the price of local manufacturers could exceed those of US suppliers by as much as 80 percent (Commission of the European Communities, 1987; Thatcher, 1999).

As equipment costs rose and service demand continued to grow, operators across the world struggled to modernize and expand their networks, waiting lists for new lines grew, corporate users complained of deficient service over saturated networks, and local manufacturers struggled to match technological developments coming from the US. These circumstances drove legislators, operators, and large corporate consumers in advanced countries to move away from the PTT model and advocate a framework based on market competition. The US initiated the shift to the market paradigm by breaking up AT&T's monopoly over services in 1984. Negotiations toward a competitive framework took place during the WTO's Uruguay Round (1986–94). An agreement came into force in 1998 in 69 jurisdictions, accounting for 90 percent of the world's telecommunications revenue (WTO, 1997).

The market paradigm involved the separation between operators and the state, leading to the partial or full privatization of PTOs. It also involved changes in price mechanisms, the vertical disintegration of equipment procurement, and generalized decreases in import duties. The result was a change in the balance of power between states and firms. States no longer had full control over operators through access to capital, equipment, or full ownership. PTOs gained leverage over civil servants with generalist profiles thanks to their technological, financial, legal expertise, and their day-to-day contact with a fast-changing market (Macher, Mayo, and Schiffer, 2011). Following a restructuring process, emerging global manufacturers gained power due to a surge in equipment demand, their sheer size, the oligopolistic nature of the sector, and their control over critical resources.

These changes did not eliminate the need for public-private coordination at the national level. Liberalization led to increased regulation of most aspects of an operator's daily functions, giving states new sources of power as regulators, legislators, and arbiters of competition. States also retained control over key areas such as licenses, spectrum allocation and management, and design and development of infrastructures (Garcia Calvo, 2021). In manufacturing, rapid technological change, rising capital costs, and the increasing concentration of the industry rose firms' dependence on resources in which states retain significant powers such as patient capital, stable demand, knowledge, and skills.

Spain and Korea responded to these trends by shifting from their former PTT models toward structures based on quid pro quo exchanges and interdependences between states and firms. Nonetheless, they pursued different strategies. The Spanish model was based on a close relationship and quid pro quo exchanges between the state and Telefonica. Through this model, the operator contributed to the state's goal of overhauling and modernizing the national telecommunications network in exchange for a policy measures that lowered the costs of internal restructuring, facilitated the divestment of the operator's industrial arm, and enabled it to successfully enter emerging service segments. However, this arrangement deprived local producers of the stable demand and patient capital they needed to upgrade. Together with the absence of a substantial, dedicated effort to support manufacturing and manufacturers' early exposure to market rigors, the result was that Telefonica thrived, but manufacturers were forced to downsize or sell their interests to foreign investors.

By contrast, the Korean strategy consisted of a series of highly sophisticated R&D programs based on a clear division of labor between the state and large manufacturers. The purpose of these programs was to enable manufacturers to develop product development capabilities and pave their entry into increasingly complex product segments. The implementation of these programs was heavily dependent on having access to patient capital and stable demand from the state-controlled PTO. As a result, Korea's manufacturers successfully upgraded, but the strategy imposed a heavy burden on KT that translated into a loss of managerial autonomy, lower profitability, late restructuring, declining market share, and the inability to take advantage of opportunities to enter new markets and profitable service segments. The following two sections develop these arguments through detailed empirical analyses.

4.3 Upgrading in the Spanish ICT Sector

This section explores the transformation of Spain's ICT sector. The first subsection characterizes structure of the industry under the PTT model and outlines firms' competitive limitations. The second shows how the relationship between the state and Telefonica evolved into a quid pro quo exchange through which the operator contributed to expand and overhaul the national telecommunications network in exchange for an asymmetric regulatory environment that enabled Telefonica to divest its industrial arm, restructure, and expand into emerging segments sheltered from competition. The third subsection contrasts this approach with government's market approach to manufacturing and discusses it consequences.

4.3.1 The Structure of the Spanish ICT Sector

In the early 1980s, the Spanish ICT industry was structured around a modified version of the PTT model: unlike most other PTOs, Telefonica was a publicly listed corporation and exercised a policy-making role. This structure derived from historical circumstances. Telefonica was funded in 1924 as a fully private corporation with foreign capital, technology, and organization (Amado Calvo, 2010). In 1945, Franco's regime purchased all foreign stock from ITT, Telefonica's foreign partner, becoming the PTO's largest shareholder with 41 percent of the stock (Government of Spain, 1969). Subsequently, Telefonica continued to be a publicly listed firm, but the state exercised control over the PTO through its stake in the operator, the presence of two government representatives at the board of directors, the appointment of the firm's CEO, and the administrative approval of changes in service tariffs (Amado Calvo, 2010). However, state control was far from absolute. In fact, by virtue of a 1946 contract between the operator and the state, the state delegated most policy-making functions directly to Telefonica (Pérez Martínez and Feijóo González, 2000; Escribano and Zaballos, 2001), whose employees remained outside the organizational structure of the state (Jordana and Sancho, 2005).

The PTO—and indirectly the state—exercised control over manufacturing. In 1983, three of the four largest manufacturers, representing 85 percent of production and 90 percent of employment, were owned jointly by Telefonica and a foreign investor (Adanero, 2006). In addition, Telefonica absorbed the lion's share of local production. In 1983, 55 percent of the sales of Telefonica's industrial arm were to the PTO, and only 15 percent to the export market (Adanero, 2006).

The Spanish ICT industry operated behind the efficiency frontier. The telecommunications network fared badly in terms of coverage, network equipment, and profitability compared to more advanced economies (Table 4.1). Access to telephony service was not universal: The number of access channels was well below those of advanced economies. Coverage also varied widely by region, ranging from 45 lines per 100 inhabitants in Madrid to only 17 in the poorest, most rural region (Lera Laso and Díaz Martínez,1986). Low coverage came hand in hand with long waiting lists for new lines and deficient quality of service. Telefonica also lagged in the adoption of state-of-the-art network equipment, especially the introduction of digital switches. Figures for investment per access channel and investment per inhabitant show that Spain was on a slower route to catch up than other late industrializing such as Korea and Ireland.

Low profitability, measured in terms of revenue per access channel, can be partly attributed to the correlation between income per capita and intensity of use of the service: in 1985, Spain's income per capita was 34 percent of that of the US (Maddison Project Database, 2018). However, an unfavorable comparison with Korea and Ireland, together with Spain's low revenue per employee, suggest that there were also limitations in operational efficiency.

Electronics manufacturers also operated behind the efficiency frontier. The sector was highly atomized and firms depended for existence on Telefonica's needs, financial resources, and demand (Adanero, 2006). Manufacturers were also heavily dependent on imports of foreign technology, parts, and components (Rico González, 2006). Outputs consisted mainly of low- and mid- value-added products such answering machines and keypad telephones. Producers' capacity for innovation—a key indicator of the industry's sophistication—consisted primarily of peripheral, applied improvements

Table 4.1 Telecommunications network, profitability, and investment (1985)

Country	Standard access lines per 100 inhabitants	Percent fixed lines connected to digital exchanges (1990)	Investment per access channel	Investment per inhabitant in US$	Revenue per access channel in US$	Revenue per full time employee*
Sweden (1)	62.78	38	104.36	66.44	347.50	44,131
UK	52.93	47	73.14	38.78	358.93	45,780
US (1)	49.24	43	180.17	88.97	946.76	104,148
France (1)	40.69	75	161.94	65.89	381.55	56,743
Japan	37.48	39	152.83	57.36	474.81	69,293
Germany	32.95	12	195.74	64.49	447.22	53,889
Italy	30.74	33	159.69	49.10	363.54	57,622
Spain	24.21	28	113.84	27.56	267.69	33,400
Ireland	19.85	55	204.16	40.55	670.91	29,178
Korea (2)	18.48	46	177.65	32.84	253.39	39,413

Source: OECD Telecommunications and Internet Statistics.

* Source ITU Telecommunications statistics.

(1) Revenue per full time employee, data for 1991.

(2) Percent fixed lines connected to digital exchanges for 1991.

such as durable public phone-booths and cost-effective technical solutions to reach rural areas such as semi-digital switches (Rico González, 2006). In a few instances, Spanish producers managed to overcome the country's technological limitations to generate innovative projects. This was the case of REDT/IBERPAC, the world's first public package-switched data network. However, in a move that epitomized manufacturers' dependency, the project was abandoned due to the inability of equipment manufacturers to secure patient capital and long-term stable demand from the PTO (Infante, 2002).

4.3.2 State–Firm Coordination and Telefonica's Upgrading

Spanish governments showed a clear determination to transform the existing structure of the ICT industry along with global changes in the sector. Spain's early democratic governments (1982–96) were determined to close the gap with western Europe by universalizing and improving the quality of basic services such as healthcare, education, and utilities, including telecommunications (PSOE, 1982). However, the state was neither willing nor capable of expanding and overhauling the telecommunications network without cooperation with Telefonica. The orthodox economists that dominated Spain's generalist governments openly opposed the state's direct intervention in the economy as a matter of principle (Termes, 1991; Pérez, 1997). Carlos Solchaga, who was minister of industry (1982–85) and then minister of economics (1985–93), was widely quoted as stating that "the best industrial policy is the one that doesn't exist" (Schwartz, 1995). Furthermore, the economists' concern with lowering the public deficit meant they were unlikely to commit the vast amounts of capital necessary to universalize the public telecommunications network. Even in the absence of these views, Spanish governments would have been unable to develop an appropriate strategy for network development. This is because Spain's delegation of policy-making functions to the PTO meant the government lacked a ministry, sub ministerial agency, or specialized civil service for ICT and depended on Telefonica for talent.

Telefonica was not keen to support the state's goal of universalizing the network because network investments in Spain's poorer regions and sparsely populated areas were unlikely to generate positive returns. However, in 1985, Telefonica was eager to deploy high-capacity networks and improve quality of service to address pressing corporate demands, especially those of the banking sector. Banks consumed more than 64 percent of non-residential telecommunications services in Spain (Commission of the European Communities, 1987) and bankers occupied Telefonica's three vice-presidencies and several positions at the board of directors (Telefonica, 1983). In line with this priority, Telefonica's five-year strategy (1985–90) stated three goals: deploying high-capacity networks, developing partnerships with global technological leaders, and improving procedures and human resources (Telefonica, 1985). However, to accomplish these goals, Telefonica needed cooperation from the state.

Deploying high-capacity networks requires massive capital investments. Telefonica could obtain capital via higher service tariffs, public subsidies, or Spanish capital markets. All three avenues required authorization from the state, and Spanish orthodox economists were unlikely to give it. Struggling to lower double-digit inflation levels, Spain's economists were unlikely to approve higher service tariffs because telephony services were part of the basic price basket and therefore higher tariffs meant higher inflation. Given policy makers' opposition to state activism and their concern with public deficits, the state was unlikely to use direct subsidies or accept new issues of stock, since it was obliged to purchase additional shares to maintain its participation in the company (Amado Calvo, 2010). Issuing debt was also problematic: Telefonica was already the country's largest listed firm, and there were reasonable concerns about the risks of an excessive concentration of national savings within a single firm (Rico González, 2006).

The hierarchical integration of manufacturing and manufacturers' techno-logical limitations caused critical delays in the deployment of data networks and serious traffic congestion problems. Delays were so persistent that in 1984, one of the largest banks threatened to develop its own data network unless Telefonica immediately addressed traffic congestion problems (Infante, 2002). But seeing as the state was a controlling stakeholder, Telefonica could neither shift toward a competitive procurement policy nor divest from its industrial arm without government consent. Finally, improvements in pro-cedures and human resources were expected to involve massive layoffs of employees who were protected by lifelong, quasi-public contracts. This too required government approval.

As in the case of banking, the inability of the state and the PTO to accom-plish their goals without cooperation from the other constituted the basis for an arrangement based on quid pro quo exchanges. As part of this arrangement, Telefonica assumed strategic and financial responsibilities for the universal-ization of the network in exchange for asymmetric regulation that enabled the operator to divest its industrial arm, restructure, and expand into growing service segments unencumbered by competition. The arrangement was for-malized through Decree 2,248/1984 of November 28. The decree established the framework for the expansion of fixed telephony services and attributed the articulation of specific plans, decisions over deadlines, the development of technical solutions, and the responsibility for raising 75 percent of the necessary capital to Telefonica.

In exchange, the state sold half of its stake in Telefonica between 1985 and 1987 (De la Dehesa, 1993). Unlike the UK, where the flotation of BT in 1984 intended to set an example for a new institutional structure based on competitive markets, the main purpose of Spain's sale of Telefonica's stock was to enable the operator to raise capital in international markets. In fact, the 1987 Telecommunications Act left no doubt that Spain was not moving toward an arm's length model by stating that telecommunications continued to be "essential services, owned by the state and managed by the public sector" (Telecommunications Act, Law 31/1987 of December 18, Article 2.1).

From 1986, the state also facilitated the sale of Telefonica's industrial group and helped the operator broker partnerships with foreign investors (Amado Calvo, 2014). This enabled Telefonica to liberate a substantial amount of capital and to purchase state-of-the-art network equipment from international suppliers at global prices. Finally, the state funded generous early-retirement schemes. The implementation of these measures was facilitated by trade unions and by a tightly-knit community of telecommunications engineers affiliated to the engineering professional association.

Through the 1990s, compensation to Telefonica also took the form of asymmetric regulation that enabled the operator to establish a dominant position in the emerging mobile market. The Telecommunication Act of 1987 and its successor in 1992 maintained Telefonica's exclusivity for mobile telephony until the end of 1993. Mobile licenses were awarded through an administrative decision rather than an auction, and Telefonica obtained its license without issuing payment (Calzada and Estruch Manjón, 2011). Spain's liberalization process was also tailored to protect the incumbent. Rather than a full liberalization, the government opted for a gradual liberalization initially based on a duopoly. The second mobile operator did not start operating until 1995 (Calzada and Estruch Manjón, 2011), giving Telefonica a one-year head-start after the expiration of service exclusivity. Furthermore, when a third license was issued in 1998, the operator was a recently privatized public Spanish firm rather than an international carrier (Escribano and Zaballos, 2001).

As had been the case in the banking sector, the state prevented corporate capture by combining these asymmetric policies with measures that strengthened the government's position relative to the operator. In 1986, the state created the Directorate-General for Telecommunications (Dirección General de Telecomunicaciones [DGTel]) and the Secretary of State for Telecommunications and Information Society (Secretaría de Estado de

Telecomunicaciones y Sociedad de la Información [SETSI]), responsible for policy making, network supervision, license management, and interactions with national and international organizations (Royal Decree 1,209/1985 of June 19). During its first years, the SETSI's main aim was to develop a legal framework to substitute the contractual relationship that had ruled the interface between the state and Telefonica since 1946. SETSI's workers were part of a new, high-profile body of civil servants specialized in telecommunications.

As had been the case with progressive banks, Telefonica used this favorable institutional setup to restructure, increase competitiveness, and raise profitability. Productivity passed from 118 lines per employee in 1981 to 228 lines per employee in 1996 (Telefonica, 1996). Between 1992 and 1996 alone, net benefits from operations in Spain increased by 45 percent (Telefonica, 1996), and between 1995 and 1996, market capitalization increased by 70 percent—half the growth of the Spanish stock market in that period (Telefonica, 1999). Between 1996 and 2003, Telefonica's employment in Spain decreased from a peak of 75,500 employees to 35,000, the largest layoff of any European incumbent (Telefonica, 1996, National Commission for the Telecommunications Market, 2009). Capital from the divestment of its industrial arm enabled the operator to engage in international expansion from 1989 onward; first in Europe and North America, and after a failed experience, in Latin America, where Telefonica's most lucrative acquisition was a Brazilian operator (Telefonica, 1996).

Coordination between Telefonica and the state became less visible through the 2000s as emphasis shifted from infrastructure development to service exploitation. Nonetheless, the model was still operational in the 2010s. In response to European plans to stimulate the development of next generation access networks (NGAs), the government engaged in private negotiations with Telefonica that resulted in a modification of the Telecommunications Act (Royal Decree-Law 13/2012 of March 30). This modification enabled Telefonica to charge prices over their leased lines "that take into consideration the investment made in the network to enable the operator to receive a reasonable return on its investment" (Royal Decree-Law 13/2012 of March 30,Title II, Article 13e) a major obstacle to NGA investment. Legal change was followed by Telefonica's investment of 2,300 million euro in NGAs between 2012 and 2013 (Telefonica, 2013). The government used this investment to build momentum for a 2013 Plan to Stimulate the Development of Ultrafast Networks, which together with additional investment incentives (Law 9/2014 of May 9), stimulated investment in NGAs by multiple operators. As of 2019 Spain had one of the OECD's highest rates of fiber connections as a percentage of total broadband connections (Table 1.2).

Certain features of the telecommunications sector facilitated continuity in the Spanish model. Telecommunication services reliance on physical infra-structures and national service licenses mean that Telefonica's global clout did not strengthened the operator's position relative to the state in the same proportion, maintaining the balance of power between the two actors. Additional contributing factors included the long-term presence of key deci-sion makers such as César Alierta, Telefonica's CEO (2000–16) and the last government-appointed CEO, the common background of most telecommuni-cations professionals (until 1986, there was only one school of telecommuni-cations engineering), and the requirement for telecommunications engineers to be affiliated with the engineering professional association, which acts as an informal information hub.

4.3.3 Electronics Equipment as an Outsider Subsector

The development of complex electronics equipment required vast capital investments over long periods of time, stable demand, and access to the pub-lic network to test, scale up, and debug equipment, usually through the PTO. However, an implication of the government's reticence to use classic industrial policy tools, the economic orthodoxy of Spanish policy makers, and the government's quid pro quo arrangement with Telefonica was that the state was unlikely to compel the PTO to allocate purchasing orders to local manufacturers. On the contrary, the government sanctioned the operators' divestment from its industrial arm.

On paper, the government responded to industry demands for a classic industrial policy strategy by issuing two National Electronics Plans (1984 and 1987). The plans' goals were to stimulate demand, production, and exports and to reduce Spain's technological dependence (Government of Spain, Senate, Session 9, November 5, 1986). However, in practice, and in line with the governments' economic orthodoxy, the implementation of these plans was based on attracting foreign investment (Buesa and Molero, 1986). Between 1984 and 1986, 86 percent of investments, 95 percent of produc-tion, and 97 of exports associated with the electronics industry plan corre-sponded to activities by five foreign investors: AT&T, Fujitsu, Hewlett Packard, Ericsson, and ITT (De Diego, 1995). The government encouraged FDI through the introduction of legislation that enabled foreign investment into most manufacturing sectors under the same conditions as resident Spaniards (Government of Spain, Royal Decree-Law 1,265/1986 of June 27) and through the state's facilitation of Telefonica's divestment from its industrial arm. By contrast, there was little in the way of R&D investment to enable local firms to develop more complex outputs. In 1985, Spain invested approximately 0.6 percent of its GDP in research and development. By 2018, investment had doubled to reach 1.2 percent, but was still half the OECD average (OECD, *Main Science and Technology Indicators*, 2020).

Spain's market approach needs to be understood within its European context. In the early 1980s, every European country except France abandoned public support for electronics due to high costs and disappointing results (Thatcher, 1999). Nonetheless, Spain's strategy had a detrimental effect on manufacturers. Foreign competition increased pressure on local firms, many of which sold their interests to foreign investors, only to see their facilities downsized or repurposed for wholesaling and services, as was the case with Fujitsu's acquisition of Secoinsa. Other firms folded or shifted from hardware to software, as was the case with Amper, one of the largest producers. In those instances when foreign investment led to new manufacturing capacity, as was the case with AT&T's microelectronics plant, legal provisions limiting technological spillovers (Ministerial Order of June 5, 1985) reduced upgrading opportunities for local firms. Furthermore, the investment was short-lived and the plant closed in 2001 (Zafra Díaz, 2001).

Not all outcomes were negative. Telefonica's commitment to universalize the national network, and later the operator's international expansion, provided some manufacturers an opportunity to leverage their long-standing relationship with the operator to specialize in the development of reasonably priced, low-tech, customized network solutions (Santillana del Barrio, 1997; López, Pueyo, and Zlatanova, 2002; Rama and Ferguson, 2007). By doing so, these manufacturers carved a competitive niche that large global providers would have found unprofitable and contributed to Telefonica's competitive advantage, especially in Latin America.

However, overall, the prioritization of telecommunications services and the reliance on a market solution for manufacturing meant that Spain's manufacturing capacity as a whole declined and that the remaining firms lacked the scale necessary to compete on global markets. In 2018, electronics manufacturing accounted for only 18 percent of ICT volume of business, with the remainder corresponding to telecommunications services and software (AMETIC, 2018). In 2011, the industry was composed of 187 firms and employed 5,906 people (AMETIC, 2011). For perspective, in 2018, Samsung electronics had 102,359 regular employees in Korea (Samsumg Electronics, 2019).

4.4 Building Korean Electronics' Leaders

This section examines the transformation of Korea's ICT industry through an analysis that follows the same structure as the previous section. It shows that the state's techno-industrial structure led Korea to support a strategy that prioritized the needs of electronics manufacturers and leveraged the government's control over the PTO to favor manufacturers. This strategy, imposed a heavy toll on the telecommunications operator but did not prevent the development of world-class infrastructure.

4.4.1 The Structure of the Korean ICT Sector

In the early 1980s, the Korean ICT industry was structured around its own version of the PTT model. Until 1982, the Korean ministry of communications played the dual role of policy maker and operator (Kim, 1993). In 1982, policy making and telecommunications services provision were separated with the incorporation of the monopoly operator, Korea Telecom (KT). Telecommunications services as a whole were divided among three companies, each of which operated under monopoly conditions in its respective segment: KT provided fixed telephony services, Data Telecom Corporation (DACOM), a public–private firm created in 1982, provided data services, and from 1984, Korea Mobile Telecommunications, a KT subsidiary, offered mobile telephony services (Cho, 2002). Despite the incorporation of KT, the state continued to exercise full control over the PTO through full ownership, the appointment of board members, the approval of service tariffs, and responsibility for strategic decisions, including budgeting and equipment procurement (Larson, 1995; Oh and Larson, 2011; Mytelka, 1999).

Most Korean electronics manufacturers were private firms belonging to chaebol: In 1988, Samsung, LG, Daewoo, and Hyundai accounted for 56 percent of total electronics production (Bloom, 1992). Nonetheless, the state exerted a degree of power over manufacturers through the issue of import licenses for parts and components, dominance over the credit system, and control over KT's product specifications and procurement decisions (Lim, 1998).

The Korean ICT industry was underdeveloped. In 1980, telephone service was "woefully deficient" (Oh and Larson, 2011, p. 31); Korea had a total of 2.8 million telephone lines, or 0.7 telephones per 100 inhabitants, and a perennially long waiting list for service that led to the emergence of a black market for the installation of fixed telephones that favored the wealthy and well connected (Oh and Larson, 2011). By 1985, Korea had expanded the network considerably but service penetration was still lower than Spain's (Table 4.1). Revenue per access channel was also low. Low profitability was correlated with Korea's low income per capita, which was 22 percent of the US' in 1985 (Maddison Project Database, 2018) but was also consistent with KT's reputation as a bureaucratic and inefficient organization (Kim, 1993; Choung et al., 2016).

Electronics manufacturers also suffered from significant competitive constraints. Despite being part of large business groups with significant resources, manufacturers had a limited technological base (Bloom, 1992). In the first half of the 1980s, three local firms: LG (then known as Lucky-Goldstar), Samsung, and Daewoo produced electromechanical switches, the most complex type of pre-digital telecommunications equipment, but all of them did it under foreign license (Mytelka, 1999). Local capacity for innovation consisted mostly of knowledge transfer, absorption, and adaptation to local production conditions (Kim, 1997). In fact, in the early 1980s, manufacturers and some policy makers considered telecommunications electronics excessively risky relative to the country's technological capabilities and resources (Choung and Hwang, 2007). This is reflected in the small share of resources devoted to telecommunications electronics, which accounted for about 5 percent of Samsung's and LG's overall business (Mytelka, 1999). Instead, in 1985, Korean electronics producers specialized in the production of parts and components and consumer electronics, such as microwave ovens and video cassette recorders, which constituted 80 percent of Korea's total electronics production (Garcia Calvo, 2021).

4.4.2 Strategic Coordination and Upgrading in the Electronics Industry

The Korean governments of the early 1980s, like their Spanish counterparts, showcased a strong commitment to upgrading and aspired "to participate more actively in the world economy" (EPB, 1981, p. 14). The technological base, global scope, and excellent market prospects of ICT fitted well with this purpose, while unmet demand for telecommunications services provided a concrete goal to work against.

The government's techno-industrial structure and orientation provided the strategic capacity to implement a long-term plan for an upgrading strategy that revolved around the needs of electronics manufacturers and the industry's potential to generate revenue. The decision to support upgrading in the ICT industry emanated directly from the president in 1980 (Oh and Larson, 2011). The presidential mandate provided the impulse for the development of a bureaucratic structure capable of formulating and implementing a long-term strategy. The first step was to elevate the status of the ministry of information and communication (MIC) within the ministerial structure by giving it direct access to the president. In addition, the president appointed a trained engineer as vice-minister of communications. This vice-president was later appointed as minister of communications, setting a precedent that has since been maintained (Garcia Calvo, 2021).

The office of the president coordinated the development of a long-term strategic plan that was drafted in 1981 by the MIC with support from scholars, government officials, large firms, and public research institutes (Oh and Larson, 2011). The decision was to focus on three strategic industries: electronic switching systems for telecommunications, semiconductors, and computers (Oh and Larson, 2011). This strategy underlines the relevance of Korea's techno-industrial governments and their capacity to develop sophisticated strategies that catered to the needs of complex manufacturing industries. Digital switches are essentially computers (Chapuis and Joel, 2003), which are composed of semiconductor materials. Therefore, the focus on switches stimulated firms to enter three strategic and interrelated subsegments simultaneously, generating synergies. Furthermore, the government's control of KT enabled the state to combine this strategy with plans to overhaul the public network while leveraging KT's human, physical, and financial resources to lower the costs and risks of entering the riskiest segment, which was the production of digital switches. Moreover, digital switches are complex, software-intensive products that are built to a client's specifications, whereas semiconductors are standardized products. Therefore, by bundling within a single strategy a sophisticated output that required firms to gain new competences and a standardized output that depended on competences at which Korean firms already excelled such as absorbing foreign technology, ramping up production, and keeping costs low, policy decision makers were simultaneously nudging firms to upgrade in telecommunications electronics, hedging their bets with a potential cash-cow, and dangling a carrot in front of firms.

To implement their strategy, technical-savvy policy makers were supported by a specialized, newly created agency, the Telecommunications Policy office, which assumed responsibility for policy formulation, telecommunications manufacturing, and network development. From 1984, the Telecommunications Policy Office was restructured into four separate divisions responsible for planning, promotion, management, and information/communications

(Oh and Larson, 2011) to provide a more efficient management system to support the overhaul of the ICT industry. The office was populated by high-caliber, engineering specialists, many of whom had been educated in US schools and worked in places such as Bell Labs (Kim, 2012). Korea's strategic capabilities were further reinforced by the resources of the EBP (Oh and Larson, 2011), and by a tight-knit network of ministry affiliated think tanks, public research institutions such as the Electronics and Telecommunications Research Institute (ETRI), and a world-class technical school, the Korean Advanced Institute of Science and Technology (KAIST) (Kim and Leslie, 1998).

Despite these capabilities, the severe crisis of the early 1980s had turned social perceptions against top-down political intervention in production (Lim, 1998). In addition, Korean chaebol had become sufficiently large and gained enough market power, to prevent the state from imposing direct hierarchical control. This meant that the government's upgrading plans could not be implemented without cooperation from manufacturers. In the first half of the 1980s, the government's strategy was an attractive proposition for firms. Global demand for electronics equipment was booming (Mytelka, 1999), creating a major business opportunity. In addition, unlike electromagnetic switches, digital ones had fewer, more standardized parts and were more software intensive (Mytelka, 1999). This meant that entering the segment was easier because production required less investment in precision engineering capabilities and high-level technical skills. Furthermore, some of the fabrication technology could be bought in the market, primarily from Japanese and US firms that had started to outsource the fabrication of standardized products such as semiconductors (Bloom, 1992). Moreover, emerging GVCs represented a critical commercial opportunity, especially after the revalorization of the Yen following the Plaza Accords in 1985, created a supply gap. Finally, from the mid-1980s, the Korean Won appreciated and requests for higher wages became militant (Steers, 1999), inducing manufactures to move toward more complex outputs to remain competitive.

Not only was the entry into the equipment industry attractive for Korean firms, but individual companies were unable to make the transition into complex telecommunications equipment without cooperation from the state. As part of the four largest chaebol, large electronics manufacturers had access to capital and attracted some of the best national talent. However, the diversified nature of the chaebol made them unsuitable to develop the long-term, mission-oriented, cooperative, trial-and-error research culture necessary to generate innovation, address shortages of world-class specialized talent, develop channels to process and disseminate innovation, and plug firms into international innovation networks (Jho, 2007). In addition, increasing levels of global market concentration meant that Korean firms faced market disadvantages relative to first movers from more advanced countries.

Korean firms could have addressed these challenges through inter-firm cooperation. Nonetheless, the government had already tried to persuade LG, Samsung, and the Oriental Pacific Company to form a joint venture to produce digital switches in the 1970s and failed (Mytelka, 1999). Even if inter-firm cooperation had succeeded, manufacturers still needed the state because they depended on their ability to use the PTO to provide stable demand for their products and access to its network to test, scale up, and debug models prior to commercialization (Millman and the AT&T staff, 1983).

Korea channeled the state's developmental aspirations and the firms' needs toward an upgrading strategy based on a clear division of labor between the state and large manufacturing firms. The nature of the arrangement was defined in the Fifth Economic and Social Development Plan (1982–86), which deviated from its predecessors' hierarchical approach in stating that the role of the state was to "indicate only the general framework and direction in which (investment) choices should be made," to create "incentive systems," and to foster "technological and manpower development" (EPB, 1981, p. 14). The strategy was implemented through a series of large-scale technology development projects in which the government guaranteed local demand, assumed a large share of the costs, and coordinated research and technology diffusion while firms concentrated on product development and commercialization.

The first of these projects aimed to accelerate the development of the Time Division Exchange (TDX), a digital switching system. The government stimulated production via local content rules that obliged KT to purchase from Korean manufacturers (Oh and Larson, 2011). The prioritization of digital network expansion to rural areas provided additional incentives because the first TDX models were expected to be small capacity switches unsuitable for urban areas (Kim, 1993). The government funded the entire development process through increases in service tariffs, a dedicated telecommunications tax, bond issues, and the reprioritization of public investment (Government of the Republic of Korea, 1988; Kim, Kim, and Yoon, 1992). ETRI was responsible for conducting the research and diffusing knowledge to firms (Bloom, 1992). Simultaneously, the 1986 Industrial Development Act stimulated the development of firms' innovation capabilities through schemes that involved reductions in tariffs on imports of R&D equipment, tax exemptions to attract US-educated and experienced Korean engineers, real estate tax exemptions for R&D institutes, and tax credits for expenditures on R&D and human capital development (Ahn and Jai, 2007). Finally, in 1985, President

Chun merged two preexisting educational institutions to form KAIST, thus ensuring a steady supply of technical manpower (Kim and Leslie, 1998).

The TDX program was an export failure (Oh and Larson, 2011). However, the technical success of the project gave Korea the confidence it needed to pursue an upgrading strategy based on innovation in electronics along the lines of the approach Japan had pursued in previous decades. In addition, the project enabled Korean manufacturers to develop the capabilities necessary to enter two sectors in which they eventually developed a competitive advantage: telecommunications network equipment and semiconductors. Finally, but no less importantly, the TDX project laid the basis for a coordinated model based on a clear division of labor between the state and large electronics manufacturers.

From 1989, the coordinated approach described above found continuity through the expansion of mobile telephony. A key feature of the development of Korea's strength in this segment was the government's use of its power to choose technical standards to guarantee demand for local producers and shelter them from competition. Some features of the project also showcase the importance of Korea's governments' technical know-how. By choosing the Code-Division Multiple Access (CDMA) standard, which had not yet been developed at a commercial level, over the Time-Division Multiple Access (TDMA) standard, in which European manufacturers already had a strong market position, the government set the Korean industry on a path that involved high up-front costs, a lengthy R&D phase, and long-term royalty payments to Qualcomm, the owner of the foundational technology. In exchange, this strategy guaranteed that Korean manufacturers faced zero competition in the local market and enabled them to use Korea as a test bed for technological catch up with competing TDMA manufacturers.

Korea's approach to mobile telephony was not without drawbacks: since the EU had adopted a TDMA standard, Global System for Mobile or (GSM) in 1987 (Segan, 2020), Korea's choice of CDMA meant that Korean-made mobile phones could not be commercialized in Europe. Instead, the Korean strategy implicitly relied on potential exports to other countries, and especially the US, where Qualcomm had developed the original technology and some mobile phone companies had already adopted CDMA.

As with the TDX program, the CDMA strategy relied on a division of labor between the state and large firms. The state was responsible for research coordination, knowledge diffusion, and most of the funding. Firms made capital contributions and were responsible for the development of handsets (Lee and Lim, 2001). The strategy enabled Korean firms to enter the mobile handset market, one of the segments in which both LG and Samsung are globally competitive in 2020.

Korea's coordination model found continuity through the development of the 3G version of CDMA starting in 1996. An important difference with previous projects was that 3G was a new technology to the world. Therefore, the project involved a shift from the commercial development of existing, foreign technology, to inventing technology. However, by the late 1990s the impending liberalization of telecommunications services and the adoption of GSM by most countries made it difficult for the government to subordinate the interests of mobile operators to those of the electronics industry, causing coordination to falter (Choung et al., 2016).

Rather than abandoning its coordination model, Korea reconfigured it. From then on, Korea no longer aimed to reach the efficiency frontier, but to "stay ahead" (Mullins and Shwayri, 2016, p. 51). The scope of the model broadened, from supporting the ICT industry to using ICT as "a driving force of national development" (MIC, 2004, p. 5). Incidentally, the new objective had the side effect of consolidating the MIC as a powerhouse within Korea's government.

The IT 839 strategy, launched in 2004, epitomizes this shift. The plan aimed to "promote an effective industrial development model that creates future growth engines through strong collaboration among IT services, infrastructure and manufacturing" (MIC, 2004, p. 5). As in the past, the strategy was based on a clear division of labor between the state and local electronics firms. The state was responsible for project leadership, policy design, the development of precompetitive technology, the creation of the initial market, technical leadership, and standardization. Firms were responsible for financial investment, product development, production, and commercialization (MIC, 2004). To avoid breaching WTO rules, the state substituted direct guidance with indirect advice via public agencies such as the National Information Society Agency to define the project (Kim, 2012). Direct subsidies and patient capital were substituted for precompetitive funding, low interest loans, matching funds, and investments from the NPS. Over time, the NPS has become a large source of patient capital to the ICT sector. In 2019 it held a 21.5 percent stake in Samsung electronics (NPS, 2019).

4.4.3 Telecommunications Services and Upgrading

Korea's coordination model benefited manufacturers but imposed a heavy burden on the incumbent operator. By 1986, KT was legally obliged to invest

2 percent of its revenue on R&D, a rate that was revised upwards and was expected to reach 6 percent by 1996 (Mytelka, 1999). This obligation was the equivalent of putting KT into a straightjacket: The TDX project alone required an annual workforce of 3,320 and involved approximately one billion dollars in R&D costs (Choung et al., 2016). With its capital tightly committed to the national market, and a legal mandate to provide fixed line services, KT failed to gain a strong foothold in the emerging mobile telephony market and sold its mobile subsidiary to the SK Group in 1994 (Mark and Birkinshaw, 2012). KT also failed to expand internationally until the 2010s. But even this expansion had the interests of the manufacturers in mind. For the most part, KT's international expansion has taken the form of network construction projects funded by the KDB. These projects generate demand for Korean electronics equipment and upon completion KT hands over the completed network to a local telecommunications operator.

KT's support of manufacturing also entailed a loss of managerial autonomy for the operator, caused delays in internal restructuring, and created a climate of impunity that has persisted for a long time. In 1996, KT underwent a workforce reduction, but there was little change in the company's hierarchical, seniority-based structure, bureaucratic procedures, compartmentalized divisional organization, or in its traditional culture of conformity (Mark and Birkinshaw, 2012). KT's market share and profitability declined for a decade after liberalization in 1998. Since then, KT has been mired in senior-level corruption scandals that have forced out the company's last three CEOs (Reuters, 2008; Kim, 2013; The Investor, 2018; Yonhap, 2018).

On the bright side, Korea's coordination model did not delay network development and modernization or hinder competition. Between 1985 and 1989 alone, Korea installed 5.2 million new lines—almost twice as many as Spain (International Telecommunications Union, 2010). Korea accelerated network deployment by simultaneously installing the TDX in rural areas and importing high-capacity switching systems for urban areas (Kim, 1993). Infrastructure overhaul has remained a signature component of Korea's ICT strategy through two additional plans: the Korea Information Infrastructure (KII) (1995–2005) and the Broadband Convergence Network (BcN) (2005–10).

4.5 Conclusions: Two Different Pathways to Overcoming Firms' Competitive Limitations

This chapter analyzed how Spain and Korea strategized the competitive transformation of their ICT industries, understood as telecommunications services (voice and data transmission over fixed and mobile networks) and telecommunications equipment (network and user equipment) from the 1980s. As was the case in the banking sector, these transformations were based on a system of quid pro quo exchanges underpinned by state-firm interdependencies. In the early 1980s, national governments pursued objectives related to the expansion and modernization of national networks that they could not achieve without cooperation from firms. Telecommunications operators and manufacturers faced a host of competitive deficiencies that they were unable to overcome without sustained and committed support from the state. However, in the midst of the shift to a new industry paradigm, the priorities of operators and manufacturers in Spain and Korea were not aligned. Operators stood to benefit from the disintegration of vertically integrated structures that forced them to devote vast capital and human resources to product development, sit through delays in equipment delivery that affected quality of service, and pay a high price premium. By contrast, manufacturers depended on the PTOs for the stable demand, patient capital, and access to the public network to successfully develop state-of-the-art equipment.

In this context, Spanish and Korean national governments willingly and publicly expressed their commitment to providing long-term support for the industry and honored their commitment by shifting from their pre-existing PTT models to symbiotic structures based on a division of labor and quid pro quo exchanges between governments and firms. However, Spain and Korea pursued strategies that prioritized either services or manufacturing at the expense of the other segment of the industry.

In Spain, governments dominated by orthodox economists with limited knowledge of technology and deep biases against conventional industrial policies prioritized the transformation of the incumbent telecommunications operator. As part of this strategy, they enabled Telefonica to divest from its industrial arm and to purchase equipment from global suppliers. By doing so, they favored the operator but deprived electronics manufacturers of the patient capital and stable demand they needed to develop new and complex electronics equipment.

In Korea, techno-industrial governments headed by ministers with a technical background, supported by specialized institutions in adjacent areas such as research and higher education, pursued a strategy that focused on overhauling electronics manufacturing through the development of technological competences. This strategy enabled manufactures to enter market segments for increasingly more complex products in ways that have proved durable. However, in doing so, Korea also limited growth opportunities for the incumbent operator, KT.

Through these models, Spain and Korea have developed globally competitive ICT industries. However, the misalignment between the needs of operators and manufactures means that Spain's and Korea's strategies were not without drawbacks. In all probability, Spain has missed the chance of having a globally-relevant telecommunications manufacturing industry, although Telefonica's prominence and international track record have enabled a small set of specialized suppliers to flourish. Korea has managed to have a thriving mobile telecommunications industry. However, the incumbent operator has struggled to transform and regain managerial autonomy, remaining in some ways deeply influenced by Korea's continued support for electronics manufacturers.

The next chapter examines in greater depth Spain's and Korea's approaches to manufacturing through the analysis of the automotive industry. The chapter emphasizes the integrational and self-sufficient ethos of the two countries' strategies and the implications of these strategies for industrial specialization.

5

Integration or Self-Sufficiency?

Two Approaches to Develop the Automotive Industry and Their Enduring Effects

5.1 Introduction

From the mid-1970s, the automotive sector experienced a massive transformation. New competitors, the adoption of production platforms, the rise of just-in-time, the emergence of global value chains, and greater demand for fuel-efficient vehicles transformed vertically integrated, inward oriented production structures into flexible, outward oriented, co-located clusters that operate within global value chains.

As latecomers to the industry, Spanish and Korean firms faced this transformation from a position of disadvantage compared to world-leading producers based in advanced countries. Spanish and Korean automakers or original equipment manufacturers (OEMs) depended on OEMs from advanced countries for the knowledge and know-how necessary to style and design vehicles, build prototypes, and organize complex production structures. Local OEMs also suffered from quality and process deficiencies and had yet to reach scale efficiencies. In addition, Spanish and Korean firms faced obstacles derived from the features of the two countries' institutional models. In Spain, where foreign investment was an indispensable source of technology, local OEMs, and suppliers competed directly with a growing number of better capitalized and more technologically advanced foreign rivals. In Korea, where, local OEMs aimed to develop their own technological capabilities, firms struggled to overcome their dependency from foreign partners and increase product quality.

By the 2010s, Spain and Korea had large, competitive automotive industries. According to the International Organization of Motor Vehicle Manufacturers [OICA], in 2018, the two countries were the world's ninth and seventh producers of motor vehicles respectively (OICA, 2020). The Spanish and Korean automotive sectors were comparable in terms of output, revenue, employment, and contribution to national GDP (Table 5.1). However, the structure of the

State-Firm Coordination and Upgrading: Reaching the Efficiency Frontier in Skill-, Capital-, and Knowledge-Intensive Industries in Spain and South Korea. Angela Garcia Calvo, Oxford University Press. © Angela Garcia Calvo 2021.
DOI: 10.1093/oso/9780198864561.003.0005

Table 5.1 Overview of Spain's and Korea's automotive industries

	Spain	Korea
Production all vehicles (2017)*	2,848,335	4,114,913****
Number of plants	17	12
Local vs foreign owned	100% foreign owned	60% local (7 Kia+ Hyundai)
Percentage exports	81%	63%
Employment*	330,000	246,900
Turnover in US$ million*	82,920	72,442
Contribution to GDP	9%	7%
Investment in innovation in US$ million (2014)**	516	6,713
Of which government investment in US$ million	17	167
Exports % and or value** *	Country's largest export sector; $35.8 billion in value, 17.9% of all Spanish exports, and 4.8% of world's total exports of the automotive industry)	Country's second largest export sector $38.8 billion, about 12% of all Korean exports and 5.2% of world's automotive exports.

* Only Tier 1.
Data for Spain: Sernauto Asociación Española de Proveedores de Automoción.
Data for Korea: KAICA Korea Auto Industries Cooperative Association.

Spanish and Korean automotive sectors was very different. All of Spain's assemblers and the majority of suppliers were foreign-affiliated firms (Spanish Association of Automobile and Truck Manufacturers [ANFAC], 2019; Guillén, 2010) and the industry operated within the context of the EU-wide value chain. By contrast, Korea was home to the world's third largest automaker, HMC (OICA, 2020), which exercised control over a vast vertically integrated, local value chain.

This chapter compares the development of Spain's foreign-dominated, regionally integrated automotive industry, with the successful rise and consolidation of a local Korean OEM. The analysis becomes a conduit to contrast two models of state–firm coordination and their impact on the development of a manufacturing industry that involves high levels of technological and organizational complexity. In the first model, the state sees automotive as an instrument to propel Spain's integration in the international economy through FDI and the outsourcing of technological capacity. In the second, local OEMs are active agents of a tight quid pro quo relationship in which the largest OEM and the state prioritize the development of technological capabilities as a way to reach self-sufficiency.

As the previous two chapters, this one starts by characterizing the structure of the automotive industry to showcase the challenges faced by Spanish and Korean firms. The two subsequent sections provide empirical evidence of Spain's and Korea's models, connect them to the structure of the industry, and discuss their implications as the industry continues to transform. The final section of the chapter summarizes the findings and sets the stage for the concluding portion of the book.

5.2 The Organization and Transformation of the Automotive Industry

Until the 1970s, the global automotive sector was dominated by a handful of vertically integrated firms based in the US and Europe. Most of these firms produced high volumes of standardized vehicles at affordable prices. Along with these firms, there existed a handful of smaller, independent OEMs that competed on the basis on quality, performance, and status. Vehicle models were designed individually, producers kept large inventories of parts and components on premise, and outputs were usually destined for the domestic market (Womack et al., 1990).

In the 1970s and 1980s, the industry experienced a radical transformation. In the first half of the 1970s, US manufacturers started to expand their footprint abroad to create their own global production networks. By the middle of the decade, changes in vehicle architecture led to the emergence of platforms that provided a common structure for a number of outwardly distinct vehicle models. In the 1980s, the irruption of high-quality, competitive Japanese vehicles increased competition, generated pressure to improve vehicle quality, and forced European and American OEMs to adopt more efficient forms of production. Just-in-time production enabled large European and US automakers to lower fixed costs by shedding their supply networks and adopting tiered production structures. Tight connections and geographical colocation between OEMs and Tier 1 suppliers (suppliers that sell directly to automakers) facilitated cost management, enhanced production efficiency, and increased output quality (Womack et al.,1990). Finally, from the mid-1980s, increasing market protectionism, together with the introduction of regional trade agreements in North America (North America Free Trade

Agreement) and Europe (the EU single market), led to the emergence of regionally integrated value chains.

Spanish and Korean automakers faced these changes from a position of disadvantage relative to established OEMs from the US, Japan, and other Western European countries. Spanish and Korean OEMs depended on their counterparts from more advanced nations for technology and know-how. Most of these emerging OEMs also lacked the capacity to design their own vehicles. Those that did were still heavily dependent on foreign assistance for prototyping, product development, human skills, machinery, and equipment. Spanish and Korean suppliers also faced major technological limitations and usually imported vital parts and components such as engines, power trains, and braking systems (Amsden and Kang 1995; Green, 1992).

Spanish and Korean OEMs and suppliers had yet to reach an efficient scale (Amsden and Kang, 1995). Low production runs harmed profitability and limited the ability of OEMs to learn from experience (Amsden and Kang, 1995). Furthermore, since OEMs produced primarily for their local markets, low output levels made them vulnerable to large swings in national demand due to periodic economic crises, inflation, shortages of foreign exchange, or sudden rises in interest rates (Green, 1992; García Ruíz, 2001). Spain and Korea tried to optimize production runs by introducing barriers to the import of finished vehicles and imposing constraints on FDI. However, this strategy sheltered local OEMs from competition without necessarily solving the problem due to the limited size of the internal market.

To address this problem, Spain and Korea turned to exports. However, local OEMs specialized in the production of low cost, compact vehicles that served the needs of local, relatively unsophisticated emerging middle classes (Bueno Lastra and Ramos Pérez, 1986; San Román, 1995). These vehicles lacked in terms of quality, durability, versatility, and finish (Amsden and Kang, 1995; García Ruíz, 2001; Green, 1992). In some cases, the vehicles did not even meet the regulatory requirements of advanced countries (Green, 1992), making exports to large, lucrative markets such as the US unfeasible.

Spain and Korea addressed these limitations through two different strategies. Spain followed an integrational approach consisting of attracting FDI, integrating Spain's production within the emerging EU-wide value chain, and outsourcing technological capabilities to foreign automakers. Korea pursued a self-sufficient approach that revolved around the emergence of a local, independent OEM with a vertically integrated value chain and the development of local technological capabilities.

These two strategies were rooted in Spain's and Korea's relationships with the external environment and with their views on the role of manufacturing in upgrading. In Spain, where the government strove to become accepted by the international community and manufacturing played a secondary role relative to complex services, the government instrumentalized government-controlled automakers to achieve broader political objectives. In Korea, where the state aspired to free the country from foreign interference and the development of local manufacturing firms was the main priority, the government engaged in a quid pro quo exchange with a local OEM to fulfill public goals, enabling the emergence of an autonomous, globally competitive automaker.

Ultimately, the two countries' strategies led to the emergence of large, profitable automotive sectors. However, much of Spain's production capacity is linked to foreign investors and integrated within the EU-wide value chain whereas Korea's industry is built around a local, dominant OEM and its vertically-integrated, local value chain. As the industry faces the transition to a new paradigm and a new round of consolidation, these differences have counterintuitive implications for the future of the two industries. The following two sections explore these issues in detail.

5.3 Upgrading and Innovation in the Spanish Automotive Sector

This section analyzes the transformation of Spain's automotive industry. The first subsection characterizes the Spanish automotive sector, discusses the origins of the government's integration strategy, and showcases the instrumentalization of automakers. The second subsection, shows how the government leveraged the state-controlled automotive industry to achieve its goal of integrating with Europe and the impact of this approach on upgrading. The third subsection discusses the implications of Spain's foreign-dominated production structure as the automotive sector faces a new wave of transformation.

5.3.1 Building a Local Automotive Industry through FDI

From the 1940s, the Spanish government saw the development of the automotive industry as a strategic objective. However, the government ignored several private initiatives to establish domestic automakers and sought instead to stimulate the development of the industry through direct control (San Román, 1995; Guillén, 2010). To this effect, instead of declaring the automotive sector a national interest industry, which would have given any entrant preferential access to vital resources such as discounted credit, import licenses, and foreign exchange, the government retained the right to confer preferential status to individual firms discretionally (Roldán Rabadán, 2013; Galán, 2016). In Spain's autarkic regime, these policies had the effect of condemning private initiatives to certain failure, while favoring the establishment of local OEMs championed by the state and government elites (San Román, 1995). By the mid-1950s Spain's production structure consisted of four OEMs that had tight connections to the government: FASA, a company backed by Franco's brother in cooperation with Renault (Sánchez Sánchez, 2004), and three OEMs in which the state held a controlling stake: Seat, the country's flagship car producer, ENASA, a truck producer, and Motor Ibérica, a tractor manufacturer (García Ruíz, 2001).

The Francoist governments saw the automotive industry as an instrument to accelerate industrialization and legitimize the regime. Given Spain's capital and technological deficiencies, FDI was indispensable to develop the industry (Campa and Guillén, 1996; Varela Panache, 1972). However, FDI also had an important political dimension. After World War II, the allied powers boycotted Franco's authoritarian regime (United Nations [UN] General Assembly Resolution 39(I), 1946). International isolation had a detrimental impact on the regime's legitimacy and on the economy of an impoverished Spain. As the country emerged from international ostracism in 1953 (UN General Assembly Resolution 386 (V); ABC staff, 1953), Francoists and their critics saw foreign presence as a source of validation for Spain's dictatorial system (Guillén, 2010).

The decision to stimulate FDI was formalized in the 1959 Stabilization Plan (Decree-Law 10/1959 of July 21). The plan put an end to two decades of autarky and paved the way for liberalization measures to attract foreign investors, including the adoption of a single, convertible exchange rate, the deregulation of internal prices, a large reduction of tariffs, the partial liberalization of inward FDI, and the facilitation of profit repatriation (Pérez, 1997). In addition to these favorable measures, investors were attracted by Spain's combination of cheap and docile labor, the presence of ancillary industries, and a potentially large internal market (García Ruíz, 2001).

These measures, together with Spain's favorable conditions, accomplished their goals of attracting FDI and accelerating the development of the automotive sector. By the end of the 1960s, the four local OEMs mentioned above had foreign technical partners and four additional foreign automakers (Citroën, Chrysler, British Motor Corporation, and Daimler) had established a presence in Spain (García Ruíz, 2001; Sánchez, 2004; Basque Association of Industrial and Public Patrimony—Asociación vasca de patrimonio industrial y obra pública, 2019). The arrival of foreign investors translated into rapid growth. Between 1958 and 1972 the automotive industry grew at a cumulative annual rate of 22 percent, accounting for 13.3 percent of Spain's total growth (García Ruíz, 2001). The automotive sector became the symbol of Spain's "economic miracle" (Del Arco, 2007) and the poster child of Francoist industrialization.

But while Spain's FDI strategy fulfilled public objectives, its impact on upgrading was mixed. On the plus side, the imposition of local content rules, in conjunction with rapid increases in assembly capacity, incentivized local entrepreneurs to enter the supply industry, setting the basis for what would later become a competitive subindustry (Guillén, 2010). On the other hand, although Spain imposed a legal cap on foreign ownership (San Román,1995) the welcoming attitude to FDI and the absence of dedicated initiatives to support the development of local technological capabilities meant that local OEMs remained dependent on a steady flow of foreign technology. The development of local technological capabilities was further constraint by the fact that Spanish producers were not even exposed to state-of-the-art technologies and production methods. Due to the closed nature of the Spanish market and the unsophisticated tastes (and lack of choice) of Spanish consumers, automakers concentrated on the production of vehicle models that were already obsolete in their countries of origin, often using imported, superannuated equipment (García Ruíz, 2001; Campa y Guillén,1996). Moreover, the proliferation of automakers and the local orientation of production meant that plants did not reach efficiency scale and vehicle production runs were relatively short (García Ruíz, 2001), which limited opportunities for learning-by-doing.

5.3.2 Ramping Up Integration at the Expense of Automakers' Upgrading

From the early 1970s, the Spanish government intensified its integration efforts and continued to use FDI in the automotive industry to achieve it. Spain was not invited to participate in the creation of the European Communities in the 1950s. However, ever eager for international validation and acceptance, the Francoist regime requested membership in 1962 (Powell, 2015). The dictatorial nature of Spain's government led to expeditious rejection, but the bloc opened negotiations that resulted in a preferential trade agreement in 1970.

The EU trade agreement, together with Spain's established capacity in automotive, comparatively low labor costs, and a suitable geographical location to serve surrounding European countries attracted foreign investors to Spain (Catalán Vidal, 2007; Alvarez Gil and González de la Fe, 1997). In 1971, the government entered negotiations with Ford to establish a new plant. The agreement between the government and Ford was formalized in the so-called Ford Decrees (Decree 3,339/1972 of November 30 and Decree 3,757/1972 of December 23), which were tailor-made to suit the demands of the automaker (García Ruíz, 2001; Catalán Vidal, 2007). An important component of the decrees was the declaration of automotive as a preferential industry. This meant that Ford, and any other entrant into the automotive industry, whether foreign or domestic, could claim the same privileges as Spain's government-controlled OEMs. The measure effectively deprived local OEMs of preferential treatment, exposing them to direct competition with global automakers.

The erosion of local OEM protection, the establishment of a Ford state-of-the-art plant, and the prospect of additional investment by General Motors (GM), with which the government also started negotiations in the 1970s (Alvarez Gil and González de la Fe, 1997), put Spain on the map of global automotive production and fulfilled the government's quest for international acceptance. However, this new context also compromised the upgrading trajectory of Spanish OEMs. Seat's predicament is a case in point. The enactment of the Ford decrees led Fiat, Seat's technological partner, to reconsider its alliance with the Spanish OEM and request a renegotiation of the relationship (Catalán Vidal, 2007). The prospect of a potential exit from Fiat left Seat staring into the abyss. In the first half of the 1970s, the Spanish automaker had yet to establish its own technology department and depended on Fiat's assistance to design its vehicles (Alvarez Gil and González de la Fe, 1997). Seat also faced additional competitive limitations. Unlike Ford, which planned to produce only one model and export most of its production, Seat produced a large range of vehicles, mostly for the Spanish market. This translated into short product runs, high fixed costs, and a significant exposure to Spain's market fluctuations. In addition, Seat's financial situation was precarious: in 1974, the year Ford started commercialization vehicles produced in Spain, SEAT's margins were a mere 0.1 percent (Catalán Vidal, 2007). Finally, as the leader of a protected market, Seat had relatively little experience with real competition, which translated into a sharp drop in domestic market share once Ford products were commercialized. Between 1974 and 1979, Seat lost 20 market share points (Alvarez Gil and González de la Fe, 1997).

Seat's crisis was addressed through a series of arrangements by which GM was temporarily prevented from entering the market and Fiat agreed to take a controlling stake on Seat if and when Spain joined the EU (Catalán Vidal, 2007). In addition, Seat's technological capacities were strengthened through the launch in 1975 of a technical center where the automaker designed its first vehicle (ABC, 2015). Nonetheless, these measures did not fundamentally resolve Seat's competitive deficiencies. The agreement that prevented GM from entering the market involved Seat's takeover of ailing British Leyland's operations in Spain, putting Seat's finances under further strain (Catalán Vidal, 2007). Fiat's commitment also remained on shaky grounds and the Italian OEM exited the partnership in 1981 (Lewin, 1981). Furthermore, despite the launch of the first Seat-designed vehicle in 1975, the Spanish automaker still depended on foreign assistance for the development of engines, transmissions, and vehicle design technology for most of its models (Catalán Vidal, 2007).

More importantly, from the late 1970s, the pace of Spain's integration with the EU accelerated, sealing the fate of the Spanish OEM. The first Spanish democratic governments saw EU integration as a pathway to democratic consolidation and future growth. Spain reapplied for membership in 1977 and negotiations opened in 1979 (Ministry of External Affairs, 2020). From 1982, Spain's orthodox economists further rejected the protectionist stance of previous governments and championed a strategy based on privatizations of publicly owned firms and foreign takeovers. As discussed in Chapter 3, this strategy was accompanied by measures that enabled large banks to divest from their industrial investments, including a sizeable stake in Seat, and to charge high interest rates for loans at a time when the automaker most needed them.

Through the 1980s and 1990s Spain's integrational strategy and the orthodox economists' FDI approach succeeded in attracting significant amounts of investment to the automotive industry. Spain's upcoming EU membership, low labor costs compared to those in more advanced Western European countries, and the emergence of an EU-wide value chain (Womack et al., 1990; Pallarés-Barberá, 1998), worked in favor of the government's approach. The most notorious investor during this period was GM, which agreed to establish a new plan in 1979, expanding Spain's production capacity (Pérez, 2017). However, in the absence of a dedicated effort to support technological autonomy and address local firms' needs for patient capital, much of the investment that took place during this period involved acquisitions rather than greenfield investment. Spain's four OEMs were acquired by foreign investors. Seat was acquired by Volkswagen in 1986; Motor Iberica by Nissan and Suzuki in 1987, ENASA by Iveco-Fiat in 1990, and Renault took full control of FASA (Alvarez Gil and González de la Fe, 1997; Marimón 2006; García Ruíz, 2001).

In the absence of a dedicated effort to support upgrading, Spain's integrational approach also put suppliers in a difficult position. Unable to access the patient capital they needed to upgrade, many suppliers experienced financial difficulties and faced a choice between exiting the market or selling their interests to foreign investors. Out of the population of local suppliers active in 1972, only 50 percent were still under Spanish control in 1988, 25 percent had been acquired by foreign investors, and the remaining 25 percent had exited the market (Lagendijk, 1995). By the late 1990s, about three-quarters of Spanish suppliers were affiliated to firms based outside of Spain (Guillén, 2010).

Overall, Spain's integrational approach delivered mixed results from the point of view of upgrading. The foreign acquisition of local OEMs meant Spain had lost the opportunity of having a local, independent automaker. On a more positive note, the injection of FDI, and Spain's integration into the EU-wide value chain transformed a mid-sized sector that operated behind the efficiency frontier, into a large, competitive, outward-oriented one. In 2019, Spain produced 2.8 million vehicles, which made it Europe's second largest auto manufacturer after Germany and the world's ninth largest auto producer (OICA production statistics, 2020). Over 80 percent of Spanish-produced vehicles were exported, three-quarters of which to Europe (ANFAC, 2020). Moreover, despite the influx of FDI, a handful of local suppliers managed not only to survive, but to consolidate and expand internationally by leveraging their preexisting relationships with multiple OEMs already operating in Spain to gain contracts abroad. As of 2021, Spain was home to three of the world's largest 100 suppliers: Gestamp, Grupo Antolín, and CIE Automotive (Automotive News, 2019) as well as a number of smaller yet highly specialized, competitive suppliers.

5.3.3 The Future of an Integrated Production Structure

Until the 1990s, Spain was able to attract and retain foreign investors through a combination of public incentives, low labor costs, and a favorable geographical location. Since then, European and WTO norms have outlawed public subsidies, and the fall of the Berlin Wall and Spain's own economic dynamics have eroded Spain's cost and geographical advantage. As of 2020, the Spanish automotive sector was one of the largest contributors to the national economy, accounting for 8.5 percent of GDP and 9 percent of total employment (ANFAC, 2020). Spain has managed to maintain its production capacity through a combination of labor flexibility, adaptability, high productivity levels, and the presence of a substantial supplier industry. However, as the sector marches toward a new industry paradigm defined by electrification, autonomy, connectivity, and shared vehicles (Ehlers, 2018), this is not enough to ensure the sustainability of the industry. In fact, sharp decreases in global automotive demand in 2020 and the ensuing global restructuring could lead to a substantial scale back of foreign investment. Nissan's 2020 announcement that it will close its production plant in Barcelona (Cordero, 2020) appear to show that this is the case.

In this setting, the integration of Spain's production in the EU-wide value chain, and the high level of foreign affiliated firms, including all OEMs, could be seen as the industry's weakest point. After all, critical corporate decisions, including decisions regarding production of new vehicle models and lines of systemic innovation are taken outside the country. Furthermore, in a highly regulated industry in which national states continue to hold significant stakes in large OEMs, strategic decisions are not necessarily based on strict economic criteria and are not expected to favor Spanish production.

Despite these expectations, Spain's integration in the EU-wide value chain is likely to be a source of advantage for Spain's specialized, competitive suppliers. Reputable suppliers can benefit from well-established relationship to multiple European OEMs to get a foothold on increasingly complex segments of the industry as OEMs concentrate their resources on emerging features such as the development of batteries for electric vehicles. Suppliers can also take advantage of their relationships and experience to develop innovative outputs they may offer to multiple automakers subverting the traditional hierarchies between OEMs and suppliers. Finally, some suppliers may be able to expand their operations by offering services to emerging automakers with limited experience in vehicle design and manufacturing.

The experience of Gestamp, one of Spain's three largest suppliers, offers some insights into the advantages of EU integration for large, well-established, Spanish suppliers. Gestamp is a spinoff of Gonvarri, a steel company that has served the automotive industry since 1958 and a global leader in the production of metal structures and components (Automotive News, 2019). The shift to electric vehicles, which carry much heavier batteries, has driven OEMs to request lighter metal structures that can stand stringent crash, performance, deformation, and energy absorption tests (Gestamp, 2017). Forced to concentrate their resources on the development of electric batteries, OEMs have been willing to outsource the design and development of lighter metal structures to Tier 1 suppliers. Gestamp has jumped at the opportunity by becoming one of the first companies to invest in hot stamping, a technology that delivers high-strength and ultra-light steel products. Through the acquisition of three specialized firms—SSAB HardTech in 2004; Edscha, and Tyssen Krupp Metal Forming in 2010—Gestamp has become the global leader in hot stamping and gained scale in Europe and the US (Murphy, 2017). Gestamp has also used OEMs' willingness to outsource core design functions to enter new product segments such as skins, which are the external, most complex part of a car's metal structure. To do so, from the 2000s, Gestamp has developed capabilities in die/tool manufacturing forming, advanced assembly, and advanced finishing technologies (Gestamp, 2017). Results speak for themselves: between 2007 and 2017, Gestamp's revenue more than doubled from €3,500 million in 2007 (Guillén and García-Canal, 2010) to €8,548 million in 2017 (Gestamp, 2018).

5.4 Upgrading and Innovation in the Korea Automotive Industry

This section examines the transformation of Korea's automotive industry through an analysis that parallels that of the previous section. It shows that, whereas Spain's integrational approach and the lack of a dedicated effort to develop local technological capabilities trammeled OEM's upgrading, Korea's emphasis on self-sufficiency and local technological capabilities underpinned a cooperative, quid pro quo arrangement through which the government furthered its objectives and enabled a local OEM to become an independent, globally competitive producer.

5.4.1 Building an Automotive Industry through Cooperation

From the start, the emergence of Korea's modern, mass automotive industry was based on a combination of state incentives and private initiative. The 1962 Automobile Industry Protection Act encouraged entrepreneurs to enter the industry by banning imports of assembled vehicles, enabling duty-free imports of parts and components, and establishing policy loans (Green, 1992; Guillén, 2010; KIET, 2014).

Throughout the 1960s, local automakers operated as knockdown assembly producers and were heavily dependent on foreign OEMs for technology assistance. In the early 1970s, the four largest local OEMs assembled vehicles for foreign brands: HMC for Ford, Asia Motor for Fiat, Kia for Mazda, and Shinjin (Daewoo) for GM (Kim, 1997). In addition, Korean automakers depended on the state for the provision of patient capital and import licenses for the materials, parts and components, and machinery necessary to produce (Amsden, 1989). But despite these limitations, and in stark contrast with their Spanish counterparts, Korea's automakers exercised a degree of agency relative to the government and their foreign partners. For example, manufacturers resisted government's plans to rationalize the industry. The 1963 Plan for Automotive Industry Unification and the 1964 Automobile Production Plan envisaged a single, vertically integrated OEM that could reach economies of scale. However, upon pressure from local firms, especially the Hyundai chaebol, which sought to enter the sector, the government abandoned such plans in 1967 in favor of a strategy that enabled any qualified firm to enter the market (Back, 1990). In addition, despite their dependence on foreign technology, Korean OEMs maintained strategic control over their firms. In 1976, three of the four large Korean OEMs were 100 percent locally owned (Back, 1990).

As in Spain, the development of Korea's mass automotive production was an instrument to achieve broader political goals of industrialization and political legitimation. However, while Spain saw foreign investment and foreign presence as instruments to legitimatize a regime that had been ostracized by the international community, Korea saw the development of local technological capabilities as a way to overcome experiences of unwanted foreign intervention and dependence.

Korea's perspective was linked to the country's relationship with the US. During the Vietnam war, Korea had been the US's most staunch ally, sending two divisions (about 50,000 troops) to fight along US troops (Kwak, 2003). In exchange, the US provided Korea generous financial help, political support for Park's regime, and a military defense commitment (Kwak, 2003). However, in 1970, President Nixon's announcement that US's allies were to be responsible for their defense, together with the US's unilateral reduction of troops in Korea, left the Asian country questioning American commitment (Sakong, 1993; Lee and Markusen, 2003; Pai, 2004). President Park, who at the time was also facing internal pressures to end its regime (Back, 1990), responded by hardening its stronghold on power and reorienting production toward self-sufficiency and self-defense. In 1972, he enacted the Yushing Constitution, which transformed the regime from a soft to a hard dictatorship. Park also launched the HCI, which focused on the development of dual-purpose industries (Sakong, 1993), and established a clandestine nuclear weapons program (Taliaferro, 2019).

In line with these policies, the 1974 Long-Term Automobile Production Plan called for the development of a car model entirely produced in Korea (Green, 1992; Clifford, 1994). To achieve its goal, the government made automotive manufacturing licenses conditional on the approval of detailed plans for the development of a "people's car" that complied with detailed product specifications. The level of detail of the plan, which included aspects such as the size of the engine and production costs, and the authoritarian nature of the request suggests that automakers acted solely at the government's behest. In reality, both the initiative and the successful implementation of the plan were based on a mutually beneficial coordination arrangement between the state and the automakers, especially HMC.

In response to the government mandate, three OEMs: Kia, Shinjin/ Daewoo, and HMC, submitted plans to develop a local car. Of the three automakers, only one HMC, complied not only with the letter but also with the spirit of the government's request. Kia's entry was a version of the Mazda Brisa, produced with Mazda's assistance (Ravenhill, 2001). Shinjin/Daewoo (henceforth Daewoo/GM Korea) had established a joint venture with GM in 1972 and its first vehicle was a GM model based on GM's technology platform. By contrast, HMC developed a proprietary model, the Pony.

HMC's proposal was not are sponse to a government imposition. On the contrary, the automaker made a choice that was congruent with the firm's own ambition to become an independent automaker. HMC had entered the market as a knockdown assembler for Ford in 1967. However, the Korean automaker regarded the collaboration with the American OEM as a stepping stone, and by 1969 it initiated talks to develop a joint venture to produce engines (Hyun and Lee, 1989). In 1973, HCM withdrew from this plan after it became clear that Ford's goal was to establish a plant that would be integrated in the US's automaker's emerging global value chain, whereas HMC wanted to keep strategic control of the plant and aimed to produce full vehicles for export using Ford's technology, financial resources, and distribution network (Back, 1990; Steers, 1999). The breakdown of the joint venture with Ford left HMC with two options: find a new foreign technological partner or become an independent OEM. In 1973, HMC announced its intention to become an independent OEM (Ravenshill, 2001).

The compatibility between the state's and HMC's goals, the government's inability to further its goal to achieve self-sufficiency in the automotive sector without cooperation from the OEM, and HMC's competitive limitations, set the basis for a fruitful cooperative arrangement based on quid pro quo exchanges. Through this arrangement, the state supported HMC's upgrading (and by extension that of the whole automotive industry) via the provision of patient capital and an asymmetric regulatory environment that protected local OEMs from external competition. In response, HMC developed a proprietary technological base and delivered the final output.

Interactions between HMC and the government took place directly through a special commission linked to the presidency (Back, 1990). HMC developed the capabilities necessary to design and produce a full vehicle by sourcing technology simultaneously from multiple foreign firms. To develop the Pony, HMC sourced technology from 26 firms based in five countries and formed a team responsible for absorbing and integrating the acquired knowledge (Kim, 1997; Hyun and Lee, 1989). To support the process, in 1974 the government raised tariffs on imported cars from 150 to 250 percent while simultaneously lowering taxes by over 50 percent on locally produced cars (Lee and Mah, 2017). The automotive industry was also one of the largest recipients of policy loans (Ravenhill, 2001). Furthermore, state-owned POSCO provided steel at prices that were between 40 and 25 percent lower than those paid by Japanese and American automakers respectively (Back, 1990).

In contrast with the launch of the first Spanish-designed vehicle, which passed almost under the radar, the Korean government framed the launch of the Pony in 1975 as a major technological breakthrough. the model was a commercial success in the Korean market and established HMC as the market leader. In 1982, HMC accounted for 80–90 percent of the market (Kim, 1990). More importantly, the launch of the Pony established a pattern of collaboration between automakers, especially HMC, and the state, gave HMC confidence in its capabilities, and established the automotive industry solidly in Korea. By 1980, the auto industry accounted for 3.3 percent of Korea's manufacturing, and generated 62,889 jobs (Korea Automotive Manufacturers Association [KAMA], 2009).

5.4.2 From Fledging Independence to Full Autonomy through Cooperation

Despite the initial success of the Pony, the government and HMC were still far from fulfilling their goals of achieving technological self-sufficiency. By 1976, HMC could adapt components from multiple suppliers and combine them into its own vehicle but still needed external assistance with styling, engine and transmission design, prototyping, final drawing, production preparation, and pilot production (Amsden and Kang, 1995). HMC also suffered from high rates of defects caused by poor materials, workmanship, and low-quality parts (Guillén, 2010). Production runs were too short to reach economies of scale: in 1979, HMC produced only 71,744 vehicles (KIET, 2014). Finally, although HMC started exporting to Latin America and South East Asia, exports did not did not exceed 20,000 annual units, and HMC lacked both an established network of concessionaries and marketing skills (Guillén, 2010).

The 1980s crisis provided an opportunity to accelerate upgrading (Kim, 1997). After several years of continued growth, the second oil crisis sent the automotive industry into a tailspin. Between 1979 and 1980, domestic demand shrunk by over 50 percent and capacity utilization dropped to 26 percent (Green, 1992). The way Korea addressed this situation showcases the role of the state in framing and directing transformation, the importance of self-sufficiency, and the iterative, negotiated, flexible nature of the relationship between the state and HMC.

To survive in the context of the 1980s crisis, Korean producers needed to increase their scale. There were two main ways to achieve this: industrial rationalization and a switch to exports. The government turned its attention to rationalization first. In line with the negotiated nature of the relationship between the government and HMC, the government gave the Hyundai conglomerate the choice to specialize in either power generation, an industry that was taking off at the time, or automotive, expecting the chaebol to exit the automotive industry (Back, 1990; Steers, 1999; Ravenshill, 2001). In line with HMC's quest for autonomy, Hyundai's CEO chose automotive, a sector that despite heavy regulation provided manufacturers more autonomy than electricity, where a state-owned monopoly was responsible for production, transmission, and distribution.

The government then pursued its rationalization strategy by issuing the Automobile Industry Rationalization Act of 1981, a plan that entailed the suspension of production by the two smaller OEMs (Kia and Asia Motors), and a merger between the two largest ones (HMC and Daewoo/GM Korea). However, the government had limited success imposing a top-down plan on firms. The first part of the plan was implemented but short-lived: Asia Motors was acquired by Kia, which focused on the production of commercial vehicles until 1986, when it re-entered the passenger vehicle market (Guillén, 2010). The proposed merger between HMC and Daewoo/GM Korea never took place. HMC rejected the merger as it ran counter to its interest in maintaining strategic control and becoming an independent automaker (Kim, 1997).

In addition, the government announced a shift from import substitution to export promotion. The government set its sights in the US, where the oil crises created demand for fuel-efficient compact cars and Japan's move upmarket opened a market gap for Korea's subcompact cars (KIET, 2014). Given Korea's technological limitations and the sophistication of the US market, this policy shift served as a framework for a second round of upgrading and spurred a frantic process of improvements in auto design and engineering to reach export quality (Green, 1992).

In consonance with the cooperative structure established in the previous decade, this second round of upgrading was based on a division of labor between the state and the automakers. The government defined strategic objectives and provided generous support to fulfill them. Automakers were responsible for the development of the technology necessary to deliver an export-worthy product. As in the previous decade, HMC drove the transformation of the industry while Kia and GM Korea/Daewoo continued to rely on external assistance (Amsden and Kang, 1995). HMC overhauled its product development capabilities by continuing to source technology from multiple firms based in several countries. From its establishment to 1985, HMC signed 54 licenses from eight countries (Hyun and Lee, 1989). In addition, in 1981, HMC signed a technological assistance agreement with Mitsubishi that did not include management participation (Kim, 1997). HMC also started to develop its in-house capabilities by establishing its first technological center in 1978 (Hyun and Lee, 1989). As in the previous decade, the state supported OEMs' efforts through a combination of patient capital, market protection, and tax and price incentives that lowered the costs and risks of undertaking these transformations. In addition, the state enabled local OEMs to sell cars domestically at higher prices than abroad, effectively subsidizing production (Amsden and Kang, 1995; Green, 1992).

From the point of view of upgrading, the strategy was a success. HMC entered the US market in 1986 and took the market by storm, reaching a 7.1 percent market share of the subcompact segment (Guillén, 2010). Despite quality problems (Mundi, 2013), between 1975 and 1990 Korean auto exports grew at an average annual rate of 47 percent and by 1993, HMC was exporting 38 percent of its production (Amsden and Kang, 1995). By 1991, HMC had also developed its first engine, and by the mid-1990s, it had the proprietary technology necessary to develop new products without outside assistance (Amsden and Kang, 1995). To address quality problems, HMC established a network of research and design centers located in Korea, Germany, the US, and Japan (Kim, 1997; Chung and Kim, 2014). It also set its own network of suppliers. By 1994, Korea's six largest suppliers (Hyundai Mobis, Hyundai Wia, Hyundai Transys, Hyundai Kefico, Hanon, and Mando) had already been established (Automotive News, 2019). Four of them are affiliates of the Hyundai Chaebol, while the other two belong to the Halla Group, originally established as the Hyundai International Group.

However, as discussed in Chapter 3, in the early 1990s, the government's strategy of supporting manufacturers by providing low-cost patient capital through the banking system and President Kim Young Sam's decision to liberalize short-term capital markets sowed the seed of a major financial crisis. Liberalization brought in a torrent of foreign credit, which banks used to finance manufacturers' investment in upgrading and capacity expansion (Shin and Chang, 2003; Mo and Moon, 2003; Lee, 2003; Park, 2003). As the flow of international credit dried in 1997, the maturity mismatch between foreign borrowing and domestic lending unleashed a major financial crisis, raised alarms about the large amounts of debt accumulated by firms, and exposed problems of overcapacity and underperformance. While the problem was widespread across the economy, the automotive sector, due to its capital intensity and rapid growth, was at the center of the crisis. In 1997 the Hyundai and Daewoo chaebol's debt to equity ratios were 578 and 472 respectively (Kim, 1998) and in 1996, Korea had produced 2.8 million cars, but sold only 1.6 million (Pollack, 1997).

The crisis dealt a major blow to the automotive industry. By 1998, automakers were operating at 40 percent capacity, down from 68 percent in 1997 (Guillén, 2010). Automakers that had not invested in developing their own technological base were the most affected. Kia became Exhibit A of Korea's overexpansion and excessive borrowing. Despite Korea's overcapacity, the automaker had established a second production plant next to a preexisting 33 million-square-foot factory and aimed to produce 1.5 million cars by 2001 (Mufson, 1997). In 1997, the group's debts amounted to ₩9.75 trillion (Pollack, 1997).

Even in the midst of a massive crisis, the Korean government did not discontinue its support for automakers or forsake the negotiated nature of firm–state interactions. Automakers' chaebol were not immediately declared bankrupt. Instead, they were designated for rescue under the Capital Structure Improvement Plans. These were agreements negotiated between debtors and their banks by which the banks temporarily forwent debt repayments and issued fresh loans, enabling highly indebted and dubiously profitable firms to continue operating and even expand (Pollack, 1997). Since the state had taken control of large commercial banks (see Chapter 3), these were essentially agreements negotiated between the firms and the government using the banks as a proxy. However, since the banks and the state were separate entities, these were technically private agreements. As a result, they did not have legal force, and thereby the state had little power to force automakers to restructure (Park, 2003). The foreseeable effect was that auto-makers did not undertake the required deep restructuring and their financial situation continued to worsen, at great cost to the Korean economy. Kia and Daewoo epitomize this situation. Three months after Kia was designated for rescue, the company had only undertaken minor restructuring. As the auto-maker's financial situation deteriorated, the government announced a bailout. The announcement caused Standard & Poor's Corp.to downgrade Korea's long- and short-term foreign currency ratings and resulted in the Won's big-gest single-day drop in value (Kattoulas, 1997). Daewoo is another case in point. The group, Korea's second chaebol, continued borrowing and even expanding after being designated for rescue. In fact, in December 1997, Daewoo acquired a controlling stake in SsangYong, a smaller, debt-ridden automaker (Gadacz, 1997). By the time Daewoo was declared bankrupt in 1999, the group was US$50 billion in debt (The Economist, 1999) and its failure was "the biggest bankruptcy in Korean history" (Lee, 2003, p. 150).

Even in the case of declared bankruptcies, the government continued to support automakers. Consistent with Korea's prioritization of manufacturing over services, support usually came at the expense of the banks. To liquidate and consolidate the business activities of ailing OEMs, the government relied on so-called "Big Deals," or negotiated swaps and takeovers of subsidiaries among the largest chaebol under government guidance (Mo and Moon, 2003). These deals included generous write-offs of pre-existing debt. The takeover of HMC over Kia Motors is an example of this. Once the initial bid was accepted, HMC's creditors (the largest of which was a publicly controlled bank), agreed to a write-off of more than ₩7 trillion debt, or 71 percent of Kia's ₩9.75 trillion debt (Bloomberg News, 1998).

By the mid-2000s, the Korean automotive sector had almost assumed its current structure. Automakers that had not created their own technologi-cal platform ceased to be independent firms. Samsung, which had entered the industry in 1995 (Guillén, 2010), was acquired by Renault in 2000 (Tagliabue, 2000). Daewoo/GM Korea was fully acquired by GM in 2002 (Choe, 2006), SsanYong was acquired by SAIC in 2004 and taken over by Mahindra & Mahindra in 2011, but in late 2020 it was on the lookout for a new potential buyer (Lee and Jin, 2020; Song, 2020b). Kia was acquired by HMC, which consolidated its leadership position in the local market and increased its global scale. In 2019, HMC accounted for 81 percent of Korea's auto production (Korea Auto Industries Cooperative Association statistics, 2020) and in 2017 it was the world's third largest automaker (OICA, 2020).

5.4.3 The Future of a Self-Sufficient Production Structure

Business-government coordination faded into the background in the 2000s and the first half of the 2010s as the automotive industry rebounded and continued to grow, reaching a maximum production of 4.5 million vehicles in 2015 (OICA production statistics, 2020). Since then, Korea's vehicle production has declined from 4.5 to 3.9 million vehicles (OICA, production statistics, 2020), the only country among the world's ten largest where this was the case prior to the 2020 crisis (Jung, 2019).

In the context of a complex, hierarchically structured sector, the presence of a globally competitive, independent OEM that exercises control over its value chain, is a major source of competitive advantage for Korea's automotive industry. A local OEM provides a high degree of control over critical strategic decisions such as those related to innovation. And yet, contrary to these expectations, HMC is not at the forefront of innovation in the automotive industry and has been late to respond to the shift from internal combustion engines (ICEs) to electric and autonomous vehicles (EVs and AVs). HMC marketed its first EVs (adapted versions of preexisting ICE models) in late 2018, six years after the introduction of Tesla's Model S (Edelstein, 2019). Itis expected to launch its first dedicated platform of EVs only in 2021 (Song, 2020a). The OEM has also been criticized for entering late into AVs, leading some to contend that HMC's "competitiveness in this new area is almost zero and it will face an existential threat in the self-driving era" (Song, 2018).

Instead, since 2018, Korea has responded to the industry's transition to a new paradigm by resorting to state–firm coordination. In line with the country's preexisting pattern, the state has articulated goals, emphasized technological advancement, and provided substantial financial support while HMC remains responsible for product design and fabrication. Nonetheless, the relationship between the state and the OEM has shifted in at least two ways: from emphasizing the absorption of existing technology to creating innovation that is new to the world, and from supporting the automotive sector, to embedding it within a broader cross-industry initiative centered around clean energy.

To implement this approach, in 2018, the government launched a five-year plan to supply 16,000 hydrogen-powered vehicles and build 310 hydrogen refilling stations across the country (Cho, 2018). The plan, with a budget of ₩2.6 trillion (about US$2.6 billion), provided financial support for the development of fuel cell stacks, fuel cell storage containers, and tax incentives for purchasers of fuel-cell EVs (FCEVs). HCM responded positively to the announcement. Four months after the plan was launched, the automaker revealed its FCEV Vision 2030, which prioritizes the development of FCEVs. HMC's commitment to the implementation of its plan includes ₩8 trillion budget (US$7.1 billion) for investment in hydrogen-power systems for cars, drones, and ships by 2030 (Harris and Song, 2018).

In 2019, the government followed up on this approach by setting even more ambitious goals. The Hydrogen Economy Roadmap aims to produce 6.2 million FCEVs and roll out at least 1,200 refilling stations by 2040. More recently, the 2020 "Korean-style New Deal" stimulus package commit a further ₩15.8 trillion (US$13.2 billion) to green energy production and ₩28.9 trillion (US$24.2 billion) to eco-friendly mobility between 2020 and 2025 (Ministry of Economy and Finance, 2020). Significantly, the president's announcement of the New Deal was followed, the same day, by a televised intervention in which then-vice-chairman Chung Eui Sun endorsed the government's plan and pledged to contribute to its implementation (Nam, 2020).

As of 2021, it is still too soon to valuate these plans and gauge their impact on HMC's ability to generate competitive advantages in the field of EVs. What is clear is that the relationship between the government and automakers continues to be a driver of transformation and competitiveness in the automotive industry

5.5 Conclusions: Integration or Technological Self-Sufficiency?

This chapter compared the development and upgrading of Spain's foreign-dominated and regionally integrated automotive industry with the rise Korea's globally competitive, local OEM. Automakers in both countries faced comparable limitations in terms of technological and organizational capabilities, scale, quality, and profitability. However, the two countries addressed these problems in very different ways. The Spanish government favored a strategy that prioritized inward FDI and technological borrowing while the Korean government prioritized the development of local technological capabilities using market protection and generous financial assistance.

Spanish and Korean firms played a different role in the two models. Spain's government-controlled OEMs had little leverage and became instruments at the service of broader public goals of economic growth and European integration. By contrast, Korean OEMs, and in particular HMC, were active agents and insiders within a tight pattern of interactions with the state that enabled both actors to further their respective goals.

Spanish OEMs and the majority of suppliers were eventually acquired by foreign rivals. Nonetheless, the emergence of a powerful EU-wide value chain provided Spain the opportunity to maintain a large, and globally competitive automotive industry and to host a number of local, large, competitive suppliers. HMC's strategy of using technological partnerships as a stepping stone to develop its own internal capabilities enabled the OEM to become a global leader in the industry. Other Korean OEMs, which remained dependent on foreign automakers, engaged in overspending that eventually led them to be acquired by foreign automakers.

As of 2020, Spain and Korea had large, competitive automotive industries that are comparable in terms of size, output, and contribution to the national economies of the two countries. However, as the industry faces the transition to a new industry paradigm, the two countries' different productive structures are likely to evolve in different directions.

In Spain, foreign dominance and European integration mean that critical strategic decisions are taken outside the country. As the industry consolidates, there is a risk that some foreign-based automakers and suppliers may exit the country. Nonetheless, large, local, turnkey suppliers may thrive in the emerging context by leveraging their size and their existing relationships to multiple automakers within the EU-wide value chain. The result, however, is likely to be a contraction of Spain's automotive sector as a whole.

In Korea, the presence of a local OEM is a major advantage. However, HMC has not navigated the transition to a new paradigm effectively. Its delay in entering the EV and AV segments has led to a recent decline in Korea's automotive production and prompted a re-emergence of state–firm coordination. The terms of the relationship differ from those in the pre-1997 context. Although the government continues to set ambitious objectives and provide substantial financial support, the relationship between the state and the automaker recognizes HMC's maturity and embeds automaking within a broader strategy for clean energy and sustainable economic growth. It is still early to assess the impact of Korea's 2020 New Deal, however, a potential obstacle is the disconnect between the global scope of the mobility industry's transformation and Korea's national-level strategy.

This chapter concludes the empirical section of the book, which characterized Spain's and Korea's models. The next two chapters extend the argument to provide a broader view of the Spanish and Korean economies and issue an overall conclusion.

6

The Argument Extended

Reaching the Efficiency Frontier in Complex Industries

6.1 A General View of Spain's and Korea's Upgrading

The first two chapters of the book argued that a proper understanding of Spain's and Korea's upgrading needs to start by gauging the competitive limitations that firms face, and the reasons why state intervention is necessary to enable upgrading. The subsequent three chapters presented monographic industry analyses that discussed why, despite facing a similar set of barriers, Spain and Korea chose different ways to overcome them that resulted in two different pathways to upgrading. The cases of the banking, ICT, and automotive sectors demonstrated that Spain's and Korea's choices were based on differences in the identities and capabilities of policy decision makers in these countries, their pre-existing production structures, and the opportunities derived from external linkages with more advanced economies.

In Spain, the rise to prominence of a group of policy decision makers with a background in law and macroeconomics, the presence of a powerful, for-profit banking elite, a preeminent telecommunications operator that exercised policy functions, and a strong desire to become integrated within Europe, led Spain to pursue an integrational approach that emphasized FDI in manufacturing, technological outsourcing, and regional integration with the EU but simultaneously protected complex services and supported their competitive transformation through asymmetric regulation.

In Korea, the elevated status of public sector elites with technical backgrounds in engineering fields, the existence of a dense institutional network in areas such as higher education in technical fields and applied research, the presence of emerging, local firms in manufacturing sectors, and the legacies and opportunities derived from Korea's relationships with the US and Japan, led Korea to adopt a techno-industrial approach that pursued technological autonomy and self-sufficiency in complex manufacturing but instrumentalized complex services and deprived them of strategic autonomy.

State-Firm Coordination and Upgrading: Reaching the Efficiency Frontier in Skill-, Capital-, and Knowledge-Intensive Industries in Spain and South Korea. Angela Garcia Calvo, Oxford University Press. © Angela Garcia Calvo 2021.
DOI: 10.1093/oso/9780198864561.003.0006

Spain's and Korea's approaches enabled the two countries to reach advanced country status, raised the standard of living of their citizens, and facilitated their integration in to the global economy. However, the two countries' strategies had profound effects on national production structures. Spain became home to globally competitive firms in retail banking and telecommunications, but manufacturing capacity declined sharply. By contrast, Korea's firms in manufacturing sectors such as electronics and motor vehicles became globally competitive. But firms in complex services such as banking and telecommunications services were unable to take advantage of emerging business opportunities, did not appropriately restructure, and became ensnared in financial and corruption scandals.

The purpose of this chapter is to extend this argument to a more comprehensive view of Spain's and Korea's upgrading. The chapter accomplishes this in two ways. First, it uses additional mini-cases of industries that are comparable to those explored in the previous chapters to introduce nuances to the main argument. These analyses highlight the importance of path dependence, the role of choice in defining a national pathway to upgrading, and the systemic aspects of upgrading strategies. The chapter then uses a pointed, counterfactual comparison with Brazil to discuss broader structural and socioeconomic factors that enabled Spain and Korea to succeed where other late industrializing economies have failed. The analyses contained in this chapter perform two additional functions. They implicitly refute the liberal and developmental state perspectives more strongly. In addition, they sharpen the distinction between different pathways to upgrading and underline the tradeoffs between integrational and techno-industrial strategies.

The rest of this chapter is structured as follows. Each of the following two sections focuses on a country. Section 6.2 is dedicated to Spain and section 6.3 to Korea. These two sections are divided into two subsections, each of which is dedicated to a single industry case. Section 6.4 draws broader insights about the structural and socioeconomic conditions that enabled the two countries to succeed through a comparison with Brazil. Section 6.5 concludes.

6.2 Extending the Argument in Spain

This section expands the book's argument about the Spanish model through a brief discussion of upgrading in the electricity and aerospace and defense (ASD) industries. The trajectory of Spain's electric power companies is consistent with Spain's model of coordination and with Spain's view of complex services as profitable industries with high potential for upgrading. The particularities of the case highlight the role of path dependence in the emergence of Spain's pattern of quid pro quo exchanges between the state and firms. Spain's upgrading in the ASD sector contrasts with the country's established pattern of coordination in manufacturing and shows that despite Spain's technological limitations, an upgrading strategy based on complex manufacturing sectors was feasible. This case underscores the role of policy makers' preferences on defining a country's upgrading strategy and showcases that while context certainly shaped upgrading, policy makers ultimately made path-defining choices. Finally, the ASD sector's reliance on a combination of conventional industrial policy instruments and Spain's integrational approach suggests that, within the realm of techno-industrial and integrational approach, there is room for strategic subvariants.

6.2.1 The Roots of Coordination in the Spanish Electricity Sector

In 2020, Spain's three largest utilities, Iberdrola, Endesa, and Naturgy, surpassed the combined market capitalization of the largest six banks, becoming the largest sector in the Spanish IBEX 35 blue-chip index (Vélez, 2020). Iberdrola was the world's third largest utility by market value (Patel, 2019; Thomas and Dombey, 2020), and a global leader in renewable energy. A second company, Endesa, had become a major global utility in the 1990s, before being acquired by Italian energy giant Enel.

The presence of globally competitive Spanish utilities is not a surprise from the point of view of the book's argument. However, the early trajectory of the industry, the establishment of a system of quid pro quo exchanges between the state and private utilities in the 1940s, and the continuation of this pattern after Spain's transition to democracy showcase the role of path dependence and continuity in Spain's institutional structure. These factors also illustrate the adaptability of the Spanish model and its ability to support economic transformation under a wide range of environmental conditions.

Until the 1990s, most countries organized energy supply as a natural monopoly comprising production, distribution, and trading. Spain was different. Unlike most other countries, the electricity sector was never nationalized and was composed of numerous private companies in which foreign investors provided capital and technology while Spanish large banks held a controlling stake (Arocena, Khun, and Regibeau, 1999; Bartolomé Rodríguez, 2007). This structure had deep historical roots. During the

Francoist era, the Spanish electricity sector consisted of 17 regional utilities, most of which were privately owned (Ibeas Cubillo, 2011). Together with large banks, these companies constituted Spain's most powerful economic elite (Etchemendy, 2004).

After the Spanish civil war in 1939, the government and the utilities faced a conundrum. Spain's insufficient energy production and the absence of a national interconnected network caused frequent blackouts that thwarted government's plans for economic development (Roldán, 2013). Because most utilities were privately owned, the state could not expand existing production capacity directly to solve the problem. One possible option was to nationalize existing firms. However, as was the case in the banking and telecommunications sectors, the government lacked the in-house expertise required to manage the industry directly. From the point of view of utilities, Spain's industrial development represented an extraordinary business opportunity because an increase in economic activity could only mean higher demand for electricity. Furthermore, because the regime saw industrialization as a way to legitimize itself, the government was expected to provide favorable conditions for the expansion of utilities.

Utilities responded proactively by forming Unidad Eléctrica (UNESA), the electricity business union, in 1944 (Ibeas Cubillo, 2011). As the Big Seven and Telefonica had done in their respective sectors, the utilities used their technical knowledge, control of existing capacity, and financial expertise (through the banks) to assume, via UNESA, direct responsibility for the design, development, and integration of the national electricity network on behalf of the state (Arocena et al.,1999). In exchange for its services, UNESA negotiated with the government tariffs, fiscal incentives, and access to preferential credit (Arocena et al., 1999; Garrués-Irurzun, 2010) that made it profitable for the utilities to invest in production capacity and distribution networks. This original quid pro quo arrangement remained in place through the Francoist era and was formalized by Decree 175/1975 of February 13, where it was called the Concerted Action Regime, a name that underscores the cooperative nature of the relationship between the state and the utilities.

Spain's early democratic governments did not do away with the Concerted Action Regime. On the contrary, both the government and the firms resorted to the established structure to tackle the crises of the 1970s and 1980s. In the early 1980s, the government and the utilities faced a serious juncture. The end of cheap oil, which powered most of Spain's electricity production, and the political decision to phase out nuclear energy in 1983, imposed an urgent need to diversify into other sources of energy. Simultaneously, Spain needed to continue expanding generation capacity to meet rising demand for electric power. Given the dominance of private utilities, the government could not hope to diversify away from oil and guarantee energy security without cooperating with the power companies. However, the utilities were in the midst of a major financial crisis. As the country grew rapidly in the 1970s, they had financed increases in electricity generation capacity through foreign currency loans. The unexpected rise in oil prices and the subsequent devaluation of the Spanish peseta plunged the utilities into a serious financial crisis (ESC, 2017). The nuclear moratorium only worsened the situation because it left the utilities laden with sunk, irrecoverable investments (ESC, 2017).

Spain used the Concerted Action Regime to address these issues (Arocena et al.,1999, Arocena, Contín, and Huerta, 2002; Etchemendy, 2004; ESC, 2017; Garrués-Irurzun, 2010). Law 82/1980 of January 27, established a framework for coordinated public–private investment in renewable energy production that involved favorable fiscal conditions and public funding for research and capacity investment. In addition, in 1983 the ministry of industry and the utilities negotiated a framework to address the crisis and articulate a long-run strategy. The resulting protocol was formalized in Royal Decree 1,538/1987 of December 11. Under the terms of the protocol, the government helped ensure the financial viability of firms in exchange for the utilities' investment in new production, transport, and distribution capacity to guarantee energy security and diversify the energy mix.

In line with the terms of the framework, the government nationalized the transport network and absorbed economically unviable utilities and assets through Endesa, a public utility. In addition, the government established a cost-based tariff structure that guaranteed the financial stability of firms, compensated them for the costs of the nuclear moratorium, and incentivized investments in new capacity. Finally, the government and the firms carried on a restructuring process consisting of negotiated asset swaps and mergers among viable firms that enabled the utilities to expand their national footprint (Arocena et al., 1999; ESC, 2017). By the end of the 1980s, the power industry was dominated by four vertically integrated companies (ESC, 2017). Firms also made significant investments in energy production, transport, and distribution. Between 1980 and 1986 alone the industry invested 3.5 billion pesetas in new facilities (Marcos Fano, 2002).

State–firm cooperation continued to be at the heart of the Spanish model as the industry was liberalized in the 1990s and 2000s. The initial objectives of the EU-wide liberalization process were set in Council Directive 90/547 EEC of October 29, 1990 and the process took place through three reform packages issued in 1996, 2003, and 2009 (Ciucci, 2020). The bases for Spain's liberalization strategy were set in a protocol signed by the government and the industry in 1996 and formalized through Law 54/1997 of 28 November. The strategy was similar to the country's approach to banking and telecommunications services liberalizations in that it relied on generous financial packages to facilitate firm restructuring and encouraged a series of mergers and takeovers that favored local incumbents and blocked the potential entry of foreign rivals.

Specifically, the state agreed to cover the so-called "costs of transition to competition," which consisted primarily of amortization costs for investment in electricity generation capacity for the following ten years. Costs were covered for a fixed amount of 1.73 billion pesetas (ESC, 2017). In addition, the government supported a policy of mergers to create large, competitive utilities that could successfully withstand unwanted acquisitions. Two companies, Iberduero and Hidrola merged to form Iberdrola in 1992. Endesa acquired a number of smaller regional utilities and expanded from generation only and into transmission and distribution (Arocena et al., 1999). By 1997, Endesa and Iberdrola owned 84 percent of Spain's generation capacity (ESC, 2017). To further protect Spanish utilities from unwanted foreign acquisitions, the government enabled Endesa and Iberdrola to establish strategic alliances with Gas Natural, a company that controlled 70 percent of the market for natural gas, thereby blocking one of the most likely pathways to entry by foreign competitors (Arocena et al., 1999).

As liberalization proceeded, the state continued to protect local utilities and stimulate their competitive transformation. Endesa is the most emblematic example. As the company's privatization started in 1998, the government decided to sell it as a single entity, making it significantly more costly for potential investors to enter the market (Etchemendy, 2004). Endesa's privatization took place through a series of public offerings aimed at attracting small investors and private auctions that were expected to consolidate a hard core of domestic investors, primarily banks and savings banks (Etchemendy, 2004; Valdivielso del Real and Goyer, 2012). The government was unsuccessful in its attempt to establish a hard core of domestic investors because the banks, in line with their strategies to specialize in retail banking, were uninterested in maintaining a controlling stake in a firm whose operations were unrelated to their core business (Bulfone, 2017). The government then favored a merger between Endesa and Iberdrola that would have created a larger national champion. However, the high levels of market concentration in the energy sector condemned to failure a friendly merger between the two utilities (Carcar, 2001; Cinco Dias, 2001). In the absence of potential domestic buyers, and with the government unwilling to remain a core stakeholder, the only option was a foreign acquisition. In fact, Enel acquired Endesa in 2007 (Valdivielso del Real and Goyer, 2012).

Since the liberalization of the sector, state–firm coordination has continued to be part of the industry's framework, but specific objectives have shifted, in line with changes in public goals and the competitive environment. In 1997, and in congruence with the EU objective to double the share of renewable energy in total energy consumption, state–firm coordination focused on incentivizing investment in renewable energy, a segment that the government had started promoting in 1983. Law 54/1997 of November 27, incentivized investment in generation capacity by establishing a "special regime" that guaranteed access to the grid and put in place a feed-in tariff system, or a fixed tariff to be paid on top of market prices to cover the costs of renewable power installations. This measure, developed further through Royal Decree 2,818/1998 of December 30, effectively subsidized investment in renewable energy until it was phased out in 2012. The decree had a major impact on installed capacity. Between 1998 and 2009 alone, installed capacity in renewables surged from 2,119 MW to 25,173 MW. By 2019, it had doubled to reach 50,609 MW (Red Eléctrica de España, 1998, 2009, 2019). Spanish utilities, especially Iberdrola, were the major beneficiaries of these measures. Iberdrola took advantage of government incentives to specialize in wind energy. Between 2001 and 2009, it invested €62 billion in renewable (Iberdrola News, 2010). By 2020, the utility was a global leader in renewables (Thomas and Dombey, 2020) and had a presence in four continents.

6.2.2 Alternative Strategies to Upgrading in the Spanish ASD Sector

The aerospace and defense sector (ASD) is possibly the world's most politicized, capital-intensive, oligopolistic, global industry. Two global firms: Boeing and Airbus, control the sector. Against all expectations, Spain is home to a mid-sized, but vibrant, ASD industry. In 2019, it generated €13 billion, employed 57,600 highly qualified workers, and involved 415 firms, 15 of which had more than 250 employees (Spanish Association of Technology, Defense, Security, Aeronautics, and Space firms—Asociación Española de Empresas Tecnológicas de Defensa, Seguridad, Aeronáutica y Espacio [TEDAE] 2020). Moreover, Spanish firms are involved at all levels of the value chain, including design, engineering, production, certification, and sales (TEDAE, 2019).

The presence of a competitive ASD sector with a strong advanced manufacturing component defies the book's expectations about Spain's upgrading. It comes to show that, despite the country's technological limitations, Spanish firms in technology-intensive manufacturing industries held significant potential for upgrading and were able to thrive in the exceptional cases when they received dedicated public support. Spain's upgrading in ASD also underscores the importance of political choices in shaping a country's upgrading strategy and their impact on the resulting production structure. The fact that Spain was able to upgrade in what is one of the world's most technology-intensive sectors, suggests that Spain's actual pathway to upgrading was not the only viable strategy and that alternative options based on complex manufacturing could have also delivered upgrading. Finally, Spain's combination of classic industrial policy instruments with an integrational approach suggest that even within techno-industrial and integrational approaches to upgrading there is room for variation.

As was the case in other technology intensive industries, Spain's technological underdevelopment, chronically small military budgets, and collaboration agreements with the US meant that Spain historically relied on imported equipment or local production under foreign license to fulfill its defense and aerospace needs. This started to change in the 1970s. In 1971, Constructiones Aeronaúticas SA (CASA), presented the C-212 Aviocar, a transport plane designed and engineered in Spain (Hita Romero and Dopazo García, 2010). The Aviocar was an engineering and commercial success. Originally commissioned by the armed forces, the plane was certified for both military and civil use, remained in continuous production until 2013 (Waldron, 2013), and sold more than 450 units to over a dozen countries including advanced countries such as the US, France, and Switzerland (Ramírez, 2007; Alonso, 1980; El País staff, 1980). Moreover, CASA was not the only Spanish firm with considerable technological capabilities. In 1979, a newly established private firm, Ceselsa, aimed to develop and commercialize its own radar system (ABC staff, 1981). CASA and Ceselsa were dwarfs by international standards. However, their break into high-value-added segments highlights the potential of the local industry from a relatively early stage.

By the early 1980s, the consolidation and upgrading of the Spanish ASD sector depended on the ability of firms to achieve economies of scale and continuing to innovate. As in other manufacturing sectors, this was contingent on the ability of firms to secure patient capital and stable demand. Because of the industry's oligopolistic nature, astronomical capital investments, high R&D intensity, very long maturity rates, and its interdependent civil and defense dimensions, resources were expected to come directly from the state.

Despite Spain's orthodox economists' opposition to direct intervention in the economy, two unique circumstances enabled and persuaded policy makers to provide dedicated support to the ASD sector. Unlike all other manufacturing sectors, defense and civil aviation are ministerial competences funded directly through public budgets. As of 2020, the ASD sector receives almost all of its funding for R&D in defense and security, and 60 percent of its funding for aerospace directly from the government's budget (TEDAE, 2019). This means that, unlike other industries, the government could support the ASD sector directly. In addition, the government was willing to increase its budget in these areas because after the failed 1981 military coup, the transformation and modernization of the Spanish armed forces were critical to underpin the stability of Spain's democracy (Gómez, 1981).

Between 1982 and 1991, military budgets increased sevenfold (Fernández Puértolas, 1995). The government used the funding to undertake a state-directed effort aimed at creating companies that could compete successfully in the European sphere (González and Navas, 1989). Throughout the 1980s and 1990s, the government implemented this strategy through conventional industrial policy instruments, including nationalizations, incentivized mergers, and public procurement.

In the 1980s, the government raised its participation in key firms and encouraged concentration to increase scale and expand firms' product portfolio. The government's stake in CASA passed from 69 to 99 percent (Alonso, 1980). In addition, the government urged Ceselsa to merge with Inisel, a group of state-owned companies (Arancibia and Navas 1990). To overcome Ceselsa's opposition, the government made the allocation of a critical public contract for a surveillance system contingent on the merger (García-Hoz, 2013). Economic pressure prevailed, and the two parties reached an agreement in 1992 to form Indra, in which the government held a 63 percent stake (SEPI, 2020).

In the 1990s, the government concentrated on restructuring and preparing firms to compete while creating business opportunities through the industry's integration within the emerging EU-wide ASD sector. In 1992, CASA and Indra became part of Grupo TENEO, a public conglomerate composed of publicly participated companies with a strong competitive potential (El País staff, 1992). The purpose of this group was to prepare firms for competition by increasing their product development capacity and ensuring commercial viability. The case of Indra epitomizes its philosophy. Indra's restructuration plan involved a 15,000 million pesetas capital expansion. To support the development of Indra's technological capacity, Grupo TENEO orchestrated an agreement by France's Thomson. However, Thomson was only allowed to take a minority participation in Indra (Computer World, 1995), thereby ensuring that strategic control remained in Spain. Indra's restructuring was considered concluded in 1998, when it posted profits for the first time (Indra, 2013). In 1996, the incoming government decided to dissolve Grupo TENEO and accelerate the privatization of the firms participated by the public group (SEPI, 2020b). Unlike other manufacturing industries, where privatization usually involved the acquisition of Spanish firms by foreign investors, SEPI did not privatize Indra until 1999, once the company had become profitable.

In addition to restructuring Spanish firms and preparing them to compete, the government also worked to generate new business opportunities through the industry's integration in the emerging EU-wide ASD industry. Unlike other manufacturing sectors, where integration focused on facilitating inward FDI, which led to loss of firm's strategic autonomy, in the ASD sector, the government strived to ensure that strategic decision-making, research, and production capabilities remained in Spain. From the 1980s, Spain engaged in diplomatic efforts to ensure that Spanish firms were involved in European collaborative projects such as the Eurofighter. These projects became a source of foreign investment, often in the form of collaborations with local firms that helped enhance the technological capabilities of Spanish firms. For instance, ITP (Turbopropulsors Industry—Industria de Turbopropulsores) was established in 1989 as a partnership between Sener, a local firm, and Rolls Royce to participate in the development of the Eurofighter Typhoon's engine. As Europe stepped up its efforts to consolidate the ASD industry and create an EU-wide champion, the Spanish government continued to play an activist role. In 2000, the Spanish government took a 5.5 percent stake in the newly established EADS (European Aeronautic Defence and Space Company), Airbus' predecessor (Morrison, 2010). Although smaller than the participations of the French and German government's (El Mundo staff, 1999) Spain's stake in EADS provided a seat at the table and enabled ASD to become one of the "pillars of (Spain's) technological base and international presence" (Muñoz, 2013).

In the past two decades, the government has maintained its involvement in the sector through its participation in Airbus and the provision of legal and financial aid to Spanish firms. As of 2020, the Spanish government continues to own a 4 percent stake in Airbus (Airbus, Report of the Board of

Directors, 2020). During the 2008 crisis, the government also demonstrated its willingness to step up and provide financial support for major firms. In 2013, the government purchased a 20 percent stake in Indra from Bankia, a failed bank, becoming Indra's largest shareholder and effectively shoring up the company to prevent a potential takeover (Muñoz, 2013). In 2019, the government also showed its support for Indra's attempt to purchase ITP from Rolls Royce, a move that would have helped expand Indra's product portfolio. However, negotiations between the two companies ultimately broke down (Muñoz, 2019). Finally, in 2020, and in the midst of a global crisis that hit the ASD industry particularly hard, the Spanish government introduced legislation that requires foreign investors, including EU investors, willing to acquire over 10 percent of a listed Spanish firm or a large, non-listed company, to request authorization from the government (Royal Decree-Law 8/2020, of March 17; Royal Decree-Law 11/2020, of March 31; Royal Decree-Law 34/2020, of November 17). The purpose of these measures, which were to remain in vigor until June 2021, is to circle the wagons against hostile takeovers in strategic sectors, including ADS.

6.3 Extending the Argument in Korea

This section, like the previous one, provides a more general view of the book's argument in the Korean case through condensed analyses of two sectors: electricity and machine-tools (MT). The main goal of these analyses is to highlight the systemic aspects of Korea's approach to upgrading. Korea's upgrading in electric power stands in apparent contradiction to the book's argument. However, upon closer examination, The Korea Electric Power Corporation's (KEPCO) specialization in the design and construction of nuclear plants underlines Korea's commitment to self-sufficiency and technological upgrading and shows the extent to which Korea was willing to go to ensure that manufacturers had access to essential inputs at low prices. Korea's upgrading in the MT industry is consistent with Korea's pattern of tight state–firm cooperation and confirms the argument. In addition, the role of supplier–buyer relationships in facilitating MT upgrading, and the presence of synergies between the MT sector and other prominent Korean manufacturing industries underscores the systemic aspects of Korea's approach for transformation.

As in the previous section, this one is divided into two subsections, one for each of the two cases.

6.3.1 Systemic Elements of Upgrading: The Korean Electricity Sector

Korea is home to KEPCO, which in 2017 was the world's seventh largest power company ranked by installed generation capacity (Patel, 2019). The presence in Korea of one of the world's largest utilities stands in apparent contradiction with the book's argument that Korea's model did not provide adequate support for upgrading in complex services. Yet, in fact, KEPCO's upgrading embodies three key features of Korea's strategy: an emphasis on self-sufficiency, a focus on the development of local technological capabilities, and the public provision of abundant, affordable service inputs for manufacturing industries. Furthermore, the development of Korea's local energy production capacity shows that the country's transformation was not merely the result of picking a few winners, but rather the result of a systemic effort in which firms operating in complex services and manufacturing sectors played specific roles.

Energy is an indispensable resource for the type of capital-intensive industries that Korea's governments have incentivized since the early 1970s: steel, petrochemicals, shipbuilding, electronics, general-purpose machinery, and non-ferrous metals (Sakong, 1993). These sectors are among the world's largest energy consumers. However, Korea's poor endowment in natural resources made the country almost entirely reliant on imports to meet its energy demand. The clash between Korea's energy dependence and the country's self-sufficient, techno-industrial approach, arguably made the development of the energy sector a critical component of Korea's techno-industrial strategy. Because of its characteristics, nuclear energy was the obvious choice.

Korea's initial interest in nuclear energy followed from President Eisenhower's "Atoms for Peace" speech in 1953, which opened up nuclear research for civilian purposes to countries that did not previously have nuclear technology (Andrews-Speed, 2020). In the 1950s and 1960s, the Korean program focused primarily on academic research (Andrews-Speed, 2020). The shift to an active nuclear strategy started in the early 1970s. It was motivated by the Nixon Doctrine, the government's deep-seated fears of US abandonment, and the regime's concerns about its own hold to power (Taliaferro, 2019). Korea's development of nuclear power was also a response to the oil crises of the 1970s, which compelled the government to diversify away from imported oil and focus on nuclear energy to provide manufacturers access to a critical input at low cost (Jung and Rho, 2020; Park, 1992).

The development of Korea's nuclear technological capabilities relied on a familiar pattern in which the state established the goals and coordinated the development of specialized institutions and local technological capabilities. The government exercised these roles both directly and through KEPCO, the public monopoly responsible for national electricity generation, transportation, and distribution. Private companies were brought into the plan through their roles in project development and implementation. Firms' participation and responsibilities increased over time as their capabilities developed. This strategy enabled the state to further its goals of increasing self-sufficiency and developing local capabilities in a technology-intensive industry. As mentioned in Chapter 5, the strategy was also beneficial for manufacturing firms in a broad range of energy intensive industries such as steel, automotive, or machinery, which gained access to a critical input at low cost. In fact, since the early 1970s Korea's electricity charges have been reduced from some of the world's highest (Amsden, 1989), to some of the lowest among OECD countries (International Energy Agency [IEA], 2019).

The development of Korea's energy capacity revolved around a well-defined structure with clear goals and a consistent policy direction. The process, from its early beginnings to the maturity of the industry can be divided into four distinct phases: basic research and institutional building in the 1950s and 1960s, local capability development in the 1970s and 1980s, technological self-sufficiency in the 1990s and 2000s, and maturity and exports from the 2010s (Park, 1992; Ahn and Han, 2000; Jang, Choi, and Hong, 2013).

The first phase started with the signature of the 1956 Agreement for Cooperation between the Republic of Korea and the US (Park, 1992). During this phase, Korea focused primarily on institution building and basic research. Institution building revolved around three areas: policy, skills, and research. Policymaking was assigned to the newly created Office of Atomic Energy, which depended directly from the presidency. Skill development was based on cooperation with the US and training programs coordinated through the International Atomic Energy Agency (Park, 1992). Responsibilities for basic research were entrusted to the Korea Atomic Energy Research Institute (KAERI), a public institute established in 1959. To facilitate KAERI's learning, the government purchased a research reactor from the US to be used for learning purposes (Park, 1992).

The second phase started in the early 1970s and revolved around the development of local capacity through knowledge accumulation and additional institution building. This phase involved the construction of eight nuclear reactors under the responsibility of foreign firms (Ahn and Han, 2000).

Completion of these projects gave Korean firms the experience necessary to ramp up their knowledge. Knowledge acquisition took place through two mechanisms. The first was the transfer of technical documents, computer codes, licenses, and manpower training (Ahn and Han, 2000). In addition, knowledge accumulation took place through learning by doing via technological cooperation with foreign firms. After a first turnkey contract with Westinghouse, KEPCO adopted a strategy of collaborating with multiple suppliers from Canada, UK, and France (Ahn and Han, 2000). This strategy had the advantage of forcing Korean firms to assume responsibility for knowledge integration while minimizing firms' dependence on any individual foreign partner. It also enabled Korean firms to assume progressively more complex responsibilities rather than getting trapped in low value-added functions. In the first projects, Korean firms were only carrying out certain civil engineering functions under the direction of a foreign supplier. However, by the end of the second phase, some local firms were performing higher value-added tasks such as manufacturing related to the steam supply system and fabricating nuclear fuel (Ahn and Han, 2000; Park, 1992).

As KEPCO accumulated knowledge, it established a series of fully-owned subsidiaries to which it allocated high value-added functions. The Korea Power engineering Company (KOPEC), established in 1975, assumed responsibilities for architectural engineering. The Korea Heavy Industries and Construction Company (KHIC), established in 1980, became responsible for component design and development of manufacturing technologies. The Korea Nuclear Fuel Company, established in 1982, focused on the fabrication of nuclear fuel (Ahn and Han, 2000; Park, 1992). These firms collaborated closely with KAERI to develop the applied technology necessary to fulfill their roles (Jang, Choi, and Hong, 2013).

Despite evident progress, in the late 1980s Korean firms still needed external assistance with some aspects of civil engineering and with the main parts of nuclear reactors, steam generators, and other high-tech components (Park, 1992). Furthermore, under the terms of Korea's agreement with the US, Korea had limited capabilities to enrich and reprocess uranium. Accordingly, the third phase, between the late 1980s and the early 2000s, revolved around achieving self-sufficiency. A fundamental difference between this phase and the preceding ones was that foreign firms were no longer responsible for project completion. Instead, KEPCO assumed full responsibility for the construction of two nuclear reactors and allocated contracts to Korean firms while foreign subcontractors played only a consulting role (Ahn and Han, 2000; Jang, Choi, and Hong, 2013). By the mid-1990s Korea's technological capacities were mature enough that KEPCO designed its first homegrown nuclear reactor model (Kim, 2019). Following this achievement and forecasting its transition to maturity, the KEPCO group also started sharing its experiences and providing assistance to countries such as China and Turkey, which were starting to develop their nuclear capacities (Ahn and Han, 2000).

The fourth and last phase started in the mid-2000s and has involved the consolidation of the sector and a shift to exports. During this period Korea has continued expanding the country's nuclear capacity. As of 2020, KEPCO operates 25 reactors in Korea, has five more under construction, and four more planned (KEPCO, 2020). Nonetheless, local expansion may have reached its limit given the government's commitment to phase out nuclear power and increase the share of renewable energy (Jung, 2020). In this context, exports will likely become a major source of future growth for the industry. Korea signed its first contract to build four nuclear reactors in the United Arab Emirates in 2009 (Kim, 2019).

Despite its obvious upward trajectory, Korea's nuclear industry has suffered a series of problems not unlike those of other upstream services instrumentalized by the state. KEPCO, together with the handful of private firms that compose Korea's so-called "nuclear mafia" (Kim, 2019) has faced serious accusations of collusion, corruption, and corner-cutting. In 2013, the industry was engulfed in a major scandal regarding counterfeit reactor parts that escalated into a major investigation of graft, collusion, and warranty forgery (Hun, 2013; Kim, 2019). Ultimately, 68 people were sentenced to a cumulative 253 years of jail time, including the president of Korea Hydro and Nuclear Power, the KEPCO affiliate responsible for nuclear business (Kim, 2019). The scandal also raised concerns about the safety of Korean reactors, with some competitors claiming that Korean producers shed costly additional safety features in order to keep their costs down relative to their competition (Kim, 2019). These accusations have caused lasting damage to Korea's value chain and continued to plague the industry in 2021.

6.3.2 Cross-Sector Synergies in the Korean Machine-Tool Sector

In 2020, Korea was the world's sixth largest MT producer and the seventh largest exporter (Korea Machine Tool Manufacturer Association [KOMMA], 2019). Three of Korea's manufacturers: Doosan Infracore, Hyundai Wia, and Hwacheon, were among the world's largest producers (Rodríguez Roldán de Aranguiz, 2019; Machine MFG, 2017).

The trajectory of Korea's MT industry is not surprising from the point of view of the argument. As in other manufacturing sectors, upgrading was based on a familiar pattern of quid pro quo exchanges through which firms contributed to the fulfillment of government's goals to increase the country's self-sufficiency and technological autonomy in exchange for generous public support in the form of market protection and public-coordinated research programs. The purpose of exploring this case is to showcase synergies and cross-sector complementarities within Korea's upgrading strategy and to highlight the multiplier effects of those complementarities on national upgrading.

As an intermediary sector, the MT industry provides critical equipment to firms operating in other large Korean manufacturing sectors. In 2018, Korea was not only the world's sixth largest producer of MTs, but also the sixth largest consumer (KOMMA, 2019). Korea's two largest manufacturing sectors, automotive and electronics, account for 55 percent of Korea's demand for MTs (KOMMA, 2019). The MT industry is also a heavy consumer of electronics, especially semiconductors, thereby providing demand for one of Korea's largest industries. This is not a serendipitous outcome, but rather the result of a sophisticated, multipronged strategy.

In the 1960s, Korea's technological limitations, together with policy measures that enabled manufacturers to import machinery and equipment tax-free crowded out the development of the local MT industry (Guillén, 2010). The situation started to change in 1973, when the government declared general-purpose machinery a preferential industry, along with steel, petrochemicals, shipbuilding, electronics, non-ferrous metals, and the automotive sector (Sakong, 1993). The development of the MT industry was considered a valuable component in a strategy that supported a range of interrelated industries.

The rise of the automotive industry was particularly important for the development of the MT sector. As Korean OEMs started to produce their own vehicles in the first half of the 1970s, their demand for MTs rose, leaving them a choice between importing MTs or entering the industry directly (Guillén, 2010). The government stimulated entry into the MT sector by establishing the Changwon National Industrial Complex in 1974. The complex offered valuable resources to newly-established firms, including state-of-the-art infrastructures, living facilities for employees, a mechanical high-school, a vocational training center, a university, and an on-site research center (Markusen and Park, 1993). To further facilitate relocation to Changwon, the government offered firms low-cost land, and tax holidays (Markusen and Park, 1993).

As was the case in other sectors such as electronics, cooperation with public research centers played a significant role in the development of the MT industry. Korea's first CNC (Computer Numerical Control) machine was produced in 1977 through a collaboration between the Korea Institute of Science and Technology (KIST)—a public research center established in 1966, and a local firm (Sung and Carlsson, 2003). Policy loans also played an important role. The largest recipient was Doosan Infracore (then Daewoo Heavy Industries), which received a US$40 million loan (Jacobsson, 1984; Sung and Carlsson, 2003). Public incentives bore fruit. By the late 1970s, the two largest automakers, Hyundai and Daewoo Motors/GM Korea had entered the MT industry by establishing Hyundai Wia and Doosan Infracore (then Daewoo Heavy Industries) respectively.

In the early 1980s, Korean MT manufacturers still faced significant deficiencies in the form of technological limitations, a dearth of experienced engineering talent, lack of scale economies, and limited international experience (Jacobsson, 1984; Sung and Carlsson, 2003; Lee, Lee, Cho, and Choi, 1999). These limitations affected the quality, reliability, and precision of Korean MTs. Moreover, as automakers, their largest clients, sought to scale up, increase production efficiencies, and improve the quality of products to move into exports (see Chapter 5), the limitations of their MT providers became a binding constraint.

Despite the chaebol structure, automakers were not in a position to facilitate the upgrading of their MT affiliates, largely because they themselves faced similar limitations in terms of technological capabilities and quality (see Chapter 5). Instead, support in the 1980s and 1990s came through the state via a familiar set of instruments including import restrictions and publicly coordinated research programs. MT producers also benefited from the repatriation of US-educated engineers and technical agreements with foreign producers (Sung and Carlsson, 2003). Specifically, in the early 1980s, the government introduced import restrictions on items that could be produced locally and offered financial assistance to firms that bought Korean-made MTs, effectively subsidizing production (Jacobson, 1984; Sung and Carlsson, 2003). The established rule was that machines under a certain (very large) size, determined by the industry's trade association, had to be supplied domestically (Jacobson, 1984). Import restrictions were highly effective at providing a captive market for MT producers. Between 1981 and 1982 alone, the import share of investments in MT decreased from 85 to 31 percent in value terms (Jacobson, 1984). Not only did imports decrease, but local demand for MTs surged in tandem with the rapid expansion of the automotive and semiconductors industries, enabling MT manufacturers to reach scale efficiencies. Between 1985 and 1987, the period in which Hyundai started exporting its vehicles to the US, Korean MT production almost trebled from 566 to 1,605 machines. By 1993 it had reached 2,573 machines (Sung and Carlsson, 2003).

State support continued through the 1990s. Between 1992 and 2001, the state fostered the development of next generation machining systems through a series of three-year publicly coordinated and interdependent research programs (Lee, Lee, Cho, and Choi, 1999). These programs fell under the G7 Leading Technology Develop Program, a large-scale national R&D umbrella program that also housed the R&D programs described in Chapter 4 for the ICT industry (Oh, Lim, and Kim, 2016). R&D programs for the MT sector, as those described in Chapter 4 for ICT, involved a functional division of labor between public research institutes and private firms. The Korea Institute of Industrial Technology (KITECH) was responsible for applied research while private firms undertook product development and commercialization (Lee, Lee, Cho, and Choi, 1999).

By the early 2000s, some Korean MT producers had become globally competitive in segments, such as lathes and machining centers, a position that they continued to hold in 2021 (KOMMA, 2019). Nonetheless, there is still room for improvement. Korean producers still operate in the middle segments of the industry in terms of quality and precision (Park, 2018). None of the Korean firms are yet among the world's ten largest producers, a list that only includes Japanese, German, and US firms. In fact, Korean manufacturers of industrial products continue to rely on imports of high-precision machinery, especially from Japan (KOMMA, 2019).

6.4 The Role of Wider Socioeconomic and Structural Factors in Upgrading: A Counterfactual Comparison with Brazil

This section uses a pointed counterfactual comparison with Brazil to discuss the wider political and structural conditions that enabled Spain and Korea to upgrade where other late industrializing countries failed.

Brazil is a good counterfactual. In 1960, Brazil's average standard of living was US$210 per capita, a figure that was lower than Spain's US$396 but higher than Korea's US$155 per capita income (World Bank Development Indicators, 2020). During the 1960s and 1970s, the country experienced a rapid period of state-driven industrialization in the context of a repressive military regime. Between 1964 and 1980, Brazil's GDP grew by an annual average of 8 percent (World Bank Development Indicators, 2020), compared to Spain's and Korea's 7 and 9 percent annual average GDP growth rates during their peak growth periods (see Chapter 1). Like Spain's and Korea's, Brazil's industrialization supported the expansion of mature, heavy industries, and concentrated on fostering the development of a similar set of sectors to those of Spain and Korea, including steel, electronics, petrochemicals, general purpose machinery, and the automotive sectors (Mussachio and Lazzarini, 2016; Evans, 1995; González Duarte and Braga Rodrigues, 2017). By 1975, manufacturing value-added accounted for 25 percent of Brazil's GDP (Brooks and Kurtz, 2016) compared to 25 percent and 27 percent for Spain and Korea respectively at the height of their industrializations (see Chapter 1). Despite these auspicious signs, from the 1980s, Spain's and Korea's trajectories continued upwards while Brazil's transformation faltered. As of 2018, Brazil's GDP per capita was only US\$8,921, well below the threshold to be considered an advanced economy. Furthermore, while a number of Brazilian firms occupy prominent global positions in their respective fields, most of these firms operate in commodity sectors such as iron, soybeans, meat, and oil deposits (Brooks and Kurtz, 2016) rather than the complex sectors that underpin the economies of most advanced countries.

The focus of this analysis concentrates on three aspects that were common to the Spanish and Korean cases but were absent, or considerably weaker in the Brazilian case: the overlap between local business elites and insider industries, clearly defined goals and strategic guidelines supported by large social consensuses, and public investment in a vast array of public goods. The purpose of this contrast is to showcase the impact of these broader socioeconomic factors on policy consistency, coherence, and sustainability, and ultimately on the ability of countries such as Spain and Korea to carry out upgrading.

6.4.1 Overlap between Local Business Elites and Insider Industries

For the most part, Spain's and Korea's upgrading took place through complex sectors in which local firms already exercised a high degree of autonomy. As shown through the empirical cases in this book, decision makers at these firms had significant power within their organizations, could establish their own goals, and had internal motivations to upgrade. These features enabled firms to engage with the state as equals, to advocate for their own interests, and to use the resources they obtained to upgrade rather than hoard profits. More importantly, Spanish and Korean business elites concentrated mainly in these same sectors (Etchemendy, 2004, Chang and Park, 2004). This identification between local business elites and insider firms helped minimize political opposition even when upgrading had distributional consequences, thereby ensuring that policies remained in place as governments changed.

The contrast with Brazil highlights the importance of the overlap between insider sectors and national business elites. Brazilian industrialization was based on the establishment of a large number of state-owned enterprises (Mussachio and Lazzarini, 2014; Mussachio and Lazzarini, 2016). After a wave of privatizations in the 1990s, some of these firms remained under control of the state while several others were acquired by foreign investors. Many of the firms that have remained in public hands have been subject to political interferences that clash with the firms' strategic interests (Mussachio and Lazzarini, 2014), trammeling upgrading. In addition, most of the privatized firms have been integrated into global organizations that have limited incentives to replicate in Brazil activities they already perform efficiently in other locations, also constraining upgrading (Evans, 1995; Brooks and Kurtz, 2016).

Moreover, Brazil's vast natural resources and the country's history of colonial exploitation mean that local business elites concentrate in commodity sectors such as agriculture and food industries, whose priorities are usually different from, and sometimes create conflicts of interest with, those of more complex manufacturing sectors. For instance, while complex industries require a highly educated workforce, many commodity sectors rely on the availability of abundant, relatively unskilled labor, and when they do need skilled labor, they require different types of specializations from those required by complex industries. The dissociation between local economic elites and the countries' most complex industries has been a constant source of political conflict in Brazil, and has resulted in stop-and-go policies toward restructuring and upgrading since the 1980s (Abu-El-Haj, 2007; Nolke et al., 2020).

6.4.2 Clearly Defined Goals and Strategic Guidelines Supported by Large Social Consensuses

Spain's and Korea's strategies were based on clear goals, broadly shared social aspirations to reach advanced country status, and an enduring understanding on the fundamental lines of how to achieve those goals. As discussed in Chapter 2, in the early 1980s, Spain and Korea announced explicitly their aspirations to join the ranks of advanced countries and to occupy a prominent position in the global economy. Having clear goals enabled Spain and Korea to develop strategies and create institutions that were tailored to their purposes. Clear, long-term goals also enabled Spain and Korea to adapt policy incentives and instruments as circumstances changed without sacrificing policy consistency and continuity.

In addition, Spain's and Korea's strategies were based on clear interpretations of the functional role of pivotal service sectors such as banking, energy, and telecommunications relative to manufacturing, and on coherent integrational and techno-industrial approaches that were implemented consistently across a broad range of sectors. Such clear guidelines provided policy clarity and consistency and helped generate synergies that had a multiplier effect on upgrading.

Finally, Spain's and Korea's goals were supported by high levels of social consensus (Pérez-Díaz, 1993; Jung and Rho, 2020) stemming from societies whose broad middle-classes shared common aspirations. Broad social consensuses helped generate community acceptance for change, even when some groups experienced short-term losses. In addition, within the context of Spain's and Korea's new democratic societies, social consensuses connected government legitimacy to upgrading, making governments accountable for delivering results and forcing successive governments to sustain policy efforts that delivered on those outcomes, even when they may have been opposed to them for ideological reasons.

A comparison with Brazil helps illustrate the value of these traits. Brazilian policy makers and intellectuals knew what they did *not* want their country to become: a nation whose sovereignty was undermined by multilateral institutions and whose economic trajectory was dictated by foreign multinationals (Abu-El-Haj, 2007). However, there was less clarity about the country's positive objectives, let alone how to achieve them. The absence of clear goals translated into a transformational strategy that had lower levels of internal coherence and did not follow a visible logic or generated obvious cross-sector synergies. The outcome was the emergence of islands of excellence (Schneider, 2016; Mussachio and Lazzarini, 2014; Nolke et al., 2020) rather than systemic approach that generated synergies across a broad range of skilled sectors in services and manufacturing sectors.

Moreover, Brazil's commitment to upgrading was not as broadly supported by society as Spain's and Korea's. This is in part a consequence of Brazil's very unequal society. Despite making great progress in poverty reduction, Brazil's GINI coefficient in 2018 was 0.54, one of the world's highest (World Bank Development Indicators, 2020). Large differences in income translate into differences in economic preferences across different social groups that contribute to policy fluctuations (Stokes et al., 2013; Kitschelt, 2012).

6.4.3 Investment in Public Goods

Spain's and Korea's upgrading processes were supported by large investments in a broad range of public goods, including education, innovation, and physical infrastructures. These investments increased the quality of public goods, reduced barriers, and lowered the cost of upgrading in complex industries. In addition, investment in public goods created momentum for change and helped expand upgrading across industries with similar needs.

Brazil has made significant investments in public goods, but levels remain well below those of Spain and Korea. While the country has a good network of public universities, the rate of 25–64s with tertiary education is only 17 percent, or less than half that of Spain's and much lower than Korea's (OECD, *Education at a Glance*, 2019). Moreover, 14 percent of Brazil's 25–64s have less than primary education compared to 2 percent in Spain and virtually nil in Korea (OECD, *Education at a Glance*, 2019).

Brazil also has important pockets of innovation in fields such as biotech and oil (Brooks and Kurtz, 2016). In fact, in 2019, R&D investment represented 1.3 percent of Brazil's GDP, a slightly higher share than Spain's 1.2 percent. However, this figure is still only half the OECD average, and less than a third of Korea's investment in R&D relative to GDP. Furthermore, Brazil's number of researchers per million inhabitants is a meager 887, compared to Spain's 2,613 or Korea's 6,826 (Unesco Institute for Statistics, 2020). Moreover, unlike Spain and Korea, which emphasized applied innovation during their periods of upgrading, Brazilian R&D output tends to focus on academic outputs (Brooks and Kurtz, 2016), which are less directly applicable to upgrading.

Finally, Brazil's physical infrastructures are one of the country's most obvious binding constraints. The World Bank's Logistics Performance Index ranks Brazil 50th (out of 160 countries) in terms of the quality and quantity of its trade, transport, and communications infrastructures. Meanwhile, Spain ranks 19th and Korea the 22nd in the same index (World Bank International Scorecard, 2018). Brazil's stock of physical infrastructures is not only appreciably behind Spain's and Korea's state-of-the-art infrastructures, but it is also smaller and in worse condition than those of most countries at a similar income level (Raiser et al., 2017).

6.5 Conclusions: Upgrading in Spain and Korea

The material in these and the previous three chapters answered the questions with which this book started: How did Spain and South Korea upgrade to reach advanced country status? How did they come to host firms that are globally competitive in skill-, capital-, and knowledge-intensive industries? In the early 1980s, Spain and Korea experienced major episodes of crisis and announced ambitious goals to join the ranks of advanced countries and integrate into the global economy. By the 2010s, the two countries had significantly narrowed the gap with the world's most advanced countries, were deeply integrated into the global economy, and hosted a number of firms that stood at the top of their respective GVCs.

These outcomes were not merely the result of a market-embracing approach and sound macroeconomic policies. Neither were they the outcome of a hierarchically structured, state-directed models. Instead, this book argued that upgrading was the result of state–firm coordination models based on quid pro quo exchanges, interdependences, and mutually agreed-upon working rules that enabled states and firms in insider sectors to reach mutually beneficial outcomes. The negotiated nature of these agreements opened the door for Spain and Korea to pursue different pathways to upgrading. Spain's integrational approach was based on FDI, technological outsourcing, and regional integration with the EU. Korea's techno-industrial strategy prioritized self-sufficiency and the development of local technological capacity.

This chapter expanded the argument in two ways. The use of mini-cases brought to the fore certain nuances of the argument. The analysis of the Spanish electricity sector illustrated the role of path dependence and continuity in a coordination approach that was originally established in the 1940s. The discussion of the ASD industry showed that Spain's pathway to upgrading in complex services was the result of political choices rather than the only viable strategy. The cases of the Korean electricity and MT sectors highlighted the systemic elements of Korea's strategy and illustrated the importance of cross-sector synergies in amplifying upgrading. The second portion of this chapter used a pointed counterfactual comparison with Brazil to discuss wider socioeconomic and structural factors that enabled Spain and Korea to succeed where other countries failed. The comparison showed that in the Spanish and Korean cases, the overlap between local business elites and insider industries, the presence of clearly defined, broadly supported goals, and the state's commitment to increasing the quality of public goods paid off in the form of consistent, coherent, and sustainable policies that facilitated upgrading.

The following chapter puts an end to this book. The chapter articulates the main insights of the analysis, discusses the larger implications of the research for future studies, and considers briefly the main challenges that Spain and Korea face as they shift from upgrading to consolidating their positions as advanced economies.

7

Contributions to the Study of Late Development and Industrial Transformation

7.1 Spain and Korea Revisited

The purpose of this study has been to explain how Spain and Korea upgraded to reach advanced country status. This transformation deserved analytical attention for three reasons. Reaching advanced country status by way of increasing the complexity of the national productive structure is a relatively rare event, yet Spain and Korea were particularly successful. The two countries' different patterns of upgrading go against conventional accounts that upgrading necessarily involves an upward movement within the value chains of existing manufacturing sectors and the implicit assumption that complex services occupy a vicarious position. The focus on two countries that have efficiently navigated the transition from late industrializing economies to advanced countries challenges conventional views of the world as divided between advanced and developing economies.

The research showed that upgrading was based on quid pro quo exchanges and interdependences between states and firms. In these interdependent models, national governments and firms exercised control over their decisions and came to develop a set of mutually agreed-upon working rules that enabled both parties to reach beneficial outcomes. The analysis started by putting firms at the center, identifying the competitive limitations they faced, and the reasons why they needed states to help them build the stock of resources and capabilities necessary to develop complex advantages. It also paid attention to the identities and capabilities of public decision makers and how they shaped perceived policy priorities and the capability to design and implement different types of upgrading strategies. Finally, it considered the impact of historical and social linkages with more advanced countries on public and private preferences, market opportunities, and the likelihood of success of different strategies.

State-Firm Coordination and Upgrading: Reaching the Efficiency Frontier in Skill-, Capital-, and Knowledge-Intensive Industries in Spain and South Korea. Angela Garcia Calvo, Oxford University Press. © Angela Garcia Calvo 2021. DOI: 10.1093/oso/9780198864561.003.0007

National variation in these three elements led Spain and Korea to pursue two different pathways to upgrading. Spain pursued an integrational strategy that emphasized FDI, technological outsourcing, and regional integration within the EU. Korea pursued a techno-industrial approach that prioritized self-sufficiency and technological autonomy. These strategies enabled Spanish and Korean firms across multiple complex sectors to reach the efficiency frontier, but also shaped the production structures of the two countries resulting in different specializations in complex services and manufacturing respectively.

The remainder of this concluding chapter first reviews the book's methodological contributions and their implications for the study of upgrading. It then considers the implications of my findings for researchers and policy makers interested in late development and economic transformation in other contexts. Lastly, the chapter makes a few final considerations about Spain's and Korea's future economic prospects as they consolidate their advanced economy status.

7.2 Methodological Contributions

A central, if underlying, theme in this book is the nature of industrial transformation and the ways we should approach its study. Much has been written about industrial transformation from the point of view of either markets or states, yet this study started from the view that the classic market versus state approach is insufficient to explain processes of industrial transformation and upgrading. Instead, my starting point was to define upgrading as a coordination problem in which the key actors are states and firms.

The focus on state–firm interdependencies stands on the shoulders of an existing institutionalist literature. Among the most noteworthy contributions in the developmental literature, Evans (1995) and Weiss (1998) highlight the importance of state–firm interdependencies but fail to acknowledge firm agency. On the other hand, the Varieties of Capitalism literature (Hall and Soskice, 2001) stresses coordination and puts firms at the center but underplays the role of states. Instead, this book explored upgrading by looking at the identities and capabilities of both states and firms. The purpose of this approach is to gauge whether firms and states need each other to support upgrading and if so, what are their motivations to cooperate, what types of structures govern their relationships, and how they may foster upgrading.

The research put firms at the center of the analysis because they generate the type of wealth and high-quality jobs that underpin upgrading. However, firms operate within a context defined by two different types of institutions: those derived from the competitive dynamics of their industry, and those derived by the political dynamics of the country in which they are based. Accordingly, the book operationalized the analysis through a three-tiered structure that looked at firms, industries, and countries. Firm and industry level analyses are closely intertwined: firms are responsible for creating competitive advantages, but competitive advantages depend on skills, assets, and incentives that are determined at industry level. Accordingly, the analysis was based on a thorough understanding of industry dynamics during the period of analysis, and the performance of Spanish and Korean firms using sector-specific indicators. The combination of these two analyses provided detailed information about the types of competitive limitations Spanish and Korea firms faced relative to their peers in more advanced countries, the types of resources and capabilities they needed to overcome them, their capacity to develop them autonomously, and whether state activism was necessary to support their transformation. The country level analyses involved looking at the identities and capabilities of national governments by examining their composition, the backgrounds of policy makers, and the presence and characteristics of adjacent, specialized agencies. In parallel with the industry and firm level analyses, the purposes of the country analyses was to understand what were the goals and motivations of national governments, to gauge their capabilities and resources, and to assess whether they could achieve their objectives without cooperation from firms.

A multilevel analysis such as this has several important implications. The analysis of firms within their industries shows that firms cannot expect to reach the efficiency frontier without state support. In addition, it turns the book's broader question about upgrading into a more concrete exploration of how states and firms come together to help firms overcome a set of specific constraints. Cross-sector comparisons reveal that the needs of firms in different industries, and in some cases different segments within an industry, cannot be served simultaneously. Chapters 4 and 5 showed that firms operating in complex manufacturing sectors require large amounts of patient capital and stable demand to restructure and develop new, more complex outputs. By contrast, Chapter 3 showed that extending cheap, long-term credit to productive industry is detrimental for large bank profitability. Chapter 4 further argued that prioritizing local electronics manufacturers over global ones is a suboptimal strategy for telecommunications operators. A major consequence of these cross-sector conflicts of interest is that manufacturing and complex services are unlikely to upgrade simultaneously. Moreover, because firms are unable to upgrade without cooperation from the state, conflicts of interest between firms in manufacturing and services sectors put the state in a position to choose which types of resources to prioritize and therefore what types of sectors and firms are most likely to upgrade.

The country analyses further revealed that while national governments may have common goals, they can differ widely in how they accomplish them. Government priorities and the strategies to fulfill them stem not from the presence or absence of well-qualified civil servants, as the developmental literature points out, but from differences in the identities and capabilities of public decision makers within already sophisticated and competent civil services. The book characterized two different types of governments: generalists and techno-industrial, each dominated by ministers with different backgrounds in either economics and law, or technical fields. Chapters 3 and 4 connected Spain's view of upgrading with generalist governments dominated by a cohesive group of orthodox economists. It argued that these economists are in an advantageous position to understand the needs of firms in complex services such as banking and telecommunications but less willing, and also less well-prepared to devise the complex, detailed plans required by manufacturing industries. In addition, Chapters 4 and 5 linked Korea's strategy with governments in which the most powerful economic ministry is led by individuals with an engineering background. Chapters 3 and 4 also showed that Korea's technical-savvy governments are supported by a dense network of specialized civil servants, public research institutions, and think-tanks that put economic ministries in a privileged position to understand the limitations and the needs of firms across complex manufacturing sectors and to develop and implement cohesive plans that generate important cross-sector synergies.

Despite these differences, neither Spain's generalists nor Korea's techno-industrial governments were capable of accomplishing upgrading without cooperation from firms. Chapter 3 showed that, in the absence of an active interbank lending market, Spain's early democratic governments could not develop an autonomous macroeconomic policy without cooperation from large banks. Neither could they force private, publicly listed banks to restructure in order to have the type of competitive banking sector that could fight off speculative attacks capable of destabilizing the financial system. Similarly, Chapter 4 showed that having historically delegated policy decision-making powers to the telecommunications incumbent, the Spanish government lacked the tools to universalize the telecommunications network without cooperation from Telefonica. Likewise, Chapters 4 and 5 showed that Korea's techno industrial governments could not increase the country's technological self-sufficiency without cooperation from private firms in relevant industries such as electronics and the automotive sector.

In all of these cases, governments and insider firms had compatible objectives. Spanish large progressive banks saw restructuring as a necessity in order to survive in the EU's single market, as did the telecommunications incumbent, and both were willing to contribute to public goals in exchange for favorable legislation that took their needs into account. Korean manufacturers in complex industries saw the need to improve the quality of their products and branch out into more complex outputs in order to continue growing. Manufacturers were also willing to shift from the domestic market to exports to take advantage of new market opportunities derived from the US's emerging GVCs, and from the market gap left by Japan as it shifted upmarket in response to the Plaza Accord.

This combination of these two factors: the inability of both states and firms to accomplish their respective objectives without cooperation from the other, and the presence of compatible public and private objectives, provided the motivation for coordination models based on quid pro quo exchanges in which each actor helped further the other's goals and both together brought about upgrading.

7.3 Implications for Research on Late Development and Economic Transformation

Spain's and Korea's trajectories are intrinsically interesting, but their analysis can also help provide insights for current debates on late development and economic transformation. In particular, the arguments and detailed case analyses presented in this book have several implications for the DS literature and for historical institutionalism.

Characterizing upgrading as a coordination problem allows one to accommodate the idea of policy variation. This is because the negotiated nature of state–firm cooperation implies that countries can develop different working arrangements. Spain's and Korea's trajectories showcase this idea: historical experiences led these two countries to pursue fundamentally diverse strategies to revolve the same problem. These strategies arose from existing institutional arrangements and domestic policy priorities rather than ready-made recipes.

This brings me to a related point. Existing work on late development often portrays upgrading as a process that necessarily involves upward movements within the value chains of manufacturing sectors and large investments in innovation. It is important to recognize that this argument is anchored on the experiences of a few Asian countries. Spain's experience shows that there are alternative, viable strategies. It also suggests that to understand the full range of possible transformational strategies available to late industrializing economies we need detailed empirical evidence from countries that represent different institutional traditions and different forms of capitalism across a variety of regions.

Another important implication of the negotiated nature of upgrading strategies is that the trajectory of any given country may not be replicable elsewhere. The book's argument suggest that replication will be most difficult in countries where pre-existing production structures and linkages to advanced economies differ significantly from those in which the original strategy is implemented. This sends a clear message to policy makers in today's emerging economies: it is perfectly legitimate to use the successful experiences of other countries as a source of inspiration and information. It is also reasonable to use this book's argument as a way to learn about the importance of the state–firm interdependences in fostering economic transformation and the nature of state–firm interaction. However, Spain's and Korea's strategies are not blueprints that can be applied directly to other environments. Instead, a country should develop a strategy that reflects the local context, including the characteristics of local production and its existing or potential competitive advantages, the identity, strengths, and capabilities of its government, and that country's relationships with the rest of the world.

Which brings me to an additional point. Not only do policy makers need to adapt the main ideas behind state–firm coordination to develop strategies that fit the characteristics of their countries, but they also need to develop strategies capable of accommodating changes in tactical objectives and a broad range of implementation instruments. The empirical chapters of this book showed that the main lines of Spain's and Korea's strategies were consistent over a period of four decades despite multiple changes in government and shifts from dictatorships to democracies. Nonetheless, concrete public and private goals evolved over time, as did the instruments used to accomplish them. For instance, while Spain's quid pro quo arrangement is recognizable in the banking sector since the late 1970s, Spain's public goals for the banking sector evolved from setting the basis for an independent monetary policy in the 1980s, to restructuring large banks to ensure their competitiveness in the 1990s, and to addressing the aftermath of a major financial crisis in the late 2000s and 2010s. Banks' objectives also evolved from the elimination of preferential credit to industry, to preventing unwanted foreign acquisitions and weathering a major systemic crisis later on. Similarly, Korea's strategy for the electronics and the automotive sectors was consistently based on an idiosyncratic division of labor between the state and large firms that is still recognizable in 2021. However, early projects revolved around institution building and technology acquisition, whereas more recent ones aim to create future growth engines, generate innovation that is new to the world, and consolidate the leadership position of Korean firms in global markets. The instruments to achieve these goals have also evolved in consonance. From public R&D projects to much broader national strategies.

7.3.1 Wider Structural Conditions for Upgrading

The previous discussion brings me to my final point. Taking an institutional perspective seriously involves discussing context. However, there are different ways of taking context into account. This book argued that time, level of development, industrial structure, and external linkages affect the development of national strategies for upgrading. Chapter 6 also examined a broader set of socioeconomic and structural factors that affect the successful implementation of upgrading strategies.

7.3.1.1 Contextual Features that Shape Upgrading Strategies
Implicit to the book is the assumption that the timing of upgrading matters. Although Spain and Korea were countries with different institutional traditions, both of them industrialized and upgraded within the same time framework. Timing determines the competitive dynamics firms need to abide by and therefore the types of competitive limitations they face, and the resources they need to overcome them. The timing of upgrading also determines broader national and supranational dynamics that have a bearing on upgrading. This book specifically assumed a context of increasing global interdependence and trade, which was prevalent during the period of analysis.

When considering time, the book did not explicitly explore the role of Spain's and Korea's government transitions, largely because as discussed in Chapter 6, despite the change in government structure, there was a significant degree of path dependence. Instead, it mentioned specific aspects of these political changes when they were relevant, as was the case with the rise of Spain's orthodox economists or the country's bid for EU membership.

The book argued that Spain's and Korea's pathways to upgrading were informed by two other contextual factors: their pre-existing production structures and the opportunities derived from close linkages to advanced economies. With few exceptions, such as the case of Korea's nuclear power industry, Spain and Korea upgraded in sectors in which large local firms not only had upgrading potential, but already exercised a high degree of leadership and autonomy. This was true even in those cases where the state had a significant ownership stake, as was the case with Telefonica. Firm autonomy meant that firms could engage with the state as equals. Strategic independence also meant that insider firms had internal incentives to use the resources they obtained to become globally competitive rather than just hoard profits.

Spain's and Korea's choices were also shaped by the opportunities and threats derived from their linkages to more advanced economies closest to their spheres: Europe, the US, and Japan. Spain's determination to join the EU, together with the launch of the EU's single market, the emergence of EU-wide value chain, and state retrenchment from some manufacturing sectors such as electronics, impacted Spain's approach to manufacturing upgrading and its protective stance toward complex services. Similarly, Korea's ability to source technology from Japan and the US, the country's capacity to repatriate US-educated and experienced workers, the US's shift from local manufacturing to offshoring, and America's change of heart regarding its role in Asia, incentivized and enabled Korean firms to develop their technological capabilities and created attractive market opportunities for key manufacturing industries.

It is important to note that while these contextual factors shaped the development of national strategies for upgrading, they did not determine them. Spain and Korea did not have to center their strategic efforts in the sectors they did. After all, the types of industries both countries supported already had more competitive potential than other industries in their respective economies. Spanish manufacturers lagged further behind than large banks and utilities and could have benefited more from the state's dedicated support, as the case of the ASD sector showed. Similarly, Korean services firms, especially large banks, would not only have benefited from public support, but also a dedicated public effort could have spared the country a major financial crisis. External linkages did not determine upgrading either. There was nothing inevitable about Spain's accession to the EU. Spain's membership application had been initially rejected in the 1960s, and the country faced staunch opposition from France in the 1970s and 1980s. Similarly, Korea's decision to normalize its relationship with Japan in the 1960s was a political choice that responded to domestic pragmatic economic motives but angered a fair portion of Korea's society. In addition, the ebbs and flows of Korea's relationship with the US influenced Korea's prioritization of dual-purpose industries from the 1970s, but the decision was also undoubtedly motivated by Park's loss of social support and his desire to stamp the opposition out.

7.3.1.2 Broader Socioeconomic and Structural Factors that Affect Upgrading Implementation

Finally, the successful implementation of any given upgrading strategy is influenced by broader socioeconomic and structural factors that affect policy consistency, coherence, and sustainability. Among these factors the book highlighted the overlap between local business elites and insider industries, clear goals and strategic guidelines supported by large social consensuses, and public investment in a vast array of public goods.

An overlap between local business elites and insider industries helps ensure that national upgrading strategies are sustainable even when they do not distribute benefits equitable across all industries. This is because firms in outsider industries are likely to be weaker and less well organized. Spain's and Korea's examples suggest that such overlap is easier to attain in countries that lack natural resources, but confirming this will require further research.

The book's analysis also suggests that strategies based on clear, long-term goals and strategic guidelines are more likely to succeed. The presence of clear goals enables countries to build institutions that are tailored to a specific purpose and are therefore more likely to be efficient at fulfilling it. Clear ex-ante objectives also help ensure that upgrading strategies have a higher degree of internal coherence. Spain's and Korea's approaches to manufacturing and services were consistent across the board. This consistency helped increase cross-sector synergies that generated value at national level.

Large social consensuses help make upgrading strategies sustainable over time. Social consensus contributes to generate public and community acceptance for change, even in those instances when short-term change is not positive for some social groups. In addition, consensus helps establish a link between government legitimacy and upgrading, making successive governments accountable for delivering results and forcing them to sustain their policy efforts for a sufficiently long period of time to achieve their goals. The comparison between Spain, Korea, and Brazil suggests that widespread social support is more likely to emerge within homogeneous societies with broad middle classes that share similar aspirations.

Finally, but no less importantly, upgrading strategies are more likely to succeed when they are accompanied by meaningful investment in a broad array of public goods including education, innovation, and physical infrastructures. Such investments enable governments to create or improve the quality of socially embedded resources available to firms, thereby decreasing firms' costs of undertaking upgrading and removing some potential barriers. Nonetheless, it is unclear how much investment in public goods is necessary to support upgrading, and whether there are any specific thresholds that countries should reach in order to sufficiently lower costs and barriers to upgrading across sectors.

From a wider perspective, the importance of these socioeconomic and structural factors has two important implications. First, it suggests that behind successful strategies for economic transformation there is much more than cooperation between governments and a few large firms. Upgrading requires a systemic, coherent, sustainable effort encompassing economic actors and society as a whole. In addition, these factors underline the sheer complexity of upgrading and the importance of adopting strategies that are tailored to the needs of the societies in which transformation takes place.

7.4 Considerations about Spain's and Korea's Future Economic Prospects

A book about economic transformation could not end without some final considerations about the future prospects of Spain and Korea. In the last four decades, these two countries have come a long way. Their upgrading strategies enabled firms in a range of industries to become globally competitive and underpinned long periods of sustained economic growth that have translated into higher standards of living. But becoming an advanced economy is not static equilibrium. Moving forward, Spain and Korea will need to address disequilibria caused by their upgrading strategies and to create an environment that enables firms to continue generating new sources of competitive advantage through innovation.

7.4.1 Addressing Disequilibria Caused by Upgrading

Spain's and Korea's strategies involved prioritizing the needs of large firms in insider sectors over those of outsider sectors. The result were relatively narrow specializations in a few sectors and two-headed productive structures composed of large, world-leading competitive firms, and a population of small and micro firms that has significant trouble growing. Narrow production specializations mean that national economic growth depends on the performance of a relatively small number firms in a handful of industries, which makes Spain's, and Korea's, economies highly vulnerable to industry-specific downturns. Historically,

Spanish and Korean governments have demonstrated their willingness to support insider industries in times of crisis. However, public support for ailing large firms can impose a very heavy cost on national economies as a whole. Korea's 1997 debacle, and Spain's banking crisis in the early 2010s are examples of this.

Two-headed productive structures generate at least two additional types of adverse effects. First, they make it difficult for Spain and Korea to foster a second-generation of globally competitive firms with which to diversity their economies and decrease exposure to downturns. In addition, because SMEs are large creators of employment, the difficulties experienced by small firms translate into a dearth of stable jobs and a high concentration of those jobs within the country's population of large firms. Such situation has led Spain and Korea to have some of the OECD's highest rates of temporary employment and high levels of underemployment (see Chapter 2). As temporary employment has become entrenched, so have social inequalities and political polarization. By itself, these trends do not pose an immediate threat to the two countries' models, at least they did not until the Covid-19 crisis. A crisis-induced reduction in the availability of both career-track jobs and temporary employment can deal a major blow to these economies. Furthermore, the resulting increases in inequality may undermine Spain's and Korea's broad social consensuses making it difficult to undertake future rounds of economic transformation.

There is evidence that increases in inequality brought about by the 2008 crisis have increased social polarization in Spain and Korea. Between 2015 and 2019, Spain conducted four general elections, two of them in 2019 alone, due to the inability of the two largest political parties to reach a majority and their unwillingness to form a coalition government. The country has also seen the surge of extreme-right movements, including a political party with parliamentary representation, something that would have been unthinkable a decade earlier. In Korea too, widespread socioeconomic discontent stimulated a wave of mass rallies between 2016 and 2017, the largest since the country's transition to democracy in the 1980s. Through these demonstrations, Koreans demanded deep political and economic change, and started a movement that led to the fall of the government and paved the way for the indictment and eventual incarceration of President Park Geun Hye.

7.4.2 Generating New Competitive Advantages through Innovation

As Spain and Korea move from upgrading to consolidating their position as advanced economies, a major challenge will be to continue generating new sources of competitive advantage through innovation.

Spain's and Korea's integrational and techno-industrial strategies have generated different expectations about the two countries' capacity for innovation. It is assumed that Spain's integrational strategy sets limits to innovation. Historically, services have invested much lower amounts on R&D than manufacturing sectors. In addition, Spain's reliance on FDI means that many firms in manufacturing sectors are affiliated to foreign firms. Accordingly, key strategic decisions and high value-added architectural innovation takes place outside the country. Furthermore, at times of transformation or production scale back, there is a risk that foreign investors may exit the market or significantly reduce in-country production due to a combination of economic and political incentives. Spain's modest levels of investment in R&D as a percentage of GDP, the presence of a large portion of the population that has capped its education at relatively low levels, and a few announcements of closures in 2020 galvanize these expectations.

It is also assumed that Korea's techno-industrial strategy has prepared the country well to transition from knowledge absorption to knowledge generation. Complex manufacturing sectors make hefty investments in R&D. The presence of local, lead firms means that decisions concerning architectural innovation and production strategies are taken within country. Large firms' control over huge portions of their value chains gives them even more autonomy regarding innovation decisions, since they can implement changes relatively quickly, and face lower risks of technology leakages. These expectations are confirmed by Korea's high levels of R&D investment per GDP, world-class educational institutions, a very educated workforce, and a dense network of public and private specialized research institutions.

However, as of the writing of these pages in 2021, the immediate prospects for innovation and industrial renewal in the two countries do not fully confirm these expectations.

Large Spanish firms in complex industries seem poised to take advantage of opportunities derived from decarbonization, digitalization, and emerging industry paradigms. National commitments to decarbonization generate major opportunities for innovation in complex service industries such as electric power, and Spanish firms are well positioned to seize them. In 2020, Iberdrola, a global leader in wind energy and the world's third largest utility pledged to invest €75 billion in additional energy production capacity by 2025, most of it through organic growth (Thomas and Dombey, 2020).

Similarly, digitalization received a significant boost in 2020 as a result of the Covid-19 crisis and the surge in working from home across the world. Although some activities may eventually return back to the office the digitalization of many economic activities and the rise of platforms creates massive opportunities for telecommunications operators that own their networks and can guarantee high quality of service and data security. Telefonica, a large operator with a global presence and significant expertise is well situated to jump in on this trend. The company has plans to provide 100 percent fiber optic coverage in Spain and to turn its home base into a global digital hub (Dombey, 2020).

Key manufacturing sectors such as the automotive industry are also undergoing complex transformations derived from a shift in the existing industry paradigm. Spain's dependence on foreign-based automakers and its dependence on exports, makes the Spanish automotive industry particularly vulnerable. Nonetheless, manufacturers have demonstrated significant capacity to generate applied, cost-efficient, yet highly lucrative innovative solutions. As discussed in Chapter 5, in the past decade, Spain's large automotive suppliers have leveraged their existing relationships with multiple OEMs to enter increasingly higher value-added segments while automakers are forced to concentrate their resources on core functions such as the development of new batteries and the design of EV platforms.

Rather than a hindrance, EU integration could well be a source of support for Spain's innovation. Spain is scheduled to receive approximately 20 percent of the EU's coronavirus recovery fund's €750 billion, which will be disbursed between 2021 and 2026 (Dombey, 2020). In December 2020, Iberdrola and Telefonica were drafting proposals for concrete innovative projects to be co-financed by the fund. Similarly, the automotive industry was urging the government to help finance projects to develop battery technology, hydrogen power, smart factories, and the deployment of electricity charging points (Dombey (b), 2020).

While Spanish large firms seem to defy expectations in a positive way, some of their Korean counterparts in complex manufacturing industries appear to experience more difficulties than anticipated. This is particularly true in the automotive sector. As discussed in Chapter 5, HMC lags behind its competitors in the launch of a dedicated EV platform, which is expected to take place in 2021. As if this was not enough, in late 2020, the automaker was forced to recall tens of thousands of its Kona model after several incidents in which vehicles with batteries from LG Chem caught fire (Yang and Jin, 2020). HMC was also forced to recall 129,000 additional vehicles of three other models due to defective components that cause premature engine damage (Beresford, 2020).

Other firms have experienced a recent surge. Despite the issues just mentioned, in 2020 LG Chem emerged as one of the world's largest battery producers, with a quarter of the world's EV battery market (Financial Times, 2021).

Similarly, booming demand for mobile devices have provided a major boost for Korea' electronics manufacturers, including Samsung, whose market capitalization increased by 182 percent during 2020 (Financial Times, 2021).

Absent a safety net equivalent to Spain's participation in the EU Recovery Fund, the Korean government has also stepped up to stimulate innovation and competitive transformation. The 2020 Korean-style New Deal is one of the world's most ambitious economic transformation programs. With a projected investment of ₩2,064 trillion (US$1.8 trillion) (Government of Korea, 2021) the New Deal has the potential not just to address the fallout of the Covid-19 pandemic, but to set the bases for Korea's new wave of economic transformation. Nonetheless, the proof will be in the pudding. In the past decades, Korean presidents have championed ambitious initiatives, but not all of them have been fruitful. As shown throughout the book, successful implementation will depend on finding an equilibrium between the interests of the state, firms, and society, and on the ability to sustain public initiative for a sufficiently long period of time.

Bibliography

Government Acts, Law Reports, Cases, and Statutes

Commission of the European Communities v. Kingdom of Spain CASE C-463/00, 2003.

European Communities, 1990. "Council Directive 90/547 EEC of 29 October 1990." *Official Journal of the European Communities* No L313/30.

Judgment of the Court of 13 May 2003. Failure by a Member State to fulfil its obligations—Articles 43 EC and 56 EC—System of administrative approval relating to privatisedundertakings. (CASE C-463/00). http://curia.europa.eu/juris/liste.jsf?language=en&num=C-463/00. Accessed April 7, 2020.

Government of the Republic of Korea, 1983. "Foreign Capital Inducement Act, 1983" (Law No. 3691, 1983). Seoul: Korea.

Government of the Republic of Korea, 1988. "The revised sixth five-year economic and social development plan (1988–1991")." Seoul: Government of Korea.

Government of the Republic of Korea, Monopoly Regulation and Fair Trade Act. Law No. 3320, December 31, 1980. https://www.jftc.go.jp/eacpf/01/Korea-monopoly.pdf. Accessed April 7, 2020.

Government of the Republic of Korea, 2021. "The Korean New Deal. National strategy for a great transformation." Seoul: Government of the Republic of Korea.

Government of Spain, 1959. "Decree-Law 10/1959 of July 21 of economic organization." Official State Bulletin, 174, July 22, 1959.

Government of Spain, 1969. "II Plan of economic and social development." Madrid: Government of Spain.

Government of Spain, 1972a. "Decree 3,339/1972 of November 30 which regulates the fabrication of motor vehicles in Spain." Official State Bulletin, 293, December 7, 1972.

Government of Spain, 1972b. "Decree 3,757/1972 of December 23 that declares the automotive industry a preferential sector." Official State Bulletin, 293, January 23, 1973.

Government of Spain, 1975. "Decree 175/1975 of February 13, about the concerted regime in the electricity sector." Official State Bulletin, 40, February 15, 1975.

Government of Spain, 1977a. "Moncloa Pacts, 1977." Colección Gobierno, N 17. Servicio Central de Publicaciones/Secretaría General Técnica, Presidencia del Gobierno. ISBN: 84-500-2323-8. Depósito legal: M. 38590/1977 Imprenta Nacional del Boletín Oficial del Estado. https://www.mpr.gob.es/servicios2/publicaciones/vol17/. Accessed July 5, 2020.

Government of Spain, 1977b. "Royal Decree 1839/1977, of July 23 about the organic structure and the functions of the Ministry of Economics." Official State Bulletin, 177, July 26, 1977.

Government of Spain, 1977c. "Royal Decree 3,048/1977, of November 11 which creates the Deposit Guarantee Fund for Banking Institutions." Official State Bulletin, 283, November 26, 1977.

Government of Spain, 1978a. "Royal Decree 54/1978, of January 16 which modifies Royal Decree 3048/1977 of November 11, which created the Deposit Guarantee Fund of Banking Institutions." Official State Bulletin, 14, January 17, 1978.

Government of Spain, 1978b. "Royal Decree 1,388/1978 of June 23 that regulates the presence of foreign banks in Spain." Official State Bulletin, 150, June 24, 1978.

Government of Spain, 1979. "Organic Law 3/1979 of December 18 Autonomy Statute for the Basque Country." Official State Bulletin, 306, December 22, 1979.

Government of Spain, 1980a. "Law 30/1980 of June 21 that regulates the governance organs of the Bank of Spain." Official State Bulletin, 154, June 27, 1980.

Government of Spain, 1980b. "Law 82/1980 of December 30 about energy conservation." Official State Bulletin, 23, January 27, 1981.

Government of Spain, 1980c. "Royal Decree-Law 4/1980, of March 28 which gives legal status to the Deposit Guarantee Fund for Banking Institutions and other complementary measures." Official State Bulletin, 78, March 31, 1980.

Government of Spain, 1983. "Royal Decree-Law 8/1983 of November 30 about restructuring and reindustrializing." Official State Bulletin, 289, December 3, 1983.

Government of Spain, 1984. "Royal Decree-Law 2,248/1984 of November 28 about the expansion of telephony service to rural areas." Official State Bulletin, 307, December 24, 1984.

Government of Spain, 1985a. "Ministerial order of 5 June 1985 which regulates imports of double purpose technologies." Official State Bulletin, 41, June 13, 1985.

Government of Spain, 1985b. "Royal Decree 1,209/1985 of June 19 that partially modifies the basic organic structure of the Ministry of Transport, Tourism and Communications, creates the National Institute for the Promotion of Tourism and eliminates certain regional institutions adscribed to the department." Official State Bulletin, 176, July 24, 1985.

Government of Spain, 1986. "Royal Decree-Law 1,265/1986 of June 27 about foreign investment in Spain." Official State Bulletin, 154, June 28, 1986.

Government of Spain, 1987a. "Law 31/1987, of December 18 Communications." Official State Bulletin, 303, December 19, 1987.

Government of Spain, 1987b. "Royal Decree 1538/1987 of December 11 which determines the electric tariff for companies that manage the service." Official State Bulletin, 30, December 16, 1987.

Government of Spain, 1988a. "Law 24/1988, of July 28 about the stock market." Official State Bulletin, 181, July 7, 1988.

Government of Spain, 1988b. "Law 26/1988, of July 29 about discipline and intervention of credit institutions." Official State Bulletin, 182, Julio 30, 1988.

Government of Spain, 1989. "Law 13/1989, of May 26 about savings banks." Official State Bulletin, 129, May 31, 1980.

Government of Spain, 1995. "Law 5/1995, of March 23 of legal framework for the disposal of public participations in certain firms." Official State Bulletin, 72, March 25.

Government of Spain, 1997. "Law 54/1997 of 28 November of the electricity sector." Official State Bulletin, 285, November 28, 1997.

Government of Spain, 1998. "Royal Decree 2818/1998, of December 23, about production of renewable energy." Official State Bulletin, 312, December 30, 1998.

Government of Spain, 2006. "Law 13/2006 of May 26 that derogates Law 5/1995 of March 23 and its development and implementation." Official State Bulletin, 126, May 27 2006.

Government of Spain, 2012. "Royal Decree-Law 13/2012 of March 30 that transposes European directives about internal markets in electricity and gas and about electronic communications, and that adopts measures to correct deviations and misalignments between costs and income of the electricity and gas sectors." Official State Bulletin, 78, March 31, 2012.

Government of Spain, 2014. "Law 9/2014 of May 9 about telecommunications." Official State Bulletin, 11, May 10, 2014.

Government of Spain, 2020a. "Royal Decree-Law 8/2020, of March 17 of urgent and extraordinary measures to tackle the economic and social impact of COVID-19." Official State Bulletin, 73, March 18, 2020.

Government of Spain, 2020b. "Royal Decree-Law 11/2020, of March 31 by which the government adopts complementary urgent measures in the social and economic areas to tackle COVID-19." Official State Bulletin, 91, April 1, 2020.

Government of Spain, 2020c. "Royal Decree-Law 34/2020, of November 17 of urgent measures to support firm solvency, the energy sector, and address tax matters." Official State Bulletin, 303, November 18, 2020.

Government of Spain, Head of State, 1987. "Law 31/1987 of December 18 that organizes the telecommunications sector." Official State Bulletin, 303, December 19, 1987.

Government of Spain, Ministry of Economics, Industry and Competitiveness, 2007. "Sectoral agenda for the automotive industry." Madrid: Government of Spain.

Government of Spain, Parliament, Diary of Senate Sessions, 1986. 'Commission of industry and energy, commerce and tourism, presidency of Mr. Antonio Villalonga Riudavets Number 9. Celebrated November 5, 1986 http://www.senado.es/legis3/publicaciones/pdf/senado/ds/CS0009.PDF; Accessed 14 August 2013.

Ministry of Economy and Public Revenue, Royal Decree-Law 1265/1986 of June 27 about foreign investment in Spain. Official State Bulletin, 154, June 28, 1986.

Other Publications

ABC staff, 1953. "El tratado de Madrid es el logro mas importante de la política exterior de España escribe el New York Times." ABC. Published March 10. https://www.abc.es/archivo/periodicos/abc-madrid-19531003–15.html. Accessed July 31, 2020.

ABC staff, 1981. "La industrial española incorpora tecnología propia al control de trafico aéreo." Published January 14, 1981. https://www.abc.es/archivo/periodicos/abc-madrid-19810114-42.html. Accessed April 1, 2021.

ABC staff, 2015. "SEAT celebra el 40 aniversario de su 'centro técnico.'" ABC. Published July 27. https://www.abc.es/motor-reportajes/20150727/abci-seat-centro-tecnico-aniversario-201507271623.html. Accessed September 17, 2020.

Abu-El-Haj, Jawdat, 2007. "From interdependence to neo-mercantilism. Brazilian capitalism in the age of globalization." *Latin American Perspectives*, 156(34): 92–114.

Adanero, José Luís, 2006. "La industria de telecomunicaciones en España desde 1970." In: Rico, César (ed.), *Crónicas y testimonios de las telecomunicaciones españolas*. Madrid: Colegio Oficial de Ingenieros de Telecomunicaciones, 553–84.

Ahn, Hyeon Ju and Mah, Jai, S., 2007. "Development of technology-intensive industries in Korea." *Journal of Contemporary Asia*, 37(3): 364–79.

Ahn, J. H. and Han, K. I., 2000. "Korean experience in self-reliance for nuclear power technology (a case study in the Republic of Korea)." International Atomic Energy Agency (IAEA), IAEA-CSP—5/P.

Airbus SA, 2020. "Report of the board of directors, 2019." https://www.airbus.com/content/dam/events/annual-general-meeting/Report-of-the-Board-of-Directors-Airbus-SE-2019.pdf. Accessed October 28, 2020.

Akamatsu, Kaname, 1962. "A historical pattern of economic growth in developing countries." *Journal of DevelopingEconomies*, 1(1): 3–25.

Aliber, R. Z. (1994) "Financial reform in South Korea." In Cho, Lee-Jay and Kim, Yoon Hyung (eds.), *Korea's Political Economy*, San Francisco: Routledge, pp. 341–58.

Alonso, Ignacio, 1980. "CASA vendió 46 aviones C-212 Aviocar a una decena de países durante 1980." *El País*. Published November 27. https://elpais.com/diario/1980/11/27/economia/344127614_850215.html. Accessed October 29, 2020.

Alp, Harun, Elekdag, Selim A., and Lall, Subir, 2012. "Did Korean monetary policy help soften the impact of the global financial crisis of 2008–09?" IMF working paper WP 12/5. Washington DC: IMF.

Alvarez Gil, María José and González de la Fe, Pedro, 1997. "La internacionalización de Seat: de zona franca a Martorell pasando por Wolfburg." Work document 97–13. Department of

Business Economics. Business Economics Series, N 7. Carlos III University, Madrid. October 1997.

Amado Calvo, Angel, 2010. *Historia De Telefonica: 1924–1975*. Madrid: Fundación Telefonica.

Amado Calvo, Angel, 2014. *Telecomunicaciones y el nuevo mundo digital en España. La aportación de Standard Eléctrica*. Madrid: Fundación Telefonica.

Amsden, Alice H. and Euh, Yoon-Dae, 1993. "South Korea 1980s financial reforms. Goodbye financial repression (maybe), hello institutional restraints." *World Development*, 21(3): 379–90.

Amsden Alice H. and Kang Jong-Yeol, 1995. "Learning to be lean in an emerging economy: the case of South Korea." Prepared for IMVP Sponsors Meeting, Toronto, Canada, June 1995.

Andersen, John M., 2009. Memorandum to Ronald K. Lorentzen. https://enforcement.trade.gov/frn/summary/korea-south/E9-3288–1.pdf. Accessed July 5, 2020.

Andrews-Speed, Philip, 2020. "South Korea's nuclear power industry: recovering from scandal." *The Journal of World Energy Law & Business*, 13(1): 47–57.

Arancibia, Salvador and Navas, José Antonio, 1990. "Industria confirma a Inisel como base del sector de electrónica de defensa." *El País*. Published March 25. https://elpais.com/diario/1990/03/25/economia/638319606_850215.html. Accessed November 7, 2020.

Arocena, Pablo, Kuhn Kai-Uwe, and Regibeau, Pierre, 1999. "Regulatory reform in the Spanish electricity industry: a missed opportunity for competition." *Energy Policy*, 27(7): 387–99.

Arocena, Pablo, Contín, Ignacio, and Huerta, Emilio, 2002. "Price regulation in the Spanish energy sectors: who benefits?" *Energy Policy*, 30(10): 885–95.

Asociación de empresas de electrónica, tecnologías de la información, telecomunicaciones y contenidos digitales [AMETIC], 2018. Las Tecnologías de la Información en España, 2018. Available from: https://ametic.es/sites/default/files//datos_ti_2018.pdf. Accessed January 4, 2020.

Asociación Española de Empresas Tecnológicas de Defensa, Seguridad, Aeronáutica y Espacio [TEDAE], 2019. "Agenda for the Spanish Aerospace Industry." https://industria.gob.es/es-es/Servicios/AgendasSectoriales/Agenda%20sectorial%20de%20la%20industria%20espacial/agenda-sectorial-industria-espacial-versi%C3%B3n-final.PDF. Accessed November 6, 2020.

Asociación Española de Empresas Tecnológicas de Defensa, Seguridad, Aeronáutica y Espacio [TEDAE], 2020. https://www.tedae.org/es/que-es-tedae#0. Accessed November 6, 2020.

Asociación Multisectorial de Empresas de Tecnologías de la Información, Comunicaciones y Electrónica [AMETIC], 2011. Annual report, 2011.

Asociación Multisectorial de Empresas de Tecnologías de la Información, Comunicaciones y Electrónica [AMETIC], 2018. Annual report, 2018. https://ametic.es/sites/default/files//dossier_ametic_final.pdf. Accessed April 6, 2020.

Asociación vasca de patrimonio industrial y obra pública, 2019. http://www.patrimonioindustrialvasco.com/actividades/imosa-industrias-del-motor-s-a-de-vitoria-gasteiz-y-la-furgoneta-f-1000-dkw/. Accessed May 3, 2019.

Automotive News, 2019. "North America, Europe and the world. Top Suppliers." https://www.autonews.com/data-lists/2019-top-suppliers. Accessed July 31, 2020.

Back, Jong Gook, 1990. "Politics of late industrialization: The origins and processes of automobile industry policies in Mexico and South Korea." University of California Los Angeles, unpublished thesis.

Bank of Spain, 2009. "Modelo de supervisión del Banco de España." Madrid: Bank of Spain.

Bank of Spain, 2017. "Report on the financial and banking crisis in Spain, 2008–2014." Madrid: Bank of Spain.

Barney, Jay, 1991. "Firm resources and sustained competitive advantage." *Journal of Management*, 17 (1): 99–120.

Bartolomé Rodríguez, Isabel, 2007. "La industria eléctrica en España." *Banco de España. Estudios de Historia Económica N50*. Madrid: Bank of Spain.

Beramendi, Pablo, 2015. "Introduction". In: Bermendi, Pablo, Häusermann Silja, Kitschelt, Herbert, and Kriesi, Hanspeter (eds), *The Politics of Advanced Capitalism*. Cambridge: Cambridge University Press.

Beresford, Colin, 2020. "Hyundai recalls 129,000 cars for premature engine damage." *Car & Driver*. Published December 4. https://www.caranddriver.com/news/a34874678/hyundai-engine-bearings-recall/. Accessed December 23, 2020.

Berger, Suzanne, 2013. *Making in America: From Innovation to Market*. Cambridge, MA: MIT Press.

Bloom, Martin, 1992. *Technological Change in the Korean Electronics Industry*. Paris: Development Centre of the Organization for Economic Cooperation and Development.

Bloomberg News, 1998. "Hyundai wins auction to take over Kia motors." *New York Times*. Published October 19, 1998. https://www.nytimes.com/1998/10/19/business/hyundai-wins-auction-to-take-over-kia-motors.html. Accessed September 17, 2020.

Bonin, John P. and Imai, Masami, 2007. "Soft related lending: A tale of two Korean banks." *Journal of Banking & Finance*, 31(6): 1713–29.

Brazys, Samuel and Regan, Aidan, 2016. "These little PIIGS went to market: Enterprise policy and divergent recovery in European periphery." Working Papers 201517, Geary Institute, University College Dublin.

Breznitz, Dan, 2007. *Innovation and the State: Political Choice and Strategies for Growth in Israel, Taiwan, and Ireland*. New Haven, CT: Yale University Press.

Brooks, Sarah M. and Kurtz, Marcus J., 2016. "Natural resources and economic development in Brazil." In: Schneider, Ben Ross (ed.), *New Order and Progress: Development and Democracy in Brazil*. Oxford: Oxford University Press.

Bueno Lastra, Juán José, and Ramos Pérez, Antonio, 1986, *La industria de equipos y componentes para automoción en España*. Madrid: Bolsa de Madrid Servicio de Estudios.

Buesa, Mikel and Molero, José, 1986. "La intervención estatal en la remodelación del sistema productivo: el caso de la industria electrónica española durante los años 80." Madrid: Universidad Complutense, Work document 8,619.

Bulfone, Fabio, 2017. "The state strikes back. Industrial policy, state power and the emergence of competitive multinational enterprises in Italy and Spain." Florence: European University Institute. Unpublished thesis.

Business Korea, 2019. "Hyundai Mobis to shut down plants in China." *Business Korea*. Published March 14. http://www.businesskorea.co.kr/news/articleView.html?idxno=29970. Accessed July 13, 2019.

Calzada, Joan and Estruch Manjón, Alejandro, 2011. "Telefonía móvil en España: regulación y resultados." *Cuadernos económicos de ICE*, 81, 39–70.

Campa, José Manuel and Guillén, Mauro F., 1996. "Spain: By boom from economic integration." In: Dunning, John H. and Narula, Rajneesh, *Foreign Direct Investment and Governments. Catalysts for Economic Restructuring*. London: Routledge.

Carcar, Santiago, 2001. "Endesa e Iberdrola rompen la fusion." *El País*. Published February 5. https://elpais.com/diario/2001/02/06/economia/981414001_850215.html. Accessed September 25, 2020.

Catalán Vidal, Jordi, 2007. "The first crisis of SEAT: The veto to General Motors and the purchase of AUTHI to British Leyland (1972–1976)." *Investigaciones de Historia Economica*, 9 (Fall): 141–72.

Caves, Richard E., Frankel, Jeffrey A., and Jones, Ronald W., 2007. *World Trade and Payments. An Introduction*. Boston: Pearson.

Chang, Ha-Joon, 2002. *Kicking Away the Ladder: Development Strategy in Historical Perspective*. London: Anthem.

Chang, Ha-Joon, 2006. *The East Asian Development Experience: The Miracle, the Crisis and the Future*. Zed Books, London and New York.

Chang, Ha-Joon, 2011. "Institutions and economic development: theory, policy and history." *Journal of Institutional Economics*, 7(4): 473–98.

Chang, Ha-Joon and Park, J-H., 2004. "An alternative perspective on government policy towards the chaebol in Korea: Industrial policy, financial regulations and political democracy." In: Jwa, Sung-Hee, and Lee, Kwon (eds.), *Competition and Corporate Governance in Korea: Reforming and Restructuring the Chaebol*. Cheltenham, UK and Northampton, MA: Edward Elgar.

Chang, Paul Y., 2015. *Protest Dialectics: State Repression and South Korea's Democracy Movement, 1970–1979*. Stanford: Stanford University Press.

Chang Sea Jin, 2008. *Sony vs. Samsung. The Inside Story of the Electronics Giants' Battle for Global Supremacy*. Singapore: Wiley.

Chapuis, Robert J. and Joel, Amos E., 2003. *100 Years of Telephone Switching: Electronics, Computers and Telephone Switching (1960–1985)*. Amsterdam, Berlin, Oxford, Tokyo, Washington DC: IOS Press.

Chen, Liyan, 2015. "2015 Global 2000: the world's largest banks." *Forbes*. Published May 15, 2015. https://www.forbes.com/sites/liyanchen/2015/05/06/2015-global-2000-the-worlds-largest-banks/#6f24b7d17960. Accessed June 10, 2020.

Cheney, Peter, 2010. "Ten worst cars chosen by our readers." *Globe and Mail*. Published February 22, 2010. https://www.theglobeandmail.com/globe-drive/culture/commuting/10-worst-cars-chosen-by-our-readers/article4259461/. Accessed April 6, 2020.

Cho, Chung-Un, 2018. "Korea sets out to seize lead in hydrogen energy." *Korea Herald*. Published August 5. http://www.koreaherald.com/view.php?ud=20180805000139. Accessed July 31, 2020.

Cho, Sung-Hye, 2002. "Telecommunications and informatization in South Korea." *Network and Communications Studies NETCOM*, 16(1–2): 29–42.

Choe, Sang-Hun, 2006. "In Daewoo, GM finds gold in overall gloom." *New York Times*. Published May 23. https://www.nytimes.com/2006/05/23/business/worldbusiness/23iht-daewoo.html. Accessed September 17, 2020.

Choi, Hae Won and Fairclough, Gordon, 2004. "After credit binge in South Korea, big bill comes due." *The Wall Street Journal*. Published January 20, 2004. https://www.wsj.com/articles/SB107456002541605921. Accessed July 6, 2020.

Choi, Sungho, Hasan, Iftekhar, and Waisman, Maya, 1994. "Does corporate governance matter? Korean banks in the postfinancial crisis era." In: Hirschey, Mark, John, Kose, and Makhija, Anil K. (eds.), *Corporate Governance and Firm Performance* (*Advances in Financial Economics, Vol. 13*). Bingley: Emerald Group Publishing Limited, 217–41.

Choung, Jae-Yong and Hwang, Hye-Ran, 2007. "Developing the complex system in Korea: The case study of TDX and CDMA telecom system." *International Journal of Technological Learning, Innovation and Development*, 1(2): 204–25.

Choung, Jae-Yong, Hwang, Hye-Ran, and Choi, Jun Kyun, 2016. "Post catch-up system transition failure: The case of ICT technology development in Korea." *Asian Journal of Technology Innovation*, 24(1): 78–102.

Chung, Kyung-Won and Kim, Yu-Jin, 2014. "Hyundai Motor Company: Design takes the driver's seat." Design Management Institute case study. Distributed by Harvard Business School Publishing Boston, MA.

Cinco Días staff, 2001. "Endesa e Iberdrola rompen la fusión por las condiciones del Gobierno." *Cinco Días*. Published February 6. https://cincodias.elpais.com/cincodias/2001/02/06/empresas/981470416_850215.html. Published February 6, 2001. Accessed October 16, 2020.

Ciucci, Matteo, 2020. "European Parliament. Internal energy market." November 2020. https://www.europarl.europa.eu/factsheets/en/sheet/45/internal-energy-market. Accessed September 21, 2020.

Clifford, Mark, L., 1994. *Troubled Tiger: Businessmen, Bureaucrats, and Generals in South Korea*. New York: M. E. Sharpe.

Coe, Neil. M. and Yeung, Henry Way-Chung, 2015. *Global Production Networks. Theorizing Economic Development in an Interconnected World*. Oxford: Oxford University Press.

Commission of the European Communities, 1987a. "Green paper on the development of the common market for telecommunications services and equipment." NBER N 4,964, Brussels: Commission of the European Communities.

Computer World, 1995. "Thomson-CSF asume el control del 25% de Indra." *Computer World*. Published July 21. https://www.computerworld.es/archive/thomsoncsf-asume-el-control-del-25-de-indra. Accessed October 29, 2020.

Congress, February 9, 1993. Diario de sesiones del Congreso de los Diputados 1993. Comparecencia del Ministro D. Carlos Solchaga Catalán. IV Legislatura sesión 48, 9 febrero 1993. http://www.congreso.es/public_oficiales/L4/CONG/DS/CO/CO_597.PDF. Accessed December 22, 2020.

Consejo Superior Bancario, 1985. Anuario estadístico de la banca privada. Madrid, Consejo Superior Bancario/Asociación Española de Banca. http://www.aebanca.es/es/Publicaciones/AnuarioEstad%C3%ADstico/index.htm?pAnio=1985. AccessedDecember 22, 2020.

Cordero, Dani, 2020. "El cierre de Nissan en Barcelona pone en riesgo 25.000 empleos y 500 empresas." *El País*. Published May 20. https://elpais.com/economia/2020-05-28/nissan-comunica-oficialmente-al-gobierno-el-cierre-de-su-historica-fabrica-de-barcelona.html. Accessed December 9, 2020.

CYD report, 2018. Fundacion CYD. https://www.fundacioncyd.org/publicaciones-cyd/informe-cyd-2018/#. Accessed May 13, 2020.

de Bolle, Monica and Zettlemeyer, Jeromin, 2019. "Measuring the rise of economic nationalism." Petterson Institute for International Economics. Working paper 19–15. Washington DC. https://papers.ssrn.com/sol3/papers.cfm?abstract_id=3441747. Accessed May 1, 2020.

de Diego, Emilio, 1995. "Historia de la industria en España: la electrónica y la informática." Madrid: Actas.

de la Dehesa, Guillermo, 1993. "Las privatizaciones en España." https://www.guillermodeladehesa.com/files/las_ privatizaciones_en_espana.pdf. Accessed October 16, 2018.

del Arco, Serafí, 2007. "El coche que puso a España sobre ruedas." *El País*. Published June, 02. https://elpais.com/diario/2007/06/03/economia/1180821602_850215.html.   Accessed September 17, 2020.

Deutsche Bank, 2020. "Deutsche Bank Chronicle 1870–2010." https://www.bankgeschichte.de/en/docs/Chronik_D_Bank.pdf. Accessed December 22, 2020.

Dombey, Daniel, 2020a. "Spain's auto sector collides with Covid." *Financial Times*. Published December 23, 2020. https://www.ft.com/content/ae04ca36-4002-46dc-a6ff-fe5f98e09cdf. Accessed December 23, 2020.

Dombey, Daniel, 2020b. "Spanish companies jostle for EU recovery fund billions." *Financial Times*. Published December 16, 2020. https://www.ft.com/content/e56d8c25-a978-424d-be77-752292e72059. Accessed December 19, 2020.

Dziobek, Claudia H. and Pazarbasioglu, Ceyla, 1998. "Lessons from systemic bank restructuring: a survey of 24 countries." *IFM Economic issues N 14*. https://www.imf.org/en/Publications/WP/Issues/2016/12/30/Lessons-From-Systemic-Bank-Restructuring-A-Survey-of-24-Countries-2436. Accessed April 6, 2020.

Economic and Social Council, [ESC] (Consejo Económico y Social) 2017. "Informe. El sector eléctrico en España." Colección informes. Informe 4/2017. Madrid: Economic and Social Council.

Economic and Social Council [ESC] (Consejo Económico y Social). "Boletín de estadísticas laborales" (labor statistics for multiple years). http://www.ces.es/informes-de-referencia. Accessed April 7, 2020.

Economic Planning Board [EBP], 1981. *A Summary Draft of the Fifth Five-Year Economic and Social Development Plan*. Seoul: Economic Planning Board.

Ehlers, Claus, 2018. "Mobility of the future—connected, autonomous, shared, electric." https://www.avl.com/documents/10138/8682805/16+Ehlers.pdf. Accessed April 1, 2019.

Eichengreen, Barry, Lim, Wonhyuk, Park, Yung Chul, and Perkins, Dwight H., 2015. *The Korean Economy: From Miraculous Past to a Sustainable Future*. Cambridge MA: Harvard East Asian Monographs, 375.

El Mundo staff, 1999. "La empresa española de aeronaútica CASA sella su entrada en el gigante europeo EADS." *El Mundo*, Published December 2. https://www.elmundo.es/elmundo/1999/diciembre/02/economia/casa.html. Accessed October 30, 2020.

El País staff, 1980. "CASA entrega el primer Aviocar a Francia." *El País*. Published January 10. https://elpais.com/diario/1980/01/10/economia/316306809_850215.html. Accessed October 29, 2020.

El País staff, 1992. "Las compañías rentables del grupo INI se integran en un nuevo 'holding' denominado Teneo." Published July 11. https://elpais.com/diario/1992/07/11/economia/710805604_850215.html. Accessed October 29, 2020.

Epstein, Rachel, 2017. *Banking on Markets: The Transformation of Bank-State Ties in Europe and Beyond*. Oxford: Oxford University Press.

Ernst, Dieter, 1994. "What are the limits to the Korean model? The Korean electronics industry under pressure." *The Berkeley Roundtable on the International Economy*. University of California at Berkeley.

Escribano, Alvaro and Zaballos, Antonio G., 2001. "Evolución de la estructura de mercado de las telecomunicaciones en España." *Economistas*, 91: 336–44.

Estefanía, Joaquin, 1986. "Solchaga prepara una remodelación urgente en economía." *El País*, Published November 8, 1986. https://elpais.com/diario/1986/11/09/economia/531874802_850215.html. Accessed July 5, 2020.

Estefanía, Joaquín, 2010. "Las privatizaciones." *El País*, Published December 12, 2010. https://elPaís.com/diario/2010/12/12/domingo/1292128238_850215.html. Accessed April 4, 2020.

Etchemendy, Sebastian, 2004. "Revamping the weak, protecting the strong, and managing privatization. Governing globalization in the Spanish takeoff." *Comparative Political Studies*, 37(6): 623–51.

EU KLEMS database, 2009. http://www.euklems.net/euk09I.shtml. Accessed April 6, 2020.

European Central bank statistical data warehouse, 2009. http://sdw.ecb.europa.eu/browse.do?node=9691144. Accessed April 7, 2020.

European Commission, 2019. "Post-Programme Surveillance Report. Spain, Autumn 2019." *Institutional Paper 117*. November 2019. Brussels: European Commission.

Evans, Peter B., 1995. *Embedded Autonomy: States and Industrial Transformation*. Princeton: Princeton University Press.

Fainé Casas, Isidro, 2005. "La evolución del sistema bancario español desde la perspectiva del Fondo de Garantía de Depósitos." Revista Estabilidad Financiera N8, 107–26. https://www.bde.es/f/webbde/Secciones/Publicaciones/InformesBoletinesRevistas/Revista EstabilidadFinanciera/05/Fich/estfin08_rev.pdf.Accessed July 5, 2020.

Fatás, Antonio and Summers, Lawrence H., 2016. "The permanent effects of fiscal consolidations." *Journal of International Politics*, 112: 238–50.

Faulhaber, Gerald R., 1995. "Public policy in telecommunications: The third revolution." *Information Economics and Policy*, 7(3): 251–82.

Fernández Puértolas, Edmundo, 1995. El sector de la electrónica. Subsectores con notables diferencias. Telos (FundacionTelefonica).N41.

Financial Times staff, 2013. "South Korea tries to sell Woori for fourth time." *Financial Times*. Published June 26, 2013. https://www.ft.com/content/985b3de8-de32-11e2-b990-001 44feab7de. Accessed June 30, 2020.

Financial Times staff, 2021. "Prospering in the pandemic: 2020's top 100 companies." *Financial Times*. Published January 1, 2021. https://www.ft.com/content/f8251e5f-10a7-4f7a-9047-b438e4d7f83a. Accessed January 3, 2021.

Forbes Global 2000 list, 2020. https://www.forbes.com/global2000/#3b920e36335d. Accessed June 10, 2020.

Forbes, Naushad and Wield, David, 2002. *From Followers to Leaders. Managing Technology and Innovation in Newly Industrializing Economies*. London and New York: Routledge.

Fuentes Quintana, Enrique, 1985. "Prologue." In: Fanjul Martín, Oscar and Maravall, Fernándo. *La eficiencia del sistema bancario español*. Madrid: Alianza Liv.

Gadacz, Oles, 1997. "Shakeout continues in Korea: Daewobuyds Ssang Yong; Hyundai eyes parts giant." *Automotive News*. Published December 15. https://www.autonews.com/article/19971215/ANA/712150756/shakeout-continues-in-korea-daewoo-buys-ssangyong-hyundai-eyes-parts-giant. Accessed December 13, 2020.

Galán, Miguel, 2016. "El duro despegar del motor Diesel (I): de Rudolf Diesel a Eduardo Barreiros." Blog post. December 3, 2016. http://www.pistonudos.com/reportajes/el-duro-despegar-del-motor-diesel-i/. Accessed September 17, 2020.

Garcia Calvo, Angela, 2016. "Institutional development and bank competitive transformation in late industrializing economies: the Spanish case." *Business and Politics*, 18(1): 27–62.

Garcia Calvo, Angela, 2021. "State-firm coordination and upgrading in Spain's and Korea's ICT industries." *New Political Economy*. 26:1, 119-137DOI: 10.1080/13563467.2019.1708882.

García-Hoz, José María, 2013. "José Antonio Pérez-Nievas, o cómo cortar las alas a la tecnología Española. "*Expansión*". Published January 12.

García Ruíz, José Luís, 2001. "La evolución de la industria automovilística española, 1946–1999: una perspectiva comparada." *Revista de Historia* Industrial, 19–20: 133–64.

Garrues-Irurzun, Josean, 2010. "Market power versus regulatory power in the Spanish electricity system, 1973–1996." *Renewable and Sustainable Energy Reviews*, 14(2): 655–66.

Gereffi, Gary, Humphrey, John, and Sturgeon, Timothy, 2005. "The governance of global value chains." *Review of International Political Economy*, 12(1): 78–104.

Gerschenkron, Alexander, 1962. *Economic Backwardness in Historical Perspective*. Cambridge, MA: The Belknap Press of Harvard University Press.

Gestamp, 2017. "Public offering prospectus." https://www.gestamp.com/Investors-Shareholders/General-Information/Public-Offerings. Accessed May 6, 2019.

Gestamp, 2018. Annual Report. Gestamp.

Gilbert, Alton R. and Wilson, Paul W., 1998. "Effects of deregulation on the productivity of Korean banks." *Journal of Economics and Business*, 50(2): 133–55.

Giokas, Dimitris and Pentzaropoulos, Georgios C., 2008. "Efficiency ranking of the OECD member states in the area of telecommunications: a composite AHP/DEA study." *Telecommunications Policy*, 32(9–10): 672–85.

Global Capital, 2011. "Politicians pick a fight over Woori Bank's privatization." *Global Capital*, published July 19, 2011. https://www.globalcapital.com/article/k3cqj7bxsgy1/politicians-pick-a-fight-over-woori-banks-privatisation?FreeTrial=true. Accessed July 5, 2020.

Global Financial Centers' Index, 2020. https://www.longfinance.net/programmes/financial-centre-futures/global-financial-centres-index/gfci-27-explore-data/gfci-27-rank/. Accessed July 5, 2020.

Gómez, Carlos, 1981. "Cecsa ganó el primer concurso para el control del tráfico aéreo civil español." *El País*. Published January 14. http://elpais.com/diario/1981/01/14/economia/348274819_850215.html. Accessed November 6, 2020.

González Duarte, Roberto and Braga Rodrigues, Suzana, 2017. "Co-evolution of industry strategies and government policies: the case of the Brazilian automotive industry." *Brazilian Administration Review*. https://www.scielo.br/pdf/bar/v14n2/1807-7692-bar-14-02-e160100.pdf. Accessed November 7, 2020.

González, Enric and Navas, José Antonio, 1989. "El INI ofrece a Ceselsa, Saínco Cae y Page reordenar la electrónica military." *El País*. Published May 24. https://elpais.com/diario/1989/05/24/economia/611964018_850215.html. Accessed November 7, 2020.

Goodman, Matthew P. and Miller, Scott, 2014. "Korea became world's second-largest semiconductor manufacturer in 2013." *Business Korea*. Published January 17. http://www.businesskorea.co.kr/news/articleView.html?idxno=2980. Accessed December 4, 2020.

Green, Andrew E., 1992. "South Korea's automobile industry: Development and prospects." *Asian Survey*, 32(5): 411–28.

Green, Rory, 2019a. "Korea caught in the crossfire of trade and tech wars." *Financial Times*. Published July 13, 2019. https://www.ft.com/content/0dc5275a-a4bc-11e9-974c-ad1c6ab5efd1. Accessed May 14, 2020.

Guillén, Mauro F., 2010. *The Limits of Convergence: Globalization and Organizational Change in Argentina, South Korea and Spain*. Princeton: Princeton University Press.

Guillén, Mauro F. and García-Canal, Esteban, 2010. *The New Multinationals: Spanish Firms in a Global Context*. Cambridge: Cambridge University Press.

Guillén, Mauro F. and Tschoegl, Adrian E., 2008. *Building a Global Bank: The Transformation of Banco Santander*. Princeton NJ and Oxford UK: Princeton University Press.

Haggard, Stephan, 1990. *Pathways from the Periphery: The Politics of Growth in the Newly Industrializing Countries*. Ithaca: Cornell University Press.

Haggard, Stephan, 2018. *Developmental States*. Cambridge: Cambridge University Press.

Haggard, Stephan and Moon, Chung-in, 1990. "Institutions and economic policy: Theory and a Korean case study." *World Politics*, 42(2): 210–37.

Haggard, Stephan, Lim, Wonhyuk, and Kim, Euysung, 2003. "Introduction." In: Haggard, Stephan, Lim, Wonhyuk, and Kim, Euysung, *Economic Crisis and Corporate Restructuring in Korea*. Cambridge: Cambridge University Press.

Hall, Peter A. and Soskice, David, 2001. "An introduction to varieties of capitalism." In: Hall, Peter A. and Soskice, David (eds.), *Varieties of Capitalism: The Institutional Foundations of Comparative Advantage*. Oxford: Oxford University Press.

Hancké, Robert, 2001. *Large Firms and Institutional Change: Industrial Renewal and Economic Restructuring in France*. Oxford: Oxford University Press.

Harris, Bryan and Song, Jung-A., 2018. "Hyundai Motor Group commits $7bn to fuel-cell technology." *Financial Times*. December 11, 2018. https://www.ft.com/content/b773ff76-fd08-11e8-aebf-99e208d3e521. Accessed July 31, 2020.

Hausmann, Ricardo, Hwang, Jason, and Rodrik, Dani, 2006. "What you export matters." *Journal of Economic Growth*, 12: 1–25.

Hayek, Friedrich A., 1944. *The Road to Serfdom. Texts and Documents. The Definitive Edition*. New York and London: Routledge.

Hellman, Joel and Kaufmann, Daniel, 2001. "Confronting the challenges of state capture in transition economies." *Finance and Development*, 38(3).

Hidalgo, César A. and Hausmann, Ricardo, 2009. "The building blocks of economic complexity." *Proceedings of the National Academy of Sciences of the United States of America. June 30, 2009*, 106(26): 10570–5. https://doi.org/10.1073/pnas.0900943106. Accessed December 22, 2020.

Hita Romero, Manuel and Dopazo Garcia, César, 2010. "La innovación como motor de la ingeniería aeronáutica en España." Royal Academy of Engineering. http://www.raing.es/

sites/default/files/DISCURSO%20DE%20INGRESO%20MANUEL%20HITA.pdf. Accessed November 6, 2020.

Ho, Prudence, 2014. "South Korea's Woori privatization still faces biggest hurdle—suitors for Woori Bank." *Wall Street Journal*. Published July 9, 2014. http://www.theinvestor.co.kr/view.php?ud=20190625000638. Accessed July 5, 2020.

Hoshi, Takeo, 1995. "Evolution of the main bank system in Japan." In: Okabe Mitsuaki (ed.), *The Structure of the Japanese Economy: Studies in the Modern Japanese Economy*. London: Palgrave Macmillan, 287–322.

Hun, Choesang, 2013. "Scandal in South Korea over nuclear revelations." *New York Times*. Published August 4. ProQuest Historical Newspapers: The New York Times, p. 6.

Hyun, Young-suk, 2018. "Catch up to lead in Korea's automobile industry." Unpublished manuscript.

Hyun, Young-Suk and Lee, JinJoo, 1989. "Can Hyundai go it alone?" *Long Range Planning*, 22(2): 63–9.

Ibeas Cubillo, Diego, 2011. "Review of the history of the electric supply in Spain from the beginning up to now." Universidad Carlos III and Fachnochschule Dusseldorf. Unpublished thesis. https://e-archivo.uc3m.es/handle/10016/13718. Accessed September 22, 2020.

Iberdrola News, 2010. "Iberdrola projects investment of €18 billion to cement foundations for growth." *Iberdrola*. Published March 24, 2010. https://www.iberdrola.com/press-room/news/detail/iberdrola-projects-investments-of-18-billion-between-2010-and-2012-to-cement-foundations-for-growth-7518353720100324. Accessed November 6, 2020.

Indra, 2013. "A global innovation company." Corporate presentation (hard copy handed over by interviewee).

Infante, Jorge, 2002. "El desarrollo de la red pública y de datos en España (1971–1991): un caso de avance tecnológico en condiciones adversas." Madrid: Colegio Oficial de Ingenieros de Telecomunicaciones.

International Energy Agency (IEA), 2019. "Energy prices and taxes for OECD country." Statistics. Paris: International Energy Agency.

International Organization of Motor Vehicle Manufacturers [OICA], 2018. 2018 Production statistics. http://www.oica.net/production-statistics. Accessed April 6, 2020.

International Organization of Motor Vehicle Manufacturers [OICA], 2020. 2020 Production statistics. http://www.oica.net/production-statistics. Accessed April 6, 2020.

International Telecommunications Union [ITU], 2010. *ICT Indicators Database*, 14th edition CD-Rom.

Jacobsson, Staffan, 1984. "Industrial policy for the machine tool industries of South Korea and Taiwan." *Institute of Developmental Studies Bulletin*, 15(2). Institute of Developmental Studies, Sussex.

Jang, Seungkwon, Choi, Jong-in, and Hong, Kilpyo, 2013. "Technological learning in development of nuclear fuel tube: A case of KAERI (Korea Atomic Energy Research Institute)." *International Journal of Nuclear Knowledge Management*, 6(1): 22–34.

Jho, Whasun, 2007. "Liberalization as a development strategy: Network governance in the Korean mobile telecom market." *Governance: An International Journal of Policy, Administration, and Institutions*, 20(4): 633–54.

Johnson, Chalmers, 1982. *MITI and the Japanese Miracle: The Growth of Industrial Policy, 1925–1975*. Stanford: Stanford University Press.

Jones, Leroy P. and Sakong, Il, 1980. *Government, Business, and Entrepreneurship in Economic Development: The Korean Case*. Cambridge, MA: Council on East Asian Studies, Harvard University: distributed by Harvard University Press.

Jordana, Jacint and Sancho, David, 2005. "Policy networks and market opening: Telecommunications liberalization in Spain." *European Journal of Political Research*, 44(4): 519–46.

Jung, Juyong and Rho, Eunju, 2020. "Public acceptance of nuclear energy policies in South Korea." In: Farazmand, Ali (ed.), *Global Encyclopedia of Public Administration, Public Policy, and Governance*. Springer Nature Switzerland: Springer (Living Edition).

Jung, Ming-Hee, 2019. "Hyundai Mobis to shut down plants in China." *Business Korea*. Published March 14. http://www.businesskorea.co.kr/news/articleView.html?idxno=29970. Accessed July 13, 2019.

Jung, Suk-yee, 2020. "Moon Jae-in administration's nuclear phase-out policy reveals its own problems." *Korea Herald*. Published October 21. http://www.businesskorea.co.kr/news/articleView.html?idxno=53541. Accessed December 16, 2020.

Jwa, Sung-Hui, 2004. "The chaebol, corporate policy and Korea's development paradigm." In: Jwa, Sung-Hui and Lee Kwon-in (eds.), *Competition and Corporate Governance in Korea: Reforming and Restructuring the Chaebol*. Cheltenham UK and Northampton MA: Edward Elgar, 3–21.

Korea Automobile Manufacturers Association [KAMA] (2009). Korean Automobile Industry Annual Report 2009. Seoul: Korea Automobile Manufacturers Association.

Kattoulas, Velisarios, 1997. "Standard & Poor's cuts rating in response to Kia bailout: Panic sends South Korea reeling." *The New York Times*. Published October 25. https://www.nytimes.com/1997/10/25/business/worldbusiness/IHT-standard-poors-cuts-rating-in-response-to-kia.html. Accessed December 8, 2020.

Kaufmann, Daniel, Kraay, Aart, and Zoido-Lobaton, Pablo, 1999. *Governance Matters*. Washington DC: The World Bank. http://documents.worldbank.org/curated/en/665731468739470954/pdf/multi-page.pdf. Accessed May 15, 2020.

Khanna, Tarun and Palepu, Krishna, 2000. "Is group affiliation profitable in emerging markets? An analysis of diversified Indian business groups." *The Journal of Finance*, 55(2): 867–91.

Khanna, Tarun and Yafeh, Y., 2007. "Business groups in emerging markets: Paragons or parasites?" *Journal of Economic Literature*, 45(2): 331–72.

Kim, Byun Kook, 2003. "The politics of chaebol reform, 1980–1997." In: Haggard, Stephan, Lim, Wonhyuk, and Kim, Euysung (eds.), *Economic Crisis and Corporate Restructuring in Korea*. Cambridge: Cambridge University Press.

Kim, Cae-One, Kim, Young Kon, and Yoon, Chang-Bun, 1992. "Korean telecommunications development: achievements and cautionary lessons." *World Development*, 20(12): 1829–41.

Kim, Dong-Won and Leslie, Stuart W., 1998. "Winning markets or winning novel prizes? KAIST and the challenges of late industrialization." *Osiris, 13 Beyond Joseph Needham: Science, Technology, and Medicine in East and Southeast Asia*. 154–85.

Kim, Eun-Ju, 1993. "Telecommunications development in the Republic of Korea. An alternative model?" *Telecommunications Policy*, 17(2): 118–38.

Kim, Gang-rae and Cho, Jeehyun, 2020. "Korean gov't plan to sell Woori financial stake hits snag due to dip in price." *Pulsenews*. Published February 21, 2020. https://pulsenews.co.kr/view.php?year=2020&no=180941. Accessed June 30, 2020.

Kim, In Chul, Kim, Mahn-Kee, and Boyer, William W., 1994. "Privatization of South Korea's public enterprises." *Journal of Developing Areas*, 28(2): 157–66.

Kim, Jae Kyung, 2019. "Is Seoul's financial hub vision feasible?" *The Korea Times*. Published May, 2019. http://www.koreatimes.co.kr/www/biz/2019/05/488_203308.html. Accessed July 5, 2020.

Kim Joon-Kyung, 1998. "Debt and financial instability in Korea. Division of macroeconomics." Korea Development Institute. Working paper N.69. http://210.149.141.36/jp/archive/wor/wor069/wor069.pdf. Accessed December 8, 2020.

Kim, June Dong and Wang, Yun-jong, 1996. *Toward Liberalisation of International Direct Investment in Korea: Retrospects and Prospects*. Korea Institute for International Economic Policy paper, No. 96–02, April, Seoul: Korea Institute for International Economic Policy.

Kim, Limsu, 1997. *Imitation to Innovation: The Dynamics of Korea's Technological Learning*. Boston: Harvard Business School Press.

Kim, Max, S., 2019. "How greed and corruption blew up South Korea's nuclear industry." *MIT Technology Review*. April 22, 2019. https://www.technologyreview.com/2019/04/22/136020/how-greed-and-corruption-blew-up-south-koreas-nuclear-industry. Accessed October 6, 2020.

Kim, Peter, 2013. "Telecom giant KT raided over CEO scandal." *Korea Observer*, October 22. Available from: http://www.koreaobserver.com/kt-raided-chairmans-corruption-allegations-8298. Accessed October 18, 2018.

Kim, Sung-Young, 2012. "Transitioning from fast-follower to innovator: The institutional foundations of the Korean telecommunications sector." *Review of International Political Economy*, 19(1): 140–68.

Kim, Tae-Burn, 1990. "The Korean automotive industry." *Monthly Review*, 24: 3–17.

Kim, Yeon Hee and Rhee, So-eui, 2008. "HSBC walks away from $6.3 billion S.Korea bank buy." *Reuters*. Published September 19, 2008. https://www.reuters.com/article/us-keb-hsbc/hsbc-walks-away-from-6-3-billion-s-korea-bank-buy-idUSSEO8898320080919. Accessed July 5, 2020.

Kim, Yong Cheol, 2003. "The shadow of the Gwangju uprising in the democratization of Korean politics." *New Political Science*, 25(2): 225–40.

Kitschelt, Herbert, 2012. "Research and dialogue on programmatic parties and party systems." IDEA Project PO 134–01/2401. Durham, NC: Duke University.

Korea Auto Industries Cooperative Association [KAICA], statistics, 2020. http://www.kaica.or.kr/bbs/content.php?co_id=statics. Accessed July 31, 2020.

Korea Development Bank, 2018. Annual report. https://www.banktrack.org/download/annual_report_2018_102/191001_koreadevelopmentbankannualreport2018.pdf. Accessed July 6, 2020.

Korea Electric Power Corporation [KEPCO], 2020. "Domestic operations/construction." https://home.kepco.co.kr/kepco/EN/G/htmlView/ENGAHP002.do?menuCd=EN070202. Accessed October 16, 2020.

Korea Information Society Development Institute [KISDI], 2019. *2019ICT Industry Outlook of Korea*. http://kisdi.re.kr/kisdi/upload/attach/Outlook_2019.pdf. Accessed April 6, 2020.

Korea Institute for Industrial Economics and Trade [KIET], 1989. *Policies of Technology Transfer and Foreign Investment in Developing Countries*. Seoul: KIET.

Korea Institute for Industrial economics and Trade [KIET], 2014. *2014 Modularization of Korea's Development Experience: Korea's Automotive Industry*. Seoul: Ministry of Strategy and Finance.

Korea Machine Tool Manufacturer's Association [KOMMA], 2019. "2019–2020 Korea Machine Tool Industry." Seoul: Korea Machine Tool Manufacturer's Association.

Kwak, Tae Yang, 2003. "The Nixon doctrine and the Yushin reforms: American foreign policy, the Vietnam war, and the rise of authoritarianism in Korea, 1968-1973." *The Journal of American-East Asian Relations*, 12(1–2): 33–57.

Lagendijk, Arnoud, 1995. "The foreign takeover of the Spanish automobile industry: A growth analysis of internationalization." *Regional* Studies, 29(4): 381–93.

Larson, James F., 1995. *The Telecommunications Revolution in Korea*. Hong Kong and New York: Oxford University Press.

Lee, Dong Gull, 2003. "The restructuring of Daewoo." In: Haggard, Stephan and Kim, Euysung(eds.), *Economic Crisis and Corporate Restructuring in Korea*. Cambridge: Cambridge University Press.

Lee, Jee In and Mah, Jai S, 2017. "The role of the government in the development of the automobile industry in Korea." *Progress in Development Studies*, 17(3): 229–44.

Lee, Joyce and Jin, Hyunjoo, 2020. "SsangYong looking for buyer as Mahindra aims to cede control." *Automotive News Europe*. Published June 19. https://europe.autonews.com/automakers/ssangyong-looking-buyer-mahindra-aims-cede-control. Accessed December 13, 2020.

Lee, Keun and Lim, Chaysung, 2001. "Technological regimes, catching-up and leapfrogging: Findings from the Korean industries." *Research Policy*, 30(3): 459–83.

Lee, Y. S. and Markusen, Ann, 2003. "The South Korean defense industry in the post-cold war era." In: Markusen Ann, DiGiovanna, Sean, and Leary, Michael C. (eds.), *From Defense to Development? International Perspectives on Realizing the Peace Dividend*. London and New York: Routledge.

Lee, Youngsoo, Lee, Gyubong, Cho, Youngjoon, and Choi, Honzong, 1999. "The Korea Advanced Manufacturing System (KAMS) Project." *International Journal of Machine Tools and Manufacture*, 39(11): 1807–20.

Leff, Nathaniel H., 1978. "Industrial organization and entrepreneurship in the developing countries: The economic groups." *Economic Development and Cultural Change*, 26(4): 661–75.

León, Margarita, Choi, Young Jun, and Ahn, Jong-soon, 2016. "When flexibility meets familialism: Two tales of gendered labour markets in Spain and South Korea." *Journal of European Social Policy*, 26(4): 344–57.

Lera Laso, Emilio and Díaz Martínez, José Antonio, 1986. *El futuro de las telecomunicaciones en España: prospectivas y previsión tecnológica*. Madrid: Fundesco.

Levy, Jonah (2006). Introduction. In: Jonah Levy (ed.), *The State after Statism: New State Activities in the Age of Liberalization*. Cambridge: Harvard University Press.

Lewin, Ignacio, 1981. "Fiat ha dejado las manos libres a Seat para resolver el futuro." *El País*. Published June 27, 1981. https://elpais.com/diario/1981/06/28/economia/362527209_850215.html. Accessed December 9, 2020.

Lim, Haeran, 1998. *Korea's Growth and Industrial Transformation*. New York: St. Martin's Press.

López, Santiago M., Pueyo, Ana, and Zlatanova, Goritza, 2002. "Colaboración bajo incertidumbre: la formación de un grupo tecnológico en el sector de las telecomunicaciones." *Economia industrial*, 346: 81–96.

Loriaux, Michael, 2003. "France: A new capitalism of voice?" In: L. Weiss..(ed.), *States in the Global Economy: Bringing Domestic Institutions Back In*. Cambridge: Cambridge University Press.

Macher, Jeffrey T., Mayo, John W., and Schiffer, Mirjam, 2011. "The influence of firms on government." *The BE Journal of Economic Analysis and Policy*, 11(1): 1–27.

Machine MFG, 2017. "World's top 100 machine-tools companies." https://www.machinemfg.com/wp-content/uploads/2017/09/TOP-Press-Brake-Manufacturer-List-MachineMfg.pdf. Accessed October 16, 2020.

Maddison Project Database, 2018. Groningen Growth and Development Centre, Faculty of Economics and Business. Available from: https://www.rug.nl/ggdc/historicaldevelopment/maddison/releases/maddison-projectdatabase-2018. Accessed January 4, 2019.

Malo de Molina, José Luís, 2012. "Luis Angel Rojo en el servicio de estudios del Banco de España." In: Carlos Sebastián (ed.), *Luis Angel Rojo, Recuerdo y homenaje*. Madrid: Fundación Ramón Areces.

March, James G. and Olsen, Johan P., 1989. *Rediscovering Institutions: The Organizational Basis of Politics*. New York: The Free Press.

Marcos Fano, José María, 2002. "Historia y panorama actual del sistema eléctrico español." *Física y Sociedad, Revista del Colegio Oficial de Físicos*, N13: 10–17. https://www.cofis.es/pdf/fys/fys13/fys13_10-17.pdf.

Marimón, A., 2006. "La venta de SEAT a Volkswagen." Expansion 20 años. Expansión. Published May 27. http://www.expansion.com/especiales/20aniversario/20corporativos/seat.htm. Accessed May 2, 2019.

Mark, Ken and Birkinshaw, Julian, 2012. *KT Corporation: Transforming a State-Owned Enterprise to Create an Agile Organization*. London: London Business School.

Markusen, Ann and Park, Sam Ock, 1993. "The state as industrial locator and district builder: The Case of Changwon, South Korea." *Economic Geography*, 69(2): 157–81.

Martín Aceña, Pablo, 2005. "Los retos de la industria bancaria española." In: De Oña Navarro, Francisco (ed.), *La conformación histórica de la industria bancaria española*. Colección Mediterráneo Económico, 8. Almería: Fundación Cajamar. https://docplayer.es/5099941-Los-retos-de-la-industria-bancaria-en-espana-coordinador-francisco-de-ona-navarro.html.

Mazzucato, Mariana, 2013. *The Entrepreneurial State: Debunking Public vs. Private Sector Myths*. London: Anthem Press.

Millman, S. and the AT&T staff, 1983. "A history of engineering and science in the Bell System." *Physical Sciences (1925–1980)*. S.l.: AT&T Bell Laboratories.

Ministry of Economy and Finance Republic of Korea (MOEF), 2020. "Government Announces Overview of Korean New Deal." July 14, 2020. https://english.moef.go.kr/pc/selectTbPressCenterDtl.do?boardCd=N0001&seq=4940. Accessed December 23, 2020. Seoul: Ministry of Economy and Finance.

Ministry of External affairs. 2020. "España y la Unión Europea." http://www.exteriores.gob.es/portal/es/politicaexteriorcooperacion/unioneuropea/paginas/espue.aspx. Accessed April 8, 2021.

Ministry of Information and Communication Republic of Korea, 2004. *The Road to $20,000 GDP/Capita. IT 839 Strategy*. Seoul: Ministry of Information and Communication.

Mo, Jongryn and Moon, Chung-in, 2003. "Business-government relations under Kim Dae-jung." In: Haggard, Stephan and Kim, Euysung (eds.), *Economic Crisis and Corporate Restructuring in Korea*. Cambridge: Cambridge University Press.

Morris, Hank, 2020. "Seoul unlikely prospect for regional financial hub." *Asia Times*. Published January 31, 2020. https://asiatimes.com/2020/01/seoul-unlikely-prospect-for-regional-financial-hub/. Accessed July 5, 2020.

Morrison, Murdo, 2010. "EADS's complex ownership structure." *FlightGlobal*. Published July 20, 2010. https://www.flightglobal.com/eadss-complex-ownership-structure/94568.article. Accessed December 15, 2020.

Mufson, Steven, 1997. "Car maker symbolizes Korean crisis." *Washington Post*. Published December 18. https://www.washingtonpost.com/archive/politics/1997/12/18/car-maker-symbolizes-korean-crisis/8f5f6a71-961e-42a3-b17f-a07d6fdc5b77/. Accessed December 8, 2020.

Mullins, Paul D. and Shwayri, Sofia T., 2016. "Green cities and 'IT839': a new paradigm for economic growth in South Korea." *Journal of Urban Technology*, 23(2): 47–64.

Mundi, Simon, 2013a. "Foreign banks struggle in South Korea." *Financial Times*. Published September 18, 2013. https://www.ft.com/content/6f1d4f04-14f9-11e3-b3db-00144feabdc0. Accessed July 1, 2020.

Mundi, Simon, 2013b. "Hyundai: changing the mold." *Financial Times*. Published May 30. https://www.ft.com/content/dcd9f21e-bd73-11e2-890a-00144feab7de. Accessed July 31, 2020.

Muñoz, Araceli, 2019. "El Gobierno quiere convertir a Indra e ITP en un gigante español de la defensa." *El economista*. Published June 19, 2019. https://www.eleconomista.es/empresas-finanzas/noticias/9947786/06/19/El-Gobierno-quiere-convertir-a-Indra-e-ITP-en-un-gigante-espanol-de-la-defensa.html. Accessed December 15, 2020.

Muñoz, Ramón. 2013. "Bankia vende al Estado su 20,1% en Indra por 337 millones." *El País*. Published August 2, 2013. https://elpais.com/economia/2013/08/02/actualidad/1375468898_768446.html. Accessed April 1, 2021.

Murphy, Tom, 2017. "Stamping market heats up for Gestamp." *Wards Auto*. Published June 1. https://www.wardsauto.com/industry/stamping-market-heats-gestamp. Accessed November 21, 2019.

Musacchio, Aldo and Lazzarini, Sergio G., 2014. *Reinventing State Capitalism*. Cambridge, MA and London: Harvard University Press.

Musacchio, Aldo and Lazzarini, Sergio G., 2016. "The reinvention of state capitalism in Brazil, 1970–2012." In: Schneider, Ben Ross (ed.), *New Order and Progress: Development and Democracy in Brazil*. Oxford: Oxford University Press.

Mytelka, Lynn Krieger, 1999. *Competition, Innovation and Competitiveness in Developing Countries*. Paris: OECD.

Nam, Hyun-Woo, 2020. "Hyundai Motor, Naver to spearhead Korean new deal." *The Korea Times*, Published July 14. https://www.koreatimes.co.kr/www/tech/2020/07/419_292820.html. Accessed August, 4, 2020.

National Commission for the Telecommunications Market / Comisión Nacional del Mercado de las Telecomunicaciones [CNMT], 2009. Annual statistics. Barcelona: Comisión Nacional del Mercado de las Telecomunicaciones.

National Pension Service [NPS], 2019. Annual Report. https://fund.nps.or.kr/jsppage/fund/prs_e/prs_e_04.jsp. Accessed December 22, 2020.

National Statistic Institute [INE], 2013. Regional Accounts. Base 1986, regional macromagnitudes.

Navarro, Jaime E., 2008. "El Banco Santander vende su ciudad financiera por 1.900 millones a Propinvest." *Expansión*. Published January 25, 2008. https://www.expansion.com/2008/01/25/empresas/banca/1082507.html. Accessed December 22, 2020.

Nölke, Andreas, ten Brink, Tobias, May, Christian, and Claar, Simone, 2020. *State-Permeated Capitalism in Large Emerging Economies*. London and New York: Routledge.

Oh, Myung and Larson, James F., 2011. *Digital Development in Korea: Building an Information Society*. Abingdon, UK and New York: Routledge.

Oh, Sea-Hong, Lim, Hee Young, and Kim, Byoungsoo, 2016. "Strategy to promote the effectiveness of technology transfer of national R&D programs in Korea: Seen through the G7 Leading Technology Development program." *Procedia Computer Science*, 91: 221–9.

Organisation for Economic Cooperation and Development [OECD], 2009. *Reviews of Innovation Policy. Korea*. Paris: OECD.

Organisation for Economic Cooperation and Development [OECD], 2013. *Communications Outlook 2013*. Paris: OECD.

Organisation for Economic Cooperation and Development [OECD], 2014. *OECD Reviews of Innovation Policy: Industry and Technology Policies in Korea*. Paris: OECD.

Organisation for Economic Cooperation and Development [OECD], 2018a. *Economic Outlook for Southeast Asia, China and India 2019: Towards Smart Urban Transportation*. Paris: OECD.

Organisation for Economic Cooperation and Development [OECD], 2018b. *Economic Surveys: Korea*. OECD, Paris.

Organisation for Economic Cooperation and Development [OECD], 2018c. *Working Better with Age: Korea*. Paris: OECD.

Organisation for Economic Cooperation and Development [OECD], 2019. *Education at a Glance 2019*. Paris: OECD.

Organisation for Economic Cooperation and Development [OECD], 2020a. *Banking Income Statement and Balance Sheet Statistics Dataset*. https://stats.oecd.org/Index.aspx?DataSetCode=BPF1. Accessed July 5, 2020.

Organisation for Economic Cooperation and Development [OECD], 2020b. *Employment Dataset*. Paris: OECD.

Organisation for Economic Cooperation and Development [OECD], 2020c. *Family Database*. Paris: OECD.

Organisation for Economic Cooperation and Development [OECD], 2020d. *FDI Regulatory Restrictiveness Index*. https://stats.oecd.org/Index.aspx?datasetcode=FDIINDEX. Accessed. April 6, 2020.

Organisation for Economic Cooperation and Development [OECD], 2020e. *Health Statistics.* Paris: OECD.

Organisation for Economic Cooperation and Development [OECD], 2020f. *Labor Force Statistics.*Paris: OECD.

Organisation for Economic Cooperation and Development [OECD], 2020g. *Level of GDP per Capita and Productivity Statistics.* Paris: OECD.

Organisation for Economic Cooperation and Development [OECD], 2020h. *Main Science and Technology Indicators.* Paris: OECD.

Organisation for Economic Cooperation and Development [OECD], *National Accounts Dataset.* https://www.oecd-ilibrary.org/economics/data/oecd-national-accounts-statistics_na-data-en. Accessed April 6, 2020.

Organization of Motor Vehicle Manufacturers [OICA], 2020. *Production Statistics.* http://www.oica.net/production-statistics/. Accessed July 31, 2020.

Orphanides, Athanasios, 2015. "The Euro area crisis five years after the original sin." *Credit and Capital Markets*, 48(4): 535–65.

Oxford Analytica Daily Brief Service, 2001. "State banks bail out Hynix." *Oxford Analytica*, 13 Nov: 1.

Pai, M. K., 2004. *What Happened to the Productive Structure of Korea in the Past Three Decades?* Seoul: KIET.

Pallarés-Barberá, Montserrat, 1998. "Changing production systems: The automobile industry in Spain." *Economic Geography*, 74(4): 344–59.

Park, Chung-Taek, 1992. "The experience of nuclear power development in the Republic of Korea: Growth and future challenge." *Energy Policy*, 20(8): 721–34.

Park, Ju-Min, 2018. "South Korea to provide $3 billion in financial support for troubled auto suppliers." *Reuters*. Published December 18. https://www.reuters.com/article/us-southkorea-autos-suppliers/south-korea-to-provide-3-billion-in-financial-support-for-troubled-auto-suppliers-idUSKBN1OH0A3. Accessed July 31, 2020.

Park, Kang H. and Weber, William L., 2006. "A note on efficiency and productivity growth in the Korean Banking Industry, 1992–2002." *Journal of Banking & Finance*. 30(8): 2371–86.

Park, Kyung Suh, 2003. "Bank-led corporate restructuring." In: Haggard, Stephan and Kim, Euysung (eds.), *Economic Crisis and Corporate Restructuring in Korea*. Cambridge: Cambridge University Press.

Park, Won-An, 1996. "Financial liberalization: the Korean experience," In: Ito, Takatoshi, and Krueger, Anne O. (eds.), *Financial Deregulation and Integration in East Asia*. NBER-EASE Volume 5. Chicago: University of Chicago Press.

Park, Yung Chul, 1994. "Korea: Development and structural change in the financial sector." In: Park, Yung Chul and Patrick, Hugh T., *The Financial Development of Japan, Korea, and Taiwan: Growth, Repression, and Liberalization*. Oxford and New York: Oxford University Press.

Park, Yung Chul, 2013. "Financial development and liberalization in Korea. 1980–2011." In: Park, Yung Chul and Patrick, Hugh T.(eds.), *How Finance is Sapping the Economies of China, Japan and Korea*. New York: Columbia University Press, 225–301.

Park, Yung Chul and Kim, D.W., 1994. "Korea: Development and structural change of the banking sector." In Park, Yung Chul and Patrick, Hugh T. (eds.), *The Financial Development of Japan, Korea, and Taiwan: Growth, Repression, and Liberalization*. Oxford and New York: Oxford University Press, 188–221.

Partido Socialista Obrero Español, 1982. Programa electoral. Madrid: PSOE. http://www.psoe.es/mediacontent/2015/03/Programa-Electoral-Generales-1982.pdf. Accessed October 18, 2018.

Patel, Sonal, 2019. "The big picture: World's biggest power companies." Published in Power. 31 January. https://www.powermag.com/the-big-picture-worlds-biggest-power-companies/. Accessed September 24, 2020.

Pellicer, Miguel, 1992. "Los mercados financieros organizados en España." Servicio de estudios del Banco de España N 50. Madrid: Banco de España.

Pérez, José, 2012. "Banca central, mercados y estabilidad financiera: algunas experiencias del Banco de España (1977–1990)." In Sebastián, Carlos (ed.), *Luis Angel Rojo. Recuerdo y homenaje*. Madrid: Fundación Ramón Areces, 53–77.

Pérez, Roberto, 2017. "El gigante americano General Motors se despide de España tras 35 años de historia." ABC. Published October 1. https://www.abc.es/espana/aragon/abci-gigante-americano-general-motors-despide-espana-tras-35-anos-historia-201710010026_noticia.html. Accessed May 2, 2019.

Pérez, Sofía, 1997. *Banking on Privilege: The Politics of Spanish Financial Reform*. Ithaca and London: Cornell University Press.

Pérez-Díaz, Victor, 1993. *La primacia de la sociedad civil*. Madrid: Alianza Editorial.

Pérez Martínez, Jorge and Feijóo González, Claudio, 2000. Convergencia, competencia y regulación en los mercados de telecomunicaciones, el audiovisual e internet. Grupo de Regulación de las Telecomunicaciones [GRETEL]. Madrid: Colegio Oficial de Ingenieros de Telecomunicación.

Pollack, Andrew, 1997. "Koreans place KIA motors under bankruptcy shield." *The New York Times*. Published July 16. https://www.nytimes.com/1997/07/16/business/koreans-place-kia-motors-under-bankruptcy-shield.html. Accessed September 15, 2020.

Porter, Michael E., 1990. *The Competitive Advantage of Nations*. New York: The Free Press.

Porter, Michael, E., Sachs, Jeffrey D., and McArthur, John W., 2002. "Competitiveness and stages of economic development. The Global Competitiveness Report 2001–2002." Geneva: World Economic Forum.

Powell, Charles, 2015. "The Long Road to Europe: Spain and the European Community, 1957–1986." *Elcano Royal Institute Working Paper*. June 2015. Madrid: Elcano Royal Institute. http://www.realinstitutoelcano.org/wps/wcm/connect/6a64870048b28234b015fb735801e641/DT9-2015-Powell-Long-Road-Europe-Spain-European-Community-1957–1986.pdf?MOD=AJPERES&CACHEID=6a64870048b28234b015fb735801e641. Accessed July 16, 2020.

Preston, Paul, 1986. *The Triumph of Democracy in Spain*. London: Routledge.

Pulse News staff, 2020. "Hyundai Motor aims to roll out EV models running on exclusive EV platform." *Pulse News*. Published May 11. https://pulsenews.co.kr/view.php?year=2020&no=478349. Accessed July 31, 2020.

Raiser, Martin, Clarke, Roland, Procee, Paul, Brinceño-Garmendia, Cecilia, Kikoni, Edith, Kizito, Joseph, and Viñuela, Lorena, 2017. *Back to Planning: How to Close Brazil's Infrastructure Gap in Times of Austerity*. Report N°. 117392-BR.Washington DC: World Bank Group.

Rama, Ruth and Ferguson, Deron, 2007. "Emerging districts facing structural reform: the Madrid electronics district and the reshaping of the Spanish telecom monopoly." *Environment and planning*, 39(9): 2207–31.

Ramírez, Andrés, 2007. "CASA C-212 Aviocar." *Volavi*. Published April 1, 2007. https://volavi.co/aviacion/aviones/casa-c-212-aviocar.Accessed November 6, 2020.

Ravenhill, John, 2001. "From national champions to global partnerships: The Korean auto industry, financial crisis and globalization." *MIT Japan Program Working Paper* 01.04.

Red Eléctrica de España, 1998. "Annual Report." https://www.ree.es/sites/default/files/downloadable/inf_oper_ree_98.pdf. Accessed November 6, 2020.

Red Eléctrica de España, 2009. "Annual Report." https://www.ree.es/sites/default/files/downloadable/inf_sis_elec_ree_2009.pdf. Accessed November 6, 2020.

Red Eléctrica de España, 2019. "Annual Report." https://www.ree.es/sites/default/files/11_PUBLICACIONES/Documentos/InformesSistemaElectrico/2019/inf_sis_elec_ree_2019_v2.pdf. Accessed November 6, 2020.

Reisinger, Don, 2016. "Here's why only Apple and Samsung know how to profit off smartphones." *Fortune*, August 23, 2016. http://fortune.com/2016/08/23/apple-samsung-smartphone-profits/. Accessed April 7, 2020.

Reuters staff, 2008. "S. Korea KT CEO steps down as arrest warrant issued." *Reuters*. Published November 5. https://www.reuters.com/article/ktceo-arrest/s-korea-kt-ceo-steps-down-as-arrest-warrant-issued-idUSSEO28143820081105. Accessed October 18, 2018.

Reuters staff, 2013. "HSBC to exit from retail banking, wealth management in Korea." *Reuters*. Published July 5, 2013. https://www.reuters.com/article/us-hsbc-korea/hsbc-to-exit-from-retail-banking-wealth-management-in-korea-idUSBRE96406020130705. Accessed December 22, 2020.

Rico González, César, 2006. "El comienzo de la industria de las telecomunicaciones", in Rico González, César (ed.), *Crónicas y testimonios de las telecomunicaciones españolas*. Madrid: Colegio Oficial de Ingenieros de Telecomunicaciones, 495–540.

Rivases, Jesús, 1988. *Los banqueros del PSOE*. Madrid: Ediciones B.

Ro, Hyung-Go, 2001. "Banking industry consolidation in Korea." In: Bank for International Settlements (ed.), *The Banking Industry in the Emerging Market Economies: Competition, Consolidation and Systemic Stability*, Basel: Bank for International Settlements N 4: 93–101.

Rodríguez Roldán de Aranguiz, Markel, 2019. "El mercado de la máquina herramienta en Corea del Sur." Seoul: Oficina Económica y Comercial de la Embajada de España en Seúl.

Rodrik, Dani, 1997. *Has Globalization Gone Too Far?* Washington, DC: Institute for International Economics.

Rodrik, Dani, 2006. "Goodbye Washington Consensus, hello Washington confusion? A review of the World Bank's economic growth in the 1990s: Learning from a decade of reform." *Journal of Economic* Literature, 44(4): 973–87.

Rodrik, Dani, 2017. *Straight Talk on Trade. Ideas for a Sane World Economy*. Princeton and Oxford: Princeton University Press.

Roldán Rabadán, José, 2013. *Pegaso: del paternalismo a la desregulación. Las relaciones laborales entre 1954 y 1994*. E-book: Pensamiento Crítico. http://www.pensamientocritico.org/primera-epoca/josrol0714.pdf. Accessed August 21, 2020.

Rueschemeyer, Dietrich and Evans, Peter B., 1985. "The state and economic transformation: Toward an analysis of the conditions underlying effective intervention", in Evans, Peter B. Rueschemeyer, Dietrich, and Skocpol, Theda (eds.), *Bringing the State Back In*. Cambridge, MA: Cambridge University Press.

Sakong, Il, 1993. *Korea in the World Economy*. Washington, DC: Institute for International Economics.

Samsung Electronics, 2019. 2018 Business report for the year ended December 31, 2018. https://images.samsung.com/is/content/samsung/p5/global/ir/docs/2018_Business_Report_vF.pdf. Accessed May 25, 2020.

Sánchez Domínguez, M. Angeles, 2001. *Instrumentación de la política económica regional en Andalucía, 1946–2000. Fundamentos teóricos y evidencia empírica*. Granada: Universidad de Granada.

Sánchez Sánchez, Esther, 2004. "La implantación industrial de Renault en España: Los orígenes de FASA Renault 1950–1970." *Revista de Historia Económica*, N1: 147–75.

San Román, Elena, 1995. "El Nacimiento de SEAT: autarkia e intervencion del INI." *Revista de Historia Industrial*, N7: 141–65.

Santillana del Barrio, Ignacio, 1997. "La creación de una multinacional española." *El Caso de Telefónica. Economistas*, 73: 90–9.

Schneider, Ben Ross, 2016. "Introduction Brazil in historical, comparative, and theoretical perspective." In: Schneider, Ben Ross (ed.), *New Order and Progress: Development and Democracy in Brazil*. Oxford: Oxford University Press.

Schwartz, Pedro, 1995. "La major politica industrial es…" *El País*. Published July 14, 1995. https://elpais.com/diario/1995/07/15/economia/805759226_850215.html. Accessed May 25, 2020.

Segal, Philip and Kirk, Don, 1999. "HSBC to acquire bank in Seoul for $1 billion." *New York Times*. Published February 23, 1999. https://www.nytimes.com/1999/02/23/business/worldbusiness/IHT-hsbc-to-acquire-bank-in-seoul-for-1-billion.html. Accessed July 5, 2020.

Segan, Sasha, 2020. "CDMA vs. GSM: What's the difference?" *PC Magazine*. Published April 7. https://www.pcmag.com/news/cdma-vs-gsm-whats-the-difference. Accessed May 28, 2020.

Sen, Amartya, 1999. *Development as Freedom*. Oxford: Oxford University Press.

Shin, Jang-Sup, 2014. *The Global Financial Crisis and the Korean Economy*. London: Routledge.

Shin, Jang-Sup and Chang, Ha-Joon, 2003. *Restructuring Korea Inc.: Financial Crisis, Corporate Reform, and Institutional Transition*. London: Routledge Curzon Studies in the Growth Economies of Asia.

Smith, Rand W., 1998. *The Left's Dirty Job: The Politics of Industrial Restructuring in France and Spain*. Pittsburg: University of Pittsburg Press.

Son, Ji-hyoung, 2019. "Woori to be fully privatized by 2022: FSC." *The Korea Herald*. Published June 25, 2019. http://www.theinvestor.co.kr/view.php?ud=20190625000638. Accessed July 5, 2020.

Song, Hahzoong, 1997. "From brain drain to reverse brain drain: three decades of Korean experience." *Science, Technology and Society*, 2(2): 317–45.

Song, Jung-a, 2011. "StanChart's Korea unit scales back strike." *Financial Times*. Published August 11, 2011. https://www.ft.com/content/f2152420-ca2f-11e0-a0dc-00144feabdc0. Accessed June 29, 2020.

Song, Jung-a, 2018. "Hyundai pledges $21bn for car technology." *Financial Times*. Published January 17. https://www.ft.com/content/ced6ad5a-fb5e-11e7-9b32-d7d59aace167. Accessed June 13, 2018.

Song, Jung-a, 2019. "South Korea stimulus efforts struggling, finance minister says." *Financial Times*. Published November 13. https://www.ft.com/content/ab66dccc-05e9-11ea-a984-fbbacad9e7dd. Accessed May 15, 2020.

Song, Jung-a, 2020a. "Hyundai to develop own electric car platform and battery charging systems." *Financial Times*. Published December 2. https://www.ft.com/content/8617355c-8b90-49dc-b1d9-aa68add5d286. Accessed December 13, 2020.

Song, Jung-a, 2020b. "South Korea's Ssangyong Motor files for bankrupcy." *Financial Times*. Published December 23, 2020. https://www.ft.com/content/4e89971d-8570-4b6a-96bc-7670a7c7a039. Accessed December 23, 2020.

Spanish Association of Automobile and Truck Manufacturers [ANFAC], 2019. "Annual report," Madrid: ANFAC.

Spanish Association of Automobile and Truck Manufacturers [ANFAC], 2020. https://anfac.com/wp-content/uploads/2020/07/ANFAC_INFORME_ANUAL_2019_VC.pdf 'Annual report', Madrid: ANFAC. Accessed March 31, 2021.

State Agency for Industrial Investments Sociedad Estatal de Participaciones Industriales [SEPI], 2020b. "Ficha de historia. Grupo TENEO." http://154.58.19.200/default.aspx?cmd=0004&IdContent=347&lang=&idLanguage=&idContraste=. Accessed October 29, 2020.

State Agency for Industrial Investments Sociedad Estatal de Participaciones Industriales [SEPI] 2020c. "Indra." https://www.sepi.es/es/sectores/indra-0. Accessed October 29, 2020.

Stokes, Susan, Dunning, Thad, Nazareno, Marcelo, and Brusco, Valeria, 2013. *Brokers, Voters, and Clientelism: The Puzzle of Distributive Politics*. Cambridge Studies in Comparative Politics. New York: Cambridge University Press.

Sung, Tae Kyung and Carlsson, Bo, 2003. "The evolution of a technological system: The case of CNC machine tools in Korea." *Journal of Evolutionary Economics*, 13: 435–60.

Surdej, Eric, 2015. *Ils sont fous ces coréens!: Dix ans chez les forcenés de l'efficacité*. Paris: Calmann-Levy. https://livre.fnac.com/a7965870/Eric-Surdej-Ils-sont-fous-ces-coreens

Tagliabue, John, 2000. "Renault Agrees to buy troubled Samsung Motors of Korea. *New York Times*. Published April 22. https://www.nytimes.com/2000/04/22/business/international-business-renault-agrees-to-buy-troubled-samsung-motors-of-korea.html. Accessed September14, 2020.

Taliaferro, Jeffrey W., 2019. *Defending Frenemies: Alliances, Politics, and Nuclear Nonproliferation in US Foreign Policy*. Oxford: Oxford University Press.

Teece, David J., 2007. "Explicating dynamic capabilities: The nature and microfoundations of (sustainable) enterprise performance." *Strategic Management Journal*, 28(13): 1319–50.

Teece, David J., 2014. "The foundations of enterprise performance: dynamic and ordinary capabilities in an (economic) theory of firms." *The Academy of Management Perspectives*, 28(4): 328–52.

Teece, David J., 2018. "Business models and dynamic capabilities." *Long Range Planning*, 51(1): 40–9.

Teece, David J. and Pisano, Gary, 1998. "The dynamic capabilities of firms." In: Dosi, Giovanni, Teece, David J., and Chytry, Josef (eds.), *Technology, Organizations and Competitiveness*. Oxford: Oxford University Press.

Telefonica, 1985. Telefonica Historical Archive, Annual report. Available from: https://www.telefonica.com/en/web/about_telefonica/publications/previous-annual-reports/2015. Accessed October 18, 2018.

Telefonica, 1996. Telefonica Historical Archive, Annual report. Available from: https://www.telefonica.com/en/web/about_telefonica/publications/previous-annual-reports/2015. Accessed October 18, 2018.

Telefonica, 1999. Telefonica Historical Archive, Annual report. Available from: https://www.telefonica. Accessed October 18, 2018.

Telefonica, 2013. "Results January–June 2013." Investor relations. Madrid: Telefonica SA.

Telefonica, 2020. "Significant shareholdings." https://www.telefonica.com/en/web/shareholders-investors/share/significant-shareholdings. Accessed November 6, 2020.

Termes, Rafael, 1991. *Desde la banca*. Madrid: Rialp.

Thatcher, Mark, 1999. *The Politics of Telecommunications: National Institutions, Convergence, and Change in Britain and France*. New York: Oxford University Press.

Thatcher, Mark, 2004. Varieties of capitalism in an internationalized world: Domestic institutional change in European telecommunications." *Comparative Political Studies*, 37 (7). pp. 1–30.

Thatcher, Mark, 2007. "Reforming national regulatory institutions: the EU and cross-national variety in European network industries." In Hancke, Bob, Rhodes, Martin, and Thatcher Mark (eds.), *Beyond Varieties of Capitalism: Conflict, Contradiction, and Complementarities in the European Economy*. Oxford: Oxford University Press.

The Economist, 1999. "The death of Daewoo." *The Economist*. Published August 19. https://www.economist.com/business/1999/08/19/the-death-of-daewoo. Accessed December 11, 2020.

The Investor staff, 2018. "KT CEO Hwang grilled in illegal political fund probe." *The Investor*. Published April 17. http://www.theinvestor.co.kr/view.php?ud=20180417000652. Accessed October 18, 2018.

Thomas, Nathalie and Dombey, Daniel, 2020. "Iberdrola pledges €75bn to capitalise on energy transition." *Financial Times*. Published November 5. https://www.ft.com/content/d2f82435-c8d6-48d1-b9aa-b5c43e7df181. Accessed December 19, 2020.

Thurbon, Elizabeth, 2016. *Developmental Mindset. The Revival of Financial Activism in South Korea*. Ithaca NY: Cornell University Press.

Torrero, Antonio, 1989. "La formación de los tipos de interés y los problemas actuales de la economía española." *Economistas*, N39: 35–48.

Torrero, Antonio, 2001. "Banca e industrialización (1950–2000)." *Revista de historia industrial*, 19–20: 305–18.

Tortella, Gabriel and Garcia Ruiz, José Luís, 2003. "Banca y política durante el primer Franquismo." In: Sánchez Recio, Glicerio and Tarascón González Julio (eds.), *Los empresarios de Franco*. Barcelona: Critica, 67–100.

Ubide, Angel J. and Baliño, Tomás J. T., 1999. "The Korean financial crisis of 1997—A strategy of financial sector reform." International Monetary Fund, Working Paper 99/28. Washington DC.

Unesco Institute for Statistics, 2020. Research and Experimental Development (R&D) Statistics Survey. Data for 2016. Paris: Unesco.

United Nations (UN), 1950. "General Assembly Resolution 386(V), 1950 on Relationships of state members and specialized agencies with Spain." https://undocs.org/en/A/RES/386(V). Accessed July 21, 2020.

United Nations Conference on Trade and Development [UNCTAD]. Data Center. United Nations (UN), 1946. "General Assembly Resolution 39(I), 1946 on the Spanish Question." https://undocs.org/en/A/RES/39(I). Accessed on July 21, 2020.

United Nations Conference on Trade and Development [UNCTAD]. 2020 Data Center. UNCTAD.

US Department of the Treasury, 1979. Report to Congress on foreign government treatment of US commercial banking organizations. Washington DC: Department of the Treasury.

Valdivielso del Real, Rocío and Goyer, Michel, 2012. "Liberalization models in the electricity sector: the impact of the market for corporate control in Britain and Spain (1996-2010)." *Competition and Regulation in Network Industries*, 13(1): 71–100.

Valls, Fernándo H., 2019. "Cómo FG, Botín, Fainé, Guindos y Rajoy laminaron a Rato de Bankia en dos cenas." *La informacion*. Published January 20, 2019. https://www.lainformacion.com/empresas/rato-bankia-fg-botin-faine-guindos-rajoy/6490081/. Accessed July 5, 2020.

Varela Panache, Fernándo, 1972. "Las inversiones españolas en el extranjero." *Información Comercial Española*, 9(104): 59–64.

Vélez, Antonio, M., 2020. "Las tres eléctricas superan el valor bursátil de los seis bancos del Ibex tras la debacle del coronavirus." *El Diario.es*. Published March 2. https://www.eldiario.es/economia/electricas-superan-bursatil-ibex-coronavirus_1_1046417.html. Accessed December 14, 2020.

Vitzthum, Carlta, 2000. "States turn to 'golden shares' to block privatization." *The Wall Street Journal*. Published May 17, 2000. https://www.wsj.com/articles/SB958506600923079082. Accessed April 4, 2020.

Vives, Luís, 2010. "Telefonica: construyendo una compañía global." Case study. Barcelona: ESADE.

Wade, Robert, 1990. *Governing the Market. Economic Theory and the Role of Government in East Asian Industrialization*. Princeton and Oxford: Princeton University Press.

Wade, Robert, 1998. "The Asian debt-and-development crisis of 1997: Causes and consequences." *World Development*, 26(8): 1535–53.

Waldron, Greg, 2013. "Vietnam takes delivery of last Spanish-built C212." Flight Global. Published January 25. https://www.flightglobal.com/vietnam-takes-delivery-of-last-spanish-built-c212/108557.article. Accessed November 6, 2020.

Weiss, Linda, 1998. *The Myth of the Powerless State*. Ithaca, NY: Cornell University Press.

White, Edward, 2019. "South Korea set for one of worst growth periods in half a century." *Financial Times*. Published November 29. https://www.ft.com/content/17bc3560-1289-11ea-a225-db2f231cfeae. Accessed May 15, 2020.

Whitley, Richard, 1999. *Divergent Capitalisms: The Social Structuring and Change of Business Systems*. Oxford: Oxford University Press.

Womack, James P., Jones, Daniel T., and Roos, Daniel, 1990. *The Machine that Changed the World*. New York: Rawson Associates.

World Bank, 2016. *Taking on Inequality*. Washington, DC: World Bank Group.

World Bank, 2018. "International Scorecard, 2018. Logistics and performance index." https://lpi.worldbank.org/. Accessed November 3, 2020.

World Bank Development Indicators, 2020. https://databank.worldbank.org/source/world-development-indicators. Accessed April 7, 2020.

World Bank Global Financial Development Indicators dataset, 2019. https://datacatalog.worldbank.org/dataset/global-financial-development.

World Trade Organization, 1997. Ruggiero congratulates governments on landmark telecommunications agreement. Press release 67, February 17, 1997. https://www.wto.org/english/news_e/pres97_e/pr67_e.htm. Accessed May 31, 2020.

World Trade Organization, 2005. "DS 296: United States – Countervailing Duty Investigation on Dynamic Random Access Memory Semiconductors (DRAMS) from Korea." Accessed July 5, 2020.

World Trade Organization, 2007. Japan – Countervailing duties on Dynamic Random Access Memories from Korea (WT/DS 336) Dispute settlement reports 2007. Volume VII, pp. 2701–3102, 2703–2805. Cambridge: Cambridge University Press.

World Trade Organization, 2008. DS336: Japan—Countervailing Duties on Dynamic Random Access Memories from Korea. https://www.wto.org/english/tratop_e/dispu_e/cases_e/ds336_e.htm. Accessed July 5, 2020.

Yang, Jae-Jin, 2018. *The Political Economy of the Small Welfare State in South Korea*. Oxford: Oxford University Press.

Yonhap, 2018. "Police to quiz KT chief in illegal political fund probe." *Korea Herald*. Published April 16, 2018. http://www.koreaherald.com/view.php?ud=20180416000117. Accessed October 18, 2018.

Yonhap, 2019. "Samsung Electronics accounts for 20% of S. Korea's exports in H1." *Korea Herald*. Published August 18, 2019. http://www.koreaherald.com/view.php?ud=20190818000029. Accessed December 2, 2020.

Yonhap, 2019. "Suicide No. 1 cause of death for S. Korean teens, youths." *Korea Herald*. Published May 1, 2019. http://www.koreaherald.com/view.php?ud=20190501000216. Accessed May 17, 2020.

Yoo, Jung-ho, 1994. "South Korea's manufactured exports and industrial targeting policy." In: Yang, Shu-Chin (ed.), *Manufactured Exports of East Asian Industrializing Economies*. Armonk: ME Sharpe.

Yoo, Seong Min, 1999. "Corporate restructuring in Korea: Policy issues before and during the crisis." *Korea Development Institute working paper* N 9,903. Seoul: Korea Development Institute.

Yoon, Deok Ryong, 2011. "The Korean economic adjustment to the world financial crisis." *Asian Economic Papers*, 10(1): 106–27.

Yoon, Young Sil, 2019. "Foreign banks leaving South Korea due to stronger financial regulations." *Business Korea*. Published June 20, 2019. http://www.businesskorea.co.kr/news/articleView.html?idxno=33055. Accessed July 5, 2020.

Zafra Díaz, Juán Manuel, 2001. "Lucent cerrará su fábrica de microprocesadores en Tres Cantos por el desplome de las ventas." *El País*. Published June 28, 2001. https://elpais.com/diario/2001/06/29/economia/993765604_850215.html. Accessed May 25, 2020.

Zysman, John, 1983. *Governments, Markets, and Growth: Financial Systems and the Politics of Industrial Change*. Oxford: Martin Press.

Index